45.00

67C

TENNYSON: SEVEN ESSAYS

Tennyson

Seven Essays

Edited by

Philip Collins
Emeritus Professor of English
University of Leicester

St. Martin's Press

First published in Great Britain 1992 by
THE MACMILLAN PRESS LTD
Houndmills, Basingstoke, Hampshire RG21 2XS
and London
Companies and representatives
throughout the world

A catalogue record for this book is available
from the British Library

ISBN 0–333–45790–0

Printed in Great Britain by
Ipswich Book Co Ltd
Ipswich, Suffolk

.1791515   1–18–95

First published in the United States of America 1992 by
Scholarly and Reference Division,
ST. MARTIN'S PRESS, INC.,
175 Fifth Avenue,
New York, N.Y. 10010

ISBN 0–312–07958–3

Library of Congress Cataloging-in-Publication Data
Collins, Philip Arthur William.
Tennyson: seven essays / Philip Collins.
p. cm.
Includes index.
ISBN 0–312–07958–3
1. Tennyson, Alfred Tennyson, Baron, 1809–1892—Criticism and
interpretation.   I. Title.
PR5588.C63   1992
821 ' .8—dc20   92–9003
                                                              CIP

Contents

Foreword

These seven Tennyson Society essays, published by Tennyson's last, residual and favourite publishers Macmillan, echo in the title and range two earlier Macmillan books, *Six Tennyson Essays* by the poet's grandson Sir Charles Tennyson (1954, when books like that cost fifteen shillings), and *Studies in Tennyson* (1981), a lecture-celebration of Sir Charles's hundredth birthday which, having met with a fatal accident, he regrettably failed to attend. These essays all originated in Tennyson Society occasions, which would have rejoiced Sir Charles, who was a devoted originator and supporter of the Society; but most have been amplified or amended.

W. W. Robson is the only contributor common to the 1981 volume and the present one. Here he writes on a relatively neglected area of Tennyson's works: the ballads and their relationship with nineteenth-century traditions of balladry – 'But there are many areas of his work', he writes, 'that need reappraising.' Elsewhere (in his current *Encyclopaedia Britannica* entry on Tennyson) he asserts the importance of the 'realistic and comic aspect' of his work, and he accordingly writes with relish about the dialect poems. In 1981 he assessed 'The Present Value of Tennyson' and inevitably this is a theme underlying the present collection, published with the advantage that in recent years more accurate documentation of the life and works have become available. Christopher Ricks's magisterial Longmans Annotated English Poets edition of the *Poems* (1969) has now been succeeded by his three-volume Second Edition (1987, revised and much amplified by his and other scholars having at last obtained permission to cite the Trinity College manuscripts). Students can make their own investigations into the Trinity and other manuscripts by consulting the facsimiles being published in *The Tennyson Archive* (edited by Christopher Ricks and Aidan Day, 1987–) – a formidable project indeed, eventually to comprise thirty volumes.

Robert Bernard Martin's *Tennyson: the Unquiet Heart* (1980) has become the standard biography, in succession to those by members of the Tennyson family, and the *Letters*, disappointingly uninformative though they may be, have indispensably been edited with scholarly amplitude by Cecil Y. Lang and Edgar F. Shannon, Jr (1982–1990). Emily Tennyson's invaluable journal has been published in two overlapping editions, and other significant biographical information has appeared, such as Henry Mangles's diary, under the title *Tennyson at Aldworth* (edited by Earl A. Knies, 1984). Important critical editions of *In Memoriam* and *Maud* have appeared, and there has of course been a great deal of reassessment and reinterpretation, soon to be augmented by Centenary studies.

The present collection has contributions from a *doyen* of Tennyson studies – Jerome H. Buckley, whose 1960 book *Tennyson: the Growth of a Poet* was fairly described in *Victorian Poets: a Guide to Research* (1968) as 'the most extended study of the poet which has yet appeared' – and from scholars of succeeding generations. Topics include the more biographical and the more critical, and the more ideological and the more technical, approaches to the work: none is exclusively concerned with one approach. John Beer adds significantly to knowledge of what might have been thought a fully-examined episode in Tennyson's mental progress, his debt to his fellow Apostles, by studying the importance of Coleridge in Apostolic cerebration. He notes in particular the special meaning that the term 'Being' took on for Tennyson and his contemporaries and successors, and he reexamines the Romantic/Victorian preoccupation with notions of infinity and the numinous. Eric Griffiths too discusses Tennyson's connections with his immediate predecessors, notably Wordsworth and Shelley, and he also uses the Apostle Arthur Hallam as a guide to Tennyson's mind as manifested in 'Tears, idle tears', a poem which 'thinks rhythmically', and he considers in what sense it may be called 'a profound philosophic poem', relating these questions to the issue, controversial for Hallam and the Romantics, of the compatibility of poetry and philosophy, sentiment and idea, and sensation and reflection. Tennyson's friendship with another Cambridge contemporary, Edward FitzGerald, is discussed by Norman Page, as described below.

The 'infinity' theme recurs in Jerome Buckley's 'The Lyric in the Distance', which notes Tennyson's preoccupation with spatial and temporal remoteness (one of Buckley's books is *The Triumph of Time in Victorian Literature*), and relates this to his proclivity for 'distancing' his personal emotions in the dramatic monologues and other lyrics, early and late. Another familiar Tennyson theme, loss, is the subject of Aidan Day's essay 'The Archetype that Waits' which begins almost inevitably with 'Oh! that 'twere possible' (from which its title comes), but uses an earlier poem 'The Lover's Tale' – a strange

Shelley-influenced poem with a strange history, for it was published
in much-revised form fifty years after being written – as a way of
entry into this recurrent imaginative paradigm. He 'seeks the root in
Tennyson's own work of some of the less transparent features of *In
Memoriam*'. That poem – and another Cambridge friend and Apostle,
Richard Trench – are discussed by Isobel Armstrong who also, like
Aidan Day, then proceeds to *Maud*, both works being seen as poems
of loss and mourning. Her essay presents a wide-ranging argument
about some of the ideological influence upon those successive – but
so different, as everyone notes – major poems. Uncommonly, she
regards *In Memoriam*, not *Maud*, as the 'aberrant' item in the *oeuvre*.
The impact of current linguistic, psychological and pathological theories is considered, besides the more familiar geological dimension,
and the discussion attends to the significance of the two poems
having been written 'in radically different historical circumstances'.

In *Memoriam* figures too in Norman Page's 'Larger Hopes and the
New Hedonism' where, in an examination of the long but troubled
friendship of Tennyson and FitzGerald, *The Rubáiyát of Omar Khayyám*
is compared and contrasted with it, both being notably popular long
poems of their respective periods, both of them poems of friendship,
and both adumbrating an approach to life, with the *Rubáiyát* – 'a *fin-
de-siècle* poem born before its time' – becoming the more congenial in
outlook by the end of the century.

The collection ends with W. W. Robson on the ballads, seen in
relation to those of the Romantic period and to Victorian balladists
from Aytoun and Macaulay to Kipling. He considers not only the
earlier 'costume' ballads but also the 'popular or demotic' ones that
tend now to embarrass Tennyson's admirers. Robson concludes by
asking whether that is the proper reaction, and how Tennyson's
work will be assessed in the remaining years of the century and in
the next. The Centenary will doubtless occasion further stocktaking
exercises. Meanwhile, we hope, these Tennyson Society lectures will
help in the continuous process of reassessment of some major poems
and areas of activity.

Abbreviations   Poems are cited for the three-volume second edition of *The Poems of Tennyson*, edited by Christopher Ricks (Longman,
1987) in the form 'Rii, 285, ll. 169–70' for Volume Two, page 285.
Quotations from *In Memoriam* give section as well as line numbers.

Alfred Lord Tennyson: A Memoir, by his son [Hallam, Lord Tennyson] (2 volumes, Macmillan, 1897) is cited in the text as *Mem* followed by volume and page numbers. *Letters* refers to *The Letters of Alfred Lord Tennyson*, edited by Cecil Y. Lang and Edgar F. Shannon, Jr (Oxford: Clarendon Press, 1982–90).

Philip Collins

Notes on the Contributors

Isobel Armstrong is Professor of English, Birkbeck College, London. She formerly taught at University College, London, and at Leicester and Southampton. Her books include *The Major Victorian Poets: Reconsiderations*, *Victorian Scrutinies: Reviews of Poetry 1830–1870*, and *Living Form in Nineteenth-Century Poetry*.

John Beer is Professor of English Literature at Cambridge and Fellow of Peterhouse. He has written *Coleridge the Visionary*, *The Achievement of E. M. Forster*, *Blake's Humanism*, *Coleridge's Poetic Intelligence*, *Wordsworth and the Human Heart* and *Wordsworth in Time*, along with articles on De Quincey, Newman, Dickens, Bloomsbury and D. H. Lawrence. A volume of wide-ranging essays entitled *Romantic Influences* is in preparation.

Jerome H. Buckley is Gurney Professor Emeritus at Harvard, to which he went from Columbia. His books include *The Victorian Temper*, *Tennyson: the Growth of a Poet*, *The Triumph of Time*, *The Worlds of Victorian Fiction*, *The Turning Key*, an edition of Tennyson, and several collections of Victorian poetry and prose.

Philip Collins is Emeritus Professor of English, Leicester, and Chairman of the Tennyson Society's Executive Committee. Although he is best known for his writings on Dickens, he has written also on Tennyson and other Victorians.

Aidan Day is Lecturer in English Literature, Edinburgh; formerly Research Fellow at the Tennyson Research Centre, Lincoln, funded by the University of Hull, and past editor of the *Tennyson Research Bulletin*. With Christopher Ricks he is editing the multi-volume *Tennyson Archive* (Garland), a facsimile of the poetic manuscripts and related material. Author of *Jokerman: Reading the Lyrics of Bob Dylan*, and editor of the Penguin selected Poets *Tennyson*.

Eric Griffiths is Fellow of Trinity College, and Lecturer in English in the University of Cambridge. His recent book *The Printed Voice of Victorian Poetry* (1989) contains a chapter on 'Tennyson's Breath'.

Norman Page is Professor of English Literature, Nottingham; previously taught at the University of Alberta. He is Chairman of the Tennyson Society Publications Committee, and edited the Tennyson item in the *Interviews and Recollections* series, as well as its Byron, Henry James and D. H. Lawrence ones. He is also the author or editor of books about Jane Austen, Dickens, Wilkie Collins, Hardy, Kipling, Housman, Forster, Nabokov and Golding, and of *Speech in the English Novel*.

W. W. Robson was appointed Masson Professor of English Literature at Edinburgh in 1972, after teaching in London, Oxford and Sussex. He is the author of the Tennyson entry in the current (15th, 1974) edition of the *Encylopaedia Britannica*, of several volumes of essays including *The Definition of Literature*, and of *English as a University Subject*, *Modern English Literature* and *A Prologue to English Literature*.

1

Tennyson, Coleridge and the Cambridge Apostles

JOHN BEER

The sea is onmipresent in nineteenth-century writing – particularly where that writing approaches ultimate issues of human existence. From Matthew Arnold, enisled in his own secure identity yet seeing between himself and others 'the unplumbed, salt, estranging sea', to Tennyson, whose Ulysses hears the deep moan round with many voices but leads his comrades forth manfully, not knowing what his fate will be, it is a proving image, testing human pretensions and themes. Even those who turned to the historical Church for security in a time of trouble saw it, in Old Testament typology, as the ark which would convey them through the waves of intellectual questioning that were beginning to beat higher and higher in their civilisation.

Since the events of the mid-century had been earlier prefigured in the turbulence after the French Revolution, when the spirit of questioning rose to a final but powerful climax in some circles, it is not surprising that Coleridge in the 1790s should have found himself in the position of a Victorian doubter before his time. He too found the sea an appropriate image. Describing his state of mind as he began to glimpse the full extent of the division that was revealing itself between eighteenth-century science and philosophy on the one hand and the doctrines of established religion on the other, he wrote:

> Doubts rushed in; broke upon me *'from the fountains of the great deep'*, and fell *'from the windows of heaven'*. The fontal truths of natural religion and the books of Revelation alike contributed to the flood; and it was long ere my ark touched on an Ararat, and rested.[1]

The biblical imagery here is used with exactitude: the doctrines of natural religion and of the revealed Word of God were both 'fontal'

1

truths, the one to be sought in the great deep, the other in the heavens above; but when both were explored to their limits the result was more like the 'mighty fountain momently outforced' of *Kubla Khan*. For the rest of his life he would seek for an island in the deep which might, as the waters of doubting receded, reveal itself to be the visionary mountain-top from which the whole universe could be seen. The somewhat sketchy but pregnant account contains one more clue to the nature of the problem as he saw it: 'For a very long time indeed I could not reconcile personality with infinity; and my head was with Spinoza, though my whole heart remained with Paul and John.'

Coleridge's general account of his condition when he began to perceive how far the truths of science and the truths of revelation were at odds bears an obvious resemblance to many records by Victorian thinkers of the state in which they found themselves in the middle of the next century. The general problem was present throughout the intervening years, however. The suggestion to be advanced here is that Coleridge's long struggle to 'reconcile personality with infinity', far from being carried out in isolation, was known to some of his successors, and had an important effect on the group which came to be known as the Cambridge Apostles. So, by an oblique route, it reached the poetry of Tennyson.

To establish a connection between Coleridge the thinker and Tennyson the poet might at first sight seem to be a rather unrewarding enterprise, in view of Tennyson's own reticence on the subject. In his biography Hallam Tennyson mentions Coleridge only as someone 'for whose prose my father never much cared, but to whose poetry, especially Kubla Khan, The Ancient Mariner and Christabel, he was devoted' (*Mem*, i, 50). And if one looks through the other records one fares little better. William Allingham, for example, records the following brief conversation:

W. A.   Did you ever meet Coleridge?
T.   No, I was asked to visit him, but I wouldn't.
W. A.   Coleridge was a 'noticeable man, with large grey eyes'.
T.   Oh yes.[2]

This is unpromising, but Tennyson did have a grievance against Coleridge, whose remark that he had 'begun to write verses without very well understanding what metre is' was sometimes quoted to tease him (*Mem*, i, 50). The poems which his son names must after all have been some of the most important influences on him as a poet. There is also a further possibility: that Tennyson did not like talking about Coleridge because the name brought back too vividly memories of conversations with Arthur Hallam, reviving all the agonising ambiguities that had surrounded his death.

Tennyson's silence about Coleridge would not be so surprising were it not for the fact that he was a member of the society known as the Cambridge Apostles and that, at the time when he joined, Coleridge's was a name to be conjured with. We now know much more about the Apostles than we used to, thanks to the work of Peter Allen, Paul Levy and Joyce Green.[3] A point which they all make clear is that in the early years it was not a particularly secret society, though the members no doubt exercised a certain reserve. Even after the rule of secrecy began to be imposed it was not always fully observed. When Roger Fry was admitted in 1887 he lost little time in breaking it. In one of his letters he stated (incorrectly as it happens): 'It was started by Tennyson and Hallam I think about 1820, and has always considered itself very select.'[4] A short while later he wrote, 'Tennyson, I think I told you, is still a member and there are references to the society in *In Memoriam* which none but the duly initiated can fully understand.'

A great deal of documentation about individual Apostles survives, since many became sufficiently famous to be the subject of substantial biographies. Many, too, referred retrospectively to the society's activities in letters and diaries. Roger Fry's account, however, is one of the few that suggests the existence of an esoteric element. For the most part those who wrote about it in the nineteenth-century were intent on describing its spirit and what that had meant to them.

Of the three main accounts, each comes from a different phase and singles out a different quality as the most characteristic; a certain consistency of spirit over the years emerges, nonetheless. The most succinct is in a marginal note by Jack Kemble, contemporary of Tennyson and Hallam, and runs, 'No society ever existed in which more freedom of thought was found, consistent with the most perfect affection between the members; or in which a more complete toleration of the most opposite opinion prevailed . . .'.[5] A later account by Sir Arthur Helps, who had been elected in 1833, dwelt on the personal qualities required of an Apostle:

A man to succeed with us must be a real man, and not a 'sham', as Carlyle would say. . . . He was not to talk the talk of any clique; he was not to believe too much in any of his adventitious advantages; neither was he to disbelieve in them – for instance, to affect to be a radical because he was a lord. I confess I have no one word which will convey all that I mean; but I may tell you that, above all things, he was to be open-minded. When we voted for a man, we generally summed up by saying, 'He has an apostolic spirit in him,' and by that we really meant a great deal.[6]

The longest account was given by Henry Sidgwick, who also dwelt on their open-mindedness:

I can only describe it as the spirit of the pursuit of truth with absolute devotion and unreserve by a group of intimate friends, who were perfectly frank with each other, and indulged in any amount of humorous sarcasm and playful banter, and yet each respects the other, and when he discourses tries to learn from him and see what he sees. Absolute candour was the only duty that the tradition of the society enforced. No consistency was demanded with opinions previously held – truth as we saw it then and there was what we had to embrace and maintain, and there were no propositions so well established that an Apostle had not the right to deny or question, if he did so sincerely and not from mere love of paradox. The gravest subjects were continually debated, but gravity of treatment, as I have said, was not imposed, though sincerity was. In fact it was rather a point of the apostolic mind to understand how much suggestion and instruction may be derived from what is in form a jest – even in dealing with the gravest matters.[7]

Sidgwick, of course, belonged to a later, mid-Victorian, generation and his account shows the marks. While continuing the points established by Kemble and Helps, it sharpens them. Kemble's free-dom of thought' becomes Sidgwick's 'pursuit of truth with absolute devotion and unreserve', his 'perfect affection' Sidgwick's 'group of intimate friends, who indulged in any amount of humorous sarcasm and playful banter' and Helps's demand that an apostle be not a sham, Sidgwick's insistence that he argue 'sincerely and not from love of paradox'. Sidgwick's account makes his generation sound at one and the same time more earnest and more bantering than their predecessors: it opens the way towards the spirit of Bloomsbury, where the banter would be still more evident while the earnestness dropped away in favour of a more generally defined 'seriousness'. Nevertheless it displays a considerable consistency with the earlier spirit as described by Kemble and Helps, a consistency which survives in accounts much later than Sidgwick's.

While the accounts I have quoted give a clear account of the spirit in which the meetings of the Apostles were conducted and throw light on cross-currents of earnestness and humour that are to be traced in Tennyson himself, they do not explain Roger Fry's allusion to 'references to the society in *In Memoriam* which none but the duly initiated can fully understand'. Twentieth-century readers, particularly those fresh from reading about the activities of the Apostles in the 1930s, might well suppose that a cult of homosexual love was being referred to. This is doubtful, however. It is unlikely that this was in the mind of Fry himself, who was writing to his mother when he made the statement; but in any case the Apostles in the nineteenth-century were a very different group from their successors in the early years of this century, when Lytton Strachey was a dominant presence. This is not to suggest that nothing of the sort ever went on; all the indications, however, are that it did not play a part in the activities of the society itself.

Pope-Hennessy's biography of Arthur Hallam's friend Monckton Milnes gives examples of the heightened language used by young men at the time, a spirit of high sentiment being dominant.[8] Henry Hallam, as is well-known, was disturbed about the possible effects on his son's reputation of further constructions being placed upon such affectionate statements and altered some of his manuscripts for publication.[9] He also sent out a coded message on the subject in his discussion of Shakespeare's sonnets in his *Introduction to the Literature of Europe*, whereupon Tennyson commented, 'Henry Hallam made a great mistake about them: they are noble.'[10]

If clues survive concerning Fry's mysterious reference to the duly initiated, they should be looked for not in the written accounts but in the strange jargon which the Apostles are known to have adopted when talking about themselves and their activities. Some are obvious enough: they would refer to themselves as the Brethren, or the Elect, or the 'wise and good', while those who did not share their views were known as 'unapostolic', or, if more blatantly philistine, as 'Stumpfs'; the trunk in which the records of the society were kept was known as the 'Ark'.[11] There was also a whimsical and self-

deprecating element in their development of such jargon: the ancho-
vies on toast which formed their traditional fare were known as
'whales', while when a member gave one of the regular Saturday-
night papers which were the staple of their discussions he was said
to be 'called to the hearthrug'.[12] Such coinages witness to a desire not
to take themselves too solemnly.

Other usages, however, suggest a further possible depth. Those
who had shown that they could be particularly profound in discussion were called 'illumers', at least in the early days.[13] Those who
were undergoing the process of vetting and discussion before being
deemed worthy to become a member were known as 'embryos', and
induction into the society was known as 'birth', while when the time
came for one of the brothers to resign from formal membership in
order to make way for new ones to be elected he was said to have
'taken wings' and to have become an 'angel'. In a more unusual
formulation the Society and its doings were known as 'Reality' or
'noumena', while everything else in the world was referred to as
'phenomena'.[14] Such formulations have an obvious Kantian flavour;
in the strangest of all the terms, one who had been admitted as a
member of the Society was said to have attained 'the category of
Being'.[15]

The metaphor of taking wings can be associated loosely with
Coleridge, who was attracted by the fact that 'psyche' in Greek
meant both soul and butterfly and used the idea of progression from
the larva to describe the spiritual development of individuals.[16] But
although the same idea is inherent in Apostolic discourse the precise
image is different. It is the last word, 'Being', that I wish to concentrate on in connection with his thought. It is at once unexpected and
elusive to an English reader: Heidegger in Germany could produce
a book entitled *Being and Time*, and Sartre in France one called *Being
and Nothingness*, but for the average Anglo–Saxon mind the word
has little or no content. From the end of the eighteenth-century,
however, the word appears constantly in Coleridge's works. Up to
that time it had been used either generally – and usually with an
adjective, as in Milton's 'intellectual being' – or reverentially, as in
Milton's 'Thou Author of all being'.[17] It was Coleridge who began to
focus more attention on the word itself, spelling it commonly with a
capital and using it often in contexts which indicated a probing,
questioning approach rather than a simply affirming one. From the
spring of 1798, when he announced to his brother that he had for
some time been devoting himself to the study of 'what our faculties

are, and what they are capable of becoming,'[18] the word recurs in his prose. Wordsworth's use was often similarly heightened, as in 'Listen! the mighty Being is awake' (of the sea), or the address in the Immortality Ode to 'Thou little Child, yet glorious in the might/ Of heaven-born freedom, on thy Being's height'.[19] The leading idea, as I take it, is of a possible correspondence between the depths or heights of being in the human and those in the divine – as in Coleridge's description of the Imagination as 'a repetition in the finite mind of the eternal act of creation in the infinite *I AM*'.[20] The only other English writer of the time who seems to use the word with anything approaching the same emphasis is Shelley; for him, however, it primarily expresses the wholeness of personality, the full sincere identity – and that is not the same.

Coleridge's views came much closer to orthodox Christianity in his later years, but there are signs that he never quite abandoned such speculations, even if he became more cautious in expressing them publicly. He was more likely to speak freely if at all in private notes and conversations, confining himself in his published works to hints and indications. For this reason, if someone is said to have been influenced by Coleridge in his later years, it is pertinent to ask what it was in Coleridge that he or she was responding to and whether it came from published works, private writings or the conversation of the man himself.

In appraising the impact of Coleridge upon the Cambridge Apostles these questions are particularly crucial, since some had privileged access to the man himself. Detailed chronology is also important, since in the early formative period their major preoccupations could alter sharply from one three-year undergraduate generation to another.

The period during which the Apostles began to take on a distinctive character was in the mid-1820s, when their proceedings were dominated by Frederick Denison Maurice, joined shortly afterwards by John Sterling. Maurice, in particular, achieved a lasting respect: in 1834 he was toasted by the London Apostles as the true 'author' of the club. (He was also, incidentally, to become Hallam Tennyson's godfather and to receive, in that capacity, one of Tennyson's finest epistolary poems.)[21] At the time when Maurice arrived in Cambridge, in 1823, Coleridge's reputation as a prose-writer was confined mainly to *The Friend*, a work in which he urged the need for a return to principle in public affairs and for the recovery of a more enlightened view of the human mind. In the 1820s he was turning increasingly to religious questions. When his influential later work, *Aids to Reflection*, was published in 1825, Maurice had already been up at Cambridge for two years. Since Maurice claimed that before he went to Cambridge he had already read and received much influence from Coleridge, he must have been thinking of *The Friend*, and perhaps the *Lay Sermons*, which emphasised the need to distinguish the Reason from the Understanding, and assigned a higher and more absolute status to the Reason as an organ for apprehending truth intuitively. Doctrines of this kind were felt to be particularly timely in an age when respect for the doctrines of utilitarianism seemed to some to be undermining the idea of the nobility of human nature.

Neither Maurice nor Sterling met Coleridge during their undergraduate days, and Maurice never did. When Sterling went down, on the other hand, he met Coleridge shortly afterwards, and was writing of him with some familiarity when he contributed to the *Athenaeum* in 1828. By this time he had attended some of the evening gatherings which were held at the Gillmans. Carlyle, describing them, in his life of Sterling, quotes Sterling's own account as follows: 'Our interview lasted for three hours, during which he talked for two hours and three quarters.'[22] Carlyle then goes on to give his own hostile account of Coleridge's conversation and the frustration of being forced to listen for so long. What he does not do is quote the rest of Sterling's sentence, which reads in full: 'I was in his company about three hours; and of that time he spoke during two and three quarters. It would have been delightful to listen as attentively, and certainly easy for him to speak just as well for the next forty-eight hours.'[23]

Sterling's concerns at this time were primarily social, and his records of Coleridge's conversation dwell on that aspect: he quotes for example Coleridge's remark, 'The division of labour has proceeded so far even in literature, that people do not think for themselves; their review thinks for them.' Sterling and Maurice alike were turning increasingly to such questions, in the context of which the figure of Coleridge seemed portentous. Soon the *London Magazine* was apparently complaining that the *Athenaeum* was in the hands of 'dreaming, half-platonic half Jacob Behmenite mystics';[24] Trench, a fellow-Apostle, wrote more sympathetically, meanwhile, of their 'Platonico–Wordsworthian–Coleridgean–anti-Utilitarian principles'.[25] Contributing to the number for 1828, Sterling wrote the first of a series of essays purporting to be by a visiting Swede, this one being devoted to his impressions of London. Viewing the city from the top of St Paul's, he contemplates its multiplicity, the thousands who are 'to moral purposes, dead and decaying', the few hundred who are prompted to a 'higher aim of being':

> But, above all, there may be even now moving among those undistinguished swarms below me, or dwelling upon that dim eminence which rises in the distance, some great and circular mind, accomplished in endowment, of all-embracing faculties, with a reason that pervades like light, and an imagination that embodies the essence of all truth in the forms of all beauty, – even such a one as C——, the brave, the charitable, the gentle, the pious, the mighty philosopher, the glorious poet.[26]

Maurice, like Sterling, saw Coleridge as a beneficent moral presence in a world that seemed increasingly in need of the kind of guidance he was offering. His desire to link such a lofty view of humanity with solid and practical concerns intensified as he went on to become one of the initiators of Christian socialism.

Although Maurice and Sterling were to maintain strong associations with the Apostles they both left Cambridge in 1827. By the autumn of 1828, the point at which both Hallam and Tennyson arrived in Cambridge, to be elected to the Society during the following year, they might be involved as fatherly presences but were not present in the flesh to influence discussion.

The social concern which they had shown was increasing, nevertheless – general enthusiasm for liberty being coupled with a growing awareness of the problems created by new economic and industrial conditions. For young men, such concerns could still be linked with enthusiasm for the poetry that had recently been written by the second generation of Romantics. A group based primarily on Trinity College could hardly fail to be aware of the effect created in Europe by Byron's support for the cause of liberation, while members such as Hallam who came up from Eton would be similarly conscious of Shelley's doctrines. When he arrived in Cambridge, Hallam was still in fact suffering as a result of his love for Anna Wintour, which had a strong Shelleyan element. In his first year he was active in promoting a published version of *Adonais* and his early poems betray the influence everywhere. During the summer immediately preceding his arrival in Cambridge, however, it was Coleridge he was reading. Although his first reaction was to describe his work as 'strong meat' and to wonder whether it did not require a stronger stomach than his own, he was soon exploring it more fully,[27] stimulated no doubt by his new *ambience*, which was receptive to the new American influences. 'The ascendant politics are Utilitarian,' he wrote to Gladstone in November, 'seasoned with a plentiful sprinkling of heterogeneous Metaphysics. Indeed the latter study is so much the rage, that scarce anyone here above the herd does not dabble in Transcendentalism, and such like.'[28] By December he was asking his friend John Frere, a nephew of John Hookham Frere, Coleridge's friend, whether he could get from Coleridge clear definitions of 'Reason, Understanding, Imagination, as he understands the words'.[29] In the same letter he reported that his father had been attacking the ideas of Coleridge and Shelley, lamenting that while they were read, Locke and Bacon would not be. He himself was determined to work out his own metaphysical creed for himself, and could not share his father's condemnation of Coleridge (he had recently been trying to buy *The Friend*).

It was R. J. Tennant, apparently, followed by Hallam and Monckton Milnes, who introduced the Society to that side of Coleridge's thoughts that bordered on and sometimes seemed to pass over into mysticism. Tennant himself is unfortunately one of the least-documented of the Apostles.[30] Hallam, however (who was actually proposed for membership by Tennant), described him in December 1829 as 'the calm earnest seeker after Truth – who sat for months at the feet of Coleridge, and impowered his own mind with some of those tones, from the world of mystery, the only real world, of which to these latter days Coleridge has been almost the only interpreter'.[31] Two or three years later, Blakesley, telling a friend that he had been seeing old friends in London, reported: 'Tennyson had his sister with him, to whom Tennant was doing the amiable in a very open way for a mystic. She is really a very fine looking person, although of a wild sort of countenance, something like what Alfred would be if he were a woman and washed.'[32] This casual reference to him as a 'mystic' provides further evidence of the way that Tennant was regarded by his friends. Hallam had written the previous year that he was keeping his authorship of the pamphlet on Professor Rossetti's Dante theories a secret, having 'no wish to earn the reputation of an Atheist or a Mystic'.[33]

It may have been through the good offices of Frere and his uncle, or of Tennant, who had attended Christ's Hospital, Coleridge's school, and had been visiting him for two or three years past, that Hallam actually met Coleridge at this time. Monckton Milnes records that he and Hallam both went to call on him – to be received, he said, rather as they might have been by Goethe or Socrates, and to be told that as young men they ought to be going to America: 'I am known there,' said Coleridge. 'I am a poor poet in England, but I am a great philosopher in America.'[34]

Hallam had certainly met Coleridge, and probably more than once, by the spring of 1829, since it was then that he wrote a poem in competition for the Cambridge prize – which Tennyson in fact won – on the subject 'Timbuctoo'. In the course of it he pictured an ideal society and then continued with lines which he glossed in a footnote as follows:

These characters are of course purely ideal, and meant to show, by way of particular diagram, that right temperament of the intellect and the heart which I have assigned to this favored nation. I cannot, however, resist the pleasure of declaring, that in the composition of the lines 'Methought I saw,' &c., my thoughts dwelt almost involuntarily on those few conversations which it is my delight to have held with that 'good old man, most eloquent,' Samuel Coleridge.[35]

The lines in question run:

Methought I saw a face whose every line
    Wore the pale cast of Thought; a good old man,
    Most eloquent, who spake of things divine.
Around him youths were gathered, who did scan
    His countenance so grand and mild; and drank
    The sweet, sad tones of Wisdom, which outran
The life-blood, coursing to the heart, and sank
    Inward from thought to thought, till they abode
    'Mid Being's dim foundations, rank by rank
With those transcendent truths, arrayed by God
    In linked armor for untiring fight,
    Whose victory is, where time hath never trod.[36]

We have no further direct record of Coleridge's doctrines as heard by Hallam and Milnes, but it is not unlikely that in the course of his exposition he referred to Heraclitus as the Greek philosopher who, with his dualism, had come closest to the truth, since we know from other sources that this was a favourite theme of his in more esoteric moments.[37] When Monckton Milnes was set to write a Latin declamation in that same year, he chose for his theme (to the amusement of Julius Hare, his tutor) 'The Truth of the Essential Dualism of Heraclitus', commenting to his family, 'as this subject penetrates to the very foundations of Coleridgian philosophy it will give me some hard Fagging'.[38]

Hallam's mention of 'Being's dim foundations' suggests that he had seen further into Coleridge's larger purposes than had those who simply read his later published works. Coleridge's emphasis on the importance of Being was, however, always available to attentive readers. Maurice, in his 1842 dedication to *The Kingdom of Christ*, spoke of his debt to him for having made him aware that 'a knowledge of The Being is the object after which we are to strive'.[39] This version of Being seems for him to have been conceived in objective terms, truly to be discovered in the Supreme Being, but to be considered primarily in the light of more practical concerns. A young man such as Hallam, on the other hand, who had steeped himself in the poetry of Shelley, where the word 'being' is a favourite one to describe human personality, would be likely to respond to the Coleridgean hints that a further depth was involved, and that there was in human nature, if we looked devotedly, an inward being which actually corresponded to that of the divine.

A particular virtue of this approach for some was that it could be regarded as Christianising the thoughts of Shelley, whose more general idea of being was so extensive as to authorise an idea of the Supreme Being which might claim superiority to the Christian version. Coleridge's, by contrast, anchored the idea in the Christianity promulgated in St John's Gospel. The following of this line of thought had indeed enabled him to return to the Church in which he had been brought up.[40] In Carlyle's hostile and mordant phrasing, he had found himself able to 'say and print to the Church of England, with its singular old rubrics and surplices at Allhallowtide, *Esto perpetua*'.[41] For young men such as Hallam, on the other hand, whose delight in the new romanticism was combined with a respect for the faith of their fathers, Coleridge's thought pointed to a possible solution for current dilemmas.

The supposition that a process of this kind took place in Hallam's mind, grafting Coleridgean ideas of Being on Shelley's, seems necessary to account for the shape of his thinking during the subsequent period; it can also be supported by a number of his statements, including some apparent echoes from Coleridge himself. At the same time, his moods were volatile, alternating between depression and exaltation, with some fears of insanity. By the autumn of 1829 his father was deeply concerned, urging him to turn his mind from 'the high metaphysical speculations, and poetic enthusiasm that were sapping its very foundations'.[42]

There are signs nevertheless that Hallam continued to be interested in Coleridge's idea of Being. By the beginning of 1830 he had read his new book *On the Constitution of the Church and State*, which contains the statement ' . . . even the 'O 'ΩN, the Supreme Being, if it were contemplated abstractly from the Absolute *Will*, whose essence it is to be causative of *all* Being, would sink into a Spinozistic Deity'. The following year, in *Theodicaea Novissima*, he wrote of Christ, 'He is God, not in that highest sense in which the Absolute, the 'O'ΩN is God: but as the object of the Infinite Being's love.'[43] The term 'O'ΩN' for God comes from the Greek version of the Old Testament but was rare in Hallam's time; the version 'the 'O'ΩN', which with its double article is particularly Coleridgean, suggests that Hallam was still paying attention to what he had to say about the nature of Being.

There are two further apparent echoes from Coleridge, both of which, as it happens, resonate into Hallam's relationship with Tennyson. The first comes when Coleridge, in *Aids to Reflection*, is passing into one of his occasional gnomic passages, suggesting that there is further esoteric wisdom that he could divulge if he had a mind to. After a long discussion of the problem of Redemption, Coleridge argues that the causative act is 'a spiritual and transcendent Mystery, "that passeth all understanding"' and that to define it by analogy with ordinary human acts of redemption is to fall into error. He continues:

> I will merely hint, to my more *learned* readers, and to the professional Students of Theology, that the origin of this error is to be sought for in the discussions of the Greek Fathers, and (at a later period) of the Schoolmen, on the obscure and *abysmal* subject of the Divine A-*seity* and the distinction between the θηλημα and the βουλη, i.e. the absolute Will, as the universal Ground of *all* Being, and the Election and purpose of God in the personal Idea, as the Father. And this view would have allowed me to express (what I believe to be) the true import and scriptural idea of Re-

demption in terms much more nearly resembling those used ordi-
narily by the Calvinistic Divines, and with a conciliative *show* of
coincidence.[44]

Discussing the same question in the *Theodicaea*, Hallam writes,

> I believe that redemption is universal, in so far as it left no obs-
> tacle between Man and God, but man's own will: that indeed is in
> the power of God's election, with whom alone rest the abysmal
> secrets of personality, but as far as Christ is concerned, his death
> was for all. . . .[45]

Without going fully into the intricacies involved, we need simply
to look at the word 'abysmal', which is used in a similar sense to
Coleridge's in 'the *abysmal* subject of the Divine A-*seity*' – where his
italics suggest that he is at one and the same time being ironically
self-deprecating and intimating profundity. It links with other statements of Coleridge about the abyss-like nature of God, which suggest that when we are most aware of the abyss within ourselves, we
are in a state which may link us to the abyss within which God is to
be found. This particular correspondence between Hallam's point
and Coleridge's is all the more striking since, although the idea of
God as containing an abyss within himself which is also source of
the fountain of life can be found elsewhere in Christian theology,[46] it
is hard to find a writer other than Coleridge who uses the word
'abysmal' in this way. Hallam's phrase 'the abysmal secrets of personality' was used in an adapted form by Tennyson a few months
later in 'The Palace of Art', moreover, at the point where the soul, in
the middle of her triumphing, is suddenly struck down. Tennyson
continued,

> Lest she should fail and perish utterly,
>   God, before whom ever lie bare
> The abysmal deeps of Personality,
>   Plagued her with sore despair.
>   (R i, 453, ll. 221–4)

The point here seems to follow Coleridge's: in the very act of
sinking into the depths of despair the soul was delivered into the
abyss of her own personality – which, being linked to the abyss of
the divine, made redemption possible.

Tennyson was deeply impressed by *Theodicaea Novissima*: it was he who put to Hallam's father the case for including it among Hallam's *Remains*.[47] It is also clear that the philosophy of love which was expounded in it corresponded closely to the idea of noble love which he was to expound in *In Memoriam*. That philosophy is also to be found in other essays by Hallam such as those on Dante, to which Tennyson's debt has been explored by others.[48] The point to be made here has to do not with the idealisation of love, which is clear enough, but with the link between that idea of love and the idea of Being outlined above which, I have contended, comes primarily from Coleridge. In the *Theodicaea*, Hallam maintains that the passion of love is grounded on a conviction of similarity, 'as though we had suddenly found a bit of ourselves that had been dropt by mischance as we descended upon earth.'[49] This is Platonic and Shelleyan but it also raises the question whether there may be other respects in which the Being of a person could be said to be related to the Being of the divine. Hallam seems to have left this issue behind him after his Cambridge days, but there are signs that during that earlier period it went deep, while still remaining subject to his Apostolic scepticism. In April 1830, for instance, when he met Emily Tennyson at Somersby for the first time, he wrote to Blakesley, 'I feel a new element of being within me – don't laugh . . . '.[50]

There is a further cluster of references which may throw light on the origin of a phrase that was to become famous. Writing about the veil of the Law as discussed by St Paul, Coleridge asks, 'What was the great point of which this Law, in its own name, offered no solution? the mystery, which it left behind the veil?'[51] The mystery, he suggests, was that of redemption. The Bible itself does not use the phrase 'behind the veil' but 'within the veil'. When Hallam met Emily Tennyson and felt 'a new element of being', the experience can be connected with his use of Coleridge's version of the Pauline phrase in a poem dated by his editor in December 1829:

> Art thou not She
> Who in my Sais-temple was a light
> Behind all veils of thought, and fantasy,
> A dim, yet beautiful Idea of one
> Perfect in womanhood, in Love alone,
> Making the earth golden in hope and joy?[52]

Hallam's editor traces the image of the Sais-temple persuasively to a story by Schiller, where the temple contains a veiled statue of Truth which a young man is forbidden to lift. If that was Hallam's source, it would link almost inevitably with Shelley's 'Lift not the painted veil' and still more with the traditional figure of the veiled Isis. In his essay on Cicero he comments that his load of prepossessions was a disadvantage to him: they were 'as the veil of the temple of Sais, hiding impenetrably "that which was, and had been, and was to be"'[53] – a clear reference to Isis. The image which expressed most naturally his awakening love for Emily was, in other words, one that extended to the nature of being itself. Hallam's sudden death just before he could marry Emily cast a shadow of grim irony over this imagery for those who survived him. In *Maud* Tennyson wrote, 'For the drift of the Maker is dark, an Isis hid by the veil' (R ii, 531, I. iv. 144); and when he wrote in *In Memoriam* about the cruelty of Nature, with her apparent disregard for the transience of all life – whether individuals or types – and showing herself 'red in tooth and claw', his final question: 'What hope of answer, or redress?/Behind the veil, behind the veil' (R ii, 373–4; lvi, 15, 27–8) carries an added plangency if it is seen to involve Hallam's own use of the veiled goddess for a Shelleyan harmony at the core of the creation corresponding to his own feelings of love. Yet there is also a suggestion which the Coleridgean echo would reinforce – that there might in the depths of divine mystery be a purpose that escapes the eye of questioning human beings.

That this delicately-poised ambiguity should then have been transposed into one of the easiest of Victorian platitudes is one of the saddest ironies of Tennyson's career. The process may have begun with Edward FitzGerald's use of the phrase in *Omar Khayyám* (1859): 'When you and I behind the Veil are past'. By the end of the century, at all events, it had become a common phrase (whether as 'behind', 'within', or 'Beyond' the veil) to describe the process of death – which it had not been, apparently, when Tennyson wrote.

I am not suggesting that Hallam became a total devotee of the Coleridgean philosophy, but that he found some of the ideas in it – and notably those about 'Being's dim foundations' – deeply engaging in ways he could reasonably be expected to discuss later with Tennyson. Back in 1828–9, he had been in a volatile state, unsettled and subject to moods of despondency. It was natural that he should turn from the imponderables of Coleridge to the poetry of Wordsworth, who seemed to offer a more substantial philosophy. By September he was quoting to Gladstone lines from *The Excursion* which set the word 'Being' in a readily acceptable context:

> One adequate support
> For the calamities of mortal life
> Exists, one only; an assured belief,
> That the procession of our fate, howe'er
> Sad or disturbed, is ordered by a Being
> Of infinite Benevolence and Power,
> Whose everlasting purposes embrace
> All accidents, converting them to good.[54]

It had not always been so. Two years before he had been fined by the Eton Society for annotating one of Wordsworth's lines irreverently.[55] Now, in the summer of 1829, it was a source of grief to him that, in spite of expounding to her the manner in which Wordsworth was 'on all objects of our double nature, Inward and outward, shedding holier light', he could not convert his friend Anne Robertson to that philosophy.[56] His enthusiasm for the Romantic poets generally was running high during the following academic year, as when he accompanied some of the other Cambridge Apostles to Oxford in the hope of converting them to the ideas of Shelley. Sterling believed that they were wrong to promote this particular hero, writing disapprovingly: 'I believe he has in his time done many of us a good deal of harm. I scarcely hold fast by anything but Shakespeare, Milton and Coleridge and I have nothing to say to any one but to read the "Aids to Reflection in the formation of a *Manly* Character" – a book the more necessary now to us all because except in England I do not see that there is a chance of any *men* being produced any where.'[57]

Events were moving rapidly in these years, for a sense of crisis was in the air. Those Apostles who argued for the pursuit of true Being in the depths of human consciousness were likely to encounter the argument that this was a dangerously indolent occupation at a time when so many problems called for direct action. Those who proclaimed the gospel of Shelley, equally, might be met with claims for the more active Byron, and this indeed seems to be precisely what happened in a very direct fashion during the summer of 1830 when, as Kemble and Trench took up the cause of the Spanish exiles and went to Gibraltar, Tennyson and Hallam visited the Pyrenees, using the occasion apparently to convey to the rebels some money that had been subscribed for them. The return of Kemble and Trench after several months was followed by a calamitous conclusion at the end of 1831 when the exiles landed in Spain, fell immediately into an ambush and were executed.[58]

In England, meanwhile, social unrest was growing, along with the agitations that gave rise to the Reform Act. In Cambridge, Hallam was present in December 1830 when local rickburnings gave rise to highly-coloured fears that the town itself was due to be attacked.[59] His own writings several times contain phrases such as 'the times that are coming on us'[60] and his instincts were with those who thought that the new reforms would bring disaster. So far from developing further any of his metaphysical speculations, his concern was now to create a synthesis which would reconcile the new with the old. In a letter to Edward Moxon in July 1831, when the latter was taking over *The Englishman's Magazine*, he wrote of a plan entertained by some of his friends to start a periodical 'with the double purpose of maintaining Conservative principles in politics, and those of the New Poetical School in literature.'[61] (He was disappointed to learn that the *Review* was on the side of reform.) In a review of Tennyson's 1830 collection of poems for the same journal he sought to bring out his originality, maintaining that 'his thoughts bear no more resemblance to Byron or Scott, Shelley or Coleridge, than to Homer or Calderon, Ferdusi or Calidas'.[62] He was also increasingly wary about cultivation of personal affection and attempts to link it with the divine. A fortnight after his letter to Moxon he wrote to Monckton Milnes disclaiming that he had any friendship, in the more lofty sense of the word, for him, and by the following May was dissociating himself from Milnes's religious beliefs, claiming 'I believe the only transcendental Knowledge possible for man is to be deduced from the written Word of God.'[63]

Coleridge's ideas were not subject to such an interdict, however, since he had explicitly attempted to link them with 'the Word of God'. One which Hallam may well have picked up from his conversation was that, from the limited point of view possible to human perception, God acquired his Being through the son. In a letter of 1826 Coleridge had twice made this point with reference to a quotation from St John's Gospel in the original Greek describing the son as 'the being in the bosom of the father'.[64] This is close to the kind of discussion that Hallam initiates in *Theodicaea Novissima*.[65] In 1829, when he was hearing Coleridge speak, it would have been particularly timely, enabling him to turn to account, by universalising, the love that he had felt for Anna Wintour; his despair at the loss of her thus opened the way both for further love and for his devotion to Dante. When Tennyson opened *In Memoriam* with the line 'Strong

Son of God, immortal Love . . . ' and added the laconic note 'This might be taken in a St John sense' (R ii, 315 and note), that may well have been what he had in mind, particularly when one recalls that the next lines, 'Whom we, that have not seen thy face,/By faith, and faith alone, embrace . . . ' could also be associated with the same verse of St John – which reads in full, 'No man hath seen God at any time; the only begotten Son, which is in the bosom of the Father, he hath declared him'.[66] The theology of *In Memoriam* may, in other words, be a little more fully and intricately thought-out than it is sometimes taken to be.

In Memoriam is not primarily a theological poem, however, nor was it for theological ideas that Tennyson primarily remembered Hallam. When the Apostles discussed the question of Being, similarly, not all of them were thinking in Christian terms. What was likely to be exciting about the idea was that it offered them a more profound way of approaching their own experiences as human beings, suggesting that in heightened states of love, and even of suffering, they were initiated into an order of reality which made better sense of their experience as a whole than did doctrines such as those of utilitarianism, based on a straightforward rationalist interpretation of common human experience. Such a view was as appealing to Monckton Milnes, whose cultivation of high sentiment led in the direction of homoerotic attachments, as it was to Hallam, with his attempts to reawaken ideas of Christian nobility.

For Tennyson such discussions must have struck further chords. There were elements in his personality that were particularly open to the idea that human experience could not be limited to the 'commonsense' evaluation of the everyday, since from an early age he had been familiar with states of mind in which his ordinary consciousness was overtaken by an impersonal state of vision. The best-known account is the one that appears in his son's *Memoir*, where he recalls

a kind of 'waking trance' (this for lack of a better word) I have frequently had quite up from boyhood when I have been all alone. This has often come upon me through repeating my own name to myself silently, till all at once as it were out of the intensity of the consciousness of individuality the individuality itself seemed to dissolve & fade away into boundless being – & this not a confused state but the clearest of the clearest, the surest of the surest, utterly beyond words – where Death was an almost laughable impossibility – the loss of personality (if so it were) seeming no extinction but the only true life.[67]

Robert Bernard Martin quotes another statement of Tennyson's in which he felt himself to be the only thing alive in a dead world: 'through excess of realising my own personality I seemed to get outside of myself.'[68] As Martin comments, these trances could be terrible as well as joyful: if they were ecstatic they were so in the strictest sense of the word. Yet they were at least fulfilling Coleridge's desire of reconciling personality with infinity.

The poetry suggests that his more trance-like moments had a twofold quality. On the one hand he seems to experience the sense of Being centrally as a sense of flowing, like the flowing of a stream. There may also be in this the suggestion of a correspondence between the flowing of the human blood-stream and the flowing of streams in the world that one notices also in the linking language and imagery of Wordsworth's 'Tintern Abbey'.[69] The other is a sense of pulsing – again as if the beating of the human heart might be related to some basic rhythm in the universe at large. Tennyson's interest in flowing things is too obvious to need illustration; his sense of pulsings emerges as early as in the adolescent poem 'Armageddon', where first he records,

> I held
> My breath and heard the beatings of my heart

and then at the end of the poem, after the vision of the Angel Mind, concludes,

> There was a beating in the atmosphere,
> An indefinable pulsation
> Inaudible to outward sense, but felt
> Through the deep heart of every living thing,
> As if the great soul of the Universe
> Heaved with tumultuous throbbings on the vast
> Suspense of some grand issue.
> (R i, 79, 85; i, 112–13, iv, 28–34)

As Christopher Ricks has pointed out, this image is picked up, though apparently in a quite different mode, in the lines 'An Idle

Rhyme', where Tennyson forswears discussion of literary fashions in favour of a more blissful and indolent state reminiscent of some moods of Keats,

> As stretched beside the river clear,
> That's round this glassy foreland curled,
> I cool my face in flowers, and hear
> The deep pulsations of the world.
> (R ii, 92, ll. 37–40)

Against this sense of inner being as pulsing and flowing, wheels and wheeling are a more ambiguous phenomenon. The wheeling of the planets can be a sublime conception, but it may also be an intimation of necessity, linking with the idea of the Wheel of Fortune and producing no more than a depressed sense of what Blake called 'the ratio of all things', repeating 'the same dull round'.[70] One can find simple examples of the contrast involved in 'Locksley Hall', where the hero's reason for asking his cousin to trust him is that 'all the current of my being sets to thee' whereas his imagery of rejection takes the form 'Let the great world spin for ever down the ringing grooves of change' and 'Better fifty years of Europe than a cycle of Cathay' (R ii, 121, 130, ll. 24, 182, 184).

The early emergence of such images into Tennyson's poetry, and the weight he gave to them, makes it likely, to say the least, that if he heard his friends discussing the idea of Being as displaying a correspondence between the profundity of the divine and the 'abysmal secrets of personality', or heard them expounding a Heraclitean dualism which suggested a fluency at the heart of things, such discussions made contact with the strange states of mind he had known when personality passed into impersonal vision, and with the sense of the abysmal, or of pulsing, or of flowing that he found characteristic of such states.

It is also possible that a more roundabout connection with Coleridge's poetry is involved: for whatever the latter may have been saying about the nature of Being at the time when Hallam heard him discoursing, he had been investigating the question in a more radical and free-ranging fashion thirty years before when he wrote the poem which Tennyson valued so much, *The Ancient Mariner*. A debate at the Union late in 1828 on the subject 'Will Mr Coleridge's poem of the Ancient Mariner or Mr Martin's acts, be most effectual in preventing Cruelty to Animals?' was opened,

according to Milnes, by some 'very deep poetical criticism' from
R. J. Tennant[71] – who, as Hallam reported, had been imbibing
Coleridge's doctrines from the man himself. It is hard to see how
debate on the poem could proceed very far without its being seen to
involve questions which went far beyond that of 'cruelty to animals'
in the simple sense.

It must still be borne in mind, however, that while Tennant may
have been expounding a mysticism based on what he had heard
from Coleridge, the debates of the Apostles were characterised by
that interplay of earnestness with light scepticism that was to remain
their most lasting characteristic; and this too comes across in
Tennyson's writing of the time.

One rarely has the chance to see the collection that Tennyson
published in 1830, *Poems, Chiefly Lyrical*, in its original form, and
many of the poems in it were subsequently dropped from later
collections, but when they are read together they are not only seen to
contain some of the ideas outlined above, but to approach them with
varying degrees of seriousness. In the poem 'A Character' (R i,
239–40), for example, Tennyson depicts in adverse terms the character of one of the Apostles, Thomas Sunderland, who was acknowledged to be one of their most brilliant orators but who seemed to
Tennyson and others to lack the true Apostolic spirit of fellowship.
Worse, he had taken over the doctrines of Wordsworth only to make
them a vehicle for his own separatist philosophy. Monckton Milnes
and Blakesley complained of his zest for 'perfect solitude' and for
'direct contemplation of the absolute'.[72] Tennyson put it more bru-
tally: whenever his character discoursed on the life in dead things or
similar Wordsworthian therapy he was 'looking as 'twere in a glass':

> With lips depressed as he were meek,
> Himself unto himself he sold:
> Upon himself himself did feed:
> Quiet, dispassionate, and cold,
> And other than his form of creed,
> With chiselled features clear and sleek.
>   (R i, 240, ll. 25–30)

At the other extreme, an outreaching to embrace all existence could,
for all its attractiveness, seem damagingly vague. In a poem 'The
Idealist' (R i, 187), not published but written into manuscripts for his
friends Allen and Heath, the identification of the philosopher with

the whole of existence is rehearsed ('I am the earth, the stars, the sun,/I am the clouds, the sea') with the conclusion, 'I am all things save souls of fellow men and very God!' The irony that seems to lurk here is akin to that of Jack Kemble who was heard to remark during a meeting of the Apostles that the universe was one thought, and he was thinking it.[73] More acutely, the 1830 collection contains a poem entitled in Greek 'Hoi Reontes' ('the flowing ones' : R i, 281), which is about the Heraclitean philosophers and their belief that everything existed in a state of flux. Its refrain is 'For all things are as they seem to all,/And all things flow like a stream'; it also contains the lines 'All men do walk in sleep, and all/Have faith in that they dream'. The pay-off comes in the comment that follows the poem: 'Argal – this very opinion is only true relatively to the flowing philosophers'. The poem gains force from this element of mockery and its hint of possible self-criticism. Tennyson is intensely drawn to things that flow and to the question of movement through time, just as he is to dreams and their relation to reality, yet he is also fully aware that this kind of speculation, if given a free rein, would be likely to end in a total relativism, far from the rock-like certainty that he, like his contemporaries, wants to find. He cannot, nevertheless, renounce his interest in flowing, or in the compulsive power of dreams at their most intense, as he shows in another, less sceptical poem of the time entitled 'The Mystic', describing human vision and its power to impress images of eternity against the transience of human experience. This includes the lines:

> He often lying broad awake, and yet
> Remaining from the body, and apart
> In intellect and power and will, hath heard
> Time flowing in the middle of the night,
> And all things creeping to a day of doom.
> (R i, 253, ll. 36–9)

Other poems in the collection such as the pair 'Nothing Will Die' and 'All Things Will Die' (R i, 247–8, 249–50) are written more lightly, in the tradition of rhetorical antithesis, putting the case for and against the idea as seen within the order of time.

Poems such as these, along with the 'Supposed Confessions of a Second-rate Sensitive Mind Not in Unity With Itself' (R i, 216–22), show Tennyson in tune with the current state of mind of the Apostles in 1829 to 1830; the cut-and-thrust of argument, including

light-hearted banter, as sustained by the majority of them, is shot
through by the vein of metaphysical questioning introduced by
Tennant and Hallam, which had sometimes spoken very directly to
him when what was being referred to seemed to correspond with
and even to explain abnormal experiences of his own.

The fact that Hallam not only shared his speculations, but in his
own personality seemed to provide an actual example of noble being, opened the issues out into a further dimension, however, which
sometimes thrust scepticism into the background. Watching him
work through his own doubts and evolve his own philosophy,
Tennyson found his own world making sense in a new way. His
most vivid account of the process was inspired by standing outside
a room in Trinity College and listening to the noise of glasses being
smashed at a rowdy party. This aroused the memory of a very
different society (almost certainly the Apostles, where much tobacco
was smoked but no wine was taken) and of Hallam in action in that
same room.

> Where once we held debate, a band
>   Of youthful friends, on mind and art,
>   And labour, and the changing mart,
> And all the framework of the land;
>
> When one would aim an arrow fair,
>   But send it slackly from the string;
>   And one would pierce an outer ring,
> And one an inner, here and there;
>
> And last the master-bowman, he,
>   Would cleave the mark. A willing ear
>   We lent him. Who, but hung to hear
> The rapt oration flowing free
>
> From point to point, with power and grace
>   And music in the bounds of law,
>   To those conclusions when we saw
> The God within him light his face,
>
> And seem to lift the form, and glow
>   In azure orbits heavenly-wise;
>   And over those ethereal eyes
> The bar of Michael Angelo.[74]

The idea of the God within him lighting his face involves the constant Romantic preoccupation with genius, inspiration and illumination, from Edward Young's assertion in his *Conjectures on Original Composition*, that 'Genius is that God within'[75] onwards. It also conveys Tennyson's sense that there were times when, in the full energy of discussion, Hallam seemed transported to another dimension of being, more akin to direct inspiration. And there are signs that this sense was one which was sustained among the Apostles: that it was not just the cut-and-thrust of candid debate that they valued, or the openness of friendship, or the sense of brotherliness that sprang up among them, but that sometimes in the height of discussion they felt themselves to be in the grip of a transcendent experience.

The doctrine of Being could issue in many forms of behaviour, acting at one extreme as a possible defence of Christianity, at the other as a more general energising power in poetry. It was of the nature of such Being that it might be revealed most readily in suffering. 'I have suffered such an extinction of Light in my mind', wrote Coleridge on one occasion, 'I have been so forsaken by all the *forms* and *colourings* of Existence, as if the *organs* of Life had been dried up; as if only simple Being remained, blind and stagnant!'[76] In some of the most haunting lines of *In Memoriam* Tennyson used a simpler, if differing, image to describe his more depressive moods. Section 1 originally opened:

> Be near me when the pulse is low,
>   When the blood creeps, and the nerves prick
>   And tingle; and the heart is sick,
> And all the wheels of Being slow.[77]

He then revised the imagery to take in the image of light which Coleridge also had used, so that the opening line read 'Be with me when my light is low'; this expanded the conception, setting up a link with the sign of hope given at the end of the section by the returning light of the physical world:

> on the low dark verge of life
> The twilight of eternal day.

In these verses Tennyson's sense of Being, closely related as we have seen to pulsations and a sense of flowing, with wheeling and cycling as a more ambiguous form of movement, opens out into that ima-

gery of glimmering or glowing light that is his most constant re-
source.

The last word to be introduced into this cluster is one that may or
may not come directly from Coleridge and Hallam but is closely
associated with the range of preoccupations we have been discussing. This word, 'Aeonian', with its suggestion of an element which is
beyond or out of time, comprehending time and even cancelling
consciousness of its workings at the height of its operation, answers
to a common Romantic theme most fully evident in Wordsworth's
Prelude. De Quincey writes of the statue of Memnon in the British
Museum as 'that sublime head which wears upon its lips a smile co-
extensive with all time and space, an Aeonian smile of gracious love
and Panlike mystery . . . '.[78] He says elsewhere that the same statue,
when he first saw it, struck him as the sublimest sight he had ever
seen, symbolic of 'the eternity which baffles all faculty of computa-
tion; the eternity which *had* been, the eternity which was to be . . . '
and as 'an emanation from some mystery of endless dawn'.[79] George
Macdonald, also, uses the word later in his supernatural writings.[80]
It may have been Coleridge who gave De Quincey this sense of the
word; certainly its conjunction with an imagery of light is very
Coleridgean. Where the idea of Being is used in conjunction both
with the word 'Æonian' and with an imagery of light one should be
alert to the possibility that a Coleridgean complex of ideas is at work,
therefore.

Tennyson's invocation of a similar cluster of images comes at one
of the crucial moments of *In Memoriam*, when he is rereading some of
Hallam's former letters:

> A hunger seized my heart; I read
>   Of that glad year which once had been,
>   In those fallen leaves which kept their green,
> The noble letters of the dead:
>
> And strangely on the silence broke
>   The silent-speaking words, and strange
>   Was love's dumb cry defying change
> To test his worth; and strangely spoke
>
> The faith, the vigour, bold to dwell
>   On doubts that drive the coward back,
>   And keen through wordy snares to track
> Suggestion to her inmost cell.

So word by word, and line by line,
    The dead man touched me from the past,
    And all at once it seemed at last
His living soul was flashed on mine,

And mine in his was wound, and whirled
    About empyreal heights of thought,
    And came on that which is, and caught
The deep pulsations of the world,

Æonian music measuring out
    The steps of Time – the shocks of Chance –
    The blows of Death. At length my trance
Was cancelled, stricken through with doubt.[81]

In one sense this is the climax to Tennyson's remembrance of Hallam in the poem. He later changed 'His living soul' to 'The Living soul' and 'mine in his' to 'mine in this', saying that the first reading troubled him as perhaps giving a wrong impression (R ii, 413n); but he had let it stand for twenty years and it is clear that that, in his own terms, is what he meant. On the other hand, the visionary experience could not last. When the trance was 'cancelled, stricken through with doubt', all that was left, as before, was the external illumination of the dawn to act as mediator between internal and external. In the same way he could rest with the more down-to-earth reflection 'I felt and feel, though left alone,/His being working in mine own,/The footsteps of his life in mine'.[82] There was also hope of a more conventional kind for the future in the promise of a new-born child to renew the pattern of nobility: 'A soul shall draw from out the vast/And strike his being into bounds' (R ii, 457; Conclusion, ll. 123–4). But while the concluding statements of the poem are formulated to meet the gaze of its more sceptical readers, the subterranean work of the poem continues through rhythms of pulsing and flowing. The movement of *In Memoriam* as a whole is that of a great eddying stream. Even the separation into short sections, each self-contained, is countered by the distinctive rhyme-scheme, in which the insistent falling-back upon the opening rhyme in each verse creates a continuous but unobtrusive eddying motion throughout the section and beyond.

A simple eddying motion would not be enough to achieve the full effect that Tennyson needs at the conclusion of his poem. As he reaches it a strong and insistent pulsation rises in the final stanzas to

suggest portentousness and even apocalypse: the last eleven stanzas
progress in fact without a single full stop, culminating in the lines

> Whereof the man, that with me trod
>   This planet, was a noble type
>   Appearing ere the times were ripe,
> That friend of mine who lives in God,
>
> That God, which ever lives and loves,
>   One God, one law, one element,
>   And one far-off divine event,
> To which the whole creation moves.

Tennyson may well have felt that in writing *In Memoriam* he had
done all he could in trying to reconcile the contradictory tides of his
own personality and that from now on he must find other modes of
expressing himself. It is only occasionally in his later writing that
one finds his speculations coming to any kind of overt statement,
even if flowings and pulsations continue to provide some of his most
characteristic effects. In the second half of the nineteenth century the
idea that it might be possible to solve the universe in a manner that
reconciled science with traditional morality recoiled under the blows
of Darwinism in its various forms. There are occasional poems in
which Tennyson revives the task of mediation, however, usually in
an oblique manner. The three most notable, 'The Ancient Sage',
'Akbar's Dream' and 'De Profundis' (R iii, 67, 138, 235) have associations with Benjamin Jowett, who had long been encouraging him to
write a visionary poem on the theme that 'All Religions are One'.[83]

Both 'The Ancient Sage' and 'Akbar's Dream' transfer the discussion of Tennyson's unusual trance-experiences to the Far East, where
the traditional experiences of great sages allow for their inclusion.
'De Profundis', on the other hand, written on the birth of Hallam
Tennyson, draws on the English tradition more directly. The imagery of flowing follows that of Wordsworth's Immortality Ode,
human life being seen as like a stream that draws out of the deep to
return eventually to it. In this poem Tennyson is again wrestling
explicitly with Coleridge's problem of reconciling personality with
infinity as he describes

                    the pain
Of this divisible-indivisible world
Among the numerable-innumerable
Sun, sun, and sun, through finite-infinite space
In finite-infinite Time – our mortal veil
And shattered phantom of that infinite One
                    (R iii, 69, ll. 42–7)

– lines which, although subtle and precise in thought, are hardly likely to be remembered as great poetry.

The Apostles, meanwhile, continued to meet, keeping alive their traditions with extraordinary consistency. It was not until the first years of this century that the temper of the society began to shift towards that of Bloomsbury. The word now used by them most frequently, meanwhile, was not 'Being' but 'Reality'. Sidgwick, for instance, recalls: 'it came to seem to me that no part of my life at Cambridge was so real to me as the Saturday evenings on which the apostolic debates were held';[84] Forster, similarly, who was a member at the turn of the century, dedicated his novel *The Longest Journey* to them ('Fratribus') and tried to convey something of the apostolic spirit in his opening chapter; the question of Reality is central both to this scene and to the novel as a whole.[85] The word 'being' did not vanish altogether from view. Virginia Woolf, for instance, whose brother Thoby had known some of the Apostles, found some of them insufferable but honoured their spirit at its best, as when she writes in her autobiographical fragments of experiences which she calls 'moments of being'.[86]

The most striking evidence of such continuity comes in the surviving typescript of a speech which Donald MacAlister, who had been elected in 1876, made at the Apostles dinner in 1908, when he rose to propose the toast of those who could not be present. Absent members, he declared, would still turn fondly to the 'hearth-rug' which was the symbolic locus of the members' weekly meetings, for it was there that each member

learned to contemplate pure being. . . . There with eyes undimmed, even by tobacco smoke, he beheld the vision of absolute truth. . . . There he mastered the art of reconciling by a phrase the most divergent of hypotheses, the most fundamentally antagonistic of antinomies. There he grew accustomed to differ from his comrades in nothing but opinion. There, upborne by the ethereal atmosphere of free and audacious enquiry, he mewed his budding wings, and discovered to his delight that, towards midnight on Saturday, he too could soar. Others might find the medium but a vacuum. . . . But he was no chimaera, for he felt his reality and knew that he was alive.[87]

At the end of the section of *Idylls of the King* entitled 'The Holy Grail', it will be recalled, King Arthur deplores the waste of effort by some of his knights in going off after the grail when they might have been doing more practical things. Although man's duty is to undertake direct and mundane tasks during the day, however, things are different by night:

> ' . . . the King must guard
> That which he rules, and is but as the hind
> To whom a space of land is given to plow.
> Who may not wander from the allotted field,
> Before his work be done; but, being done,
> Let visions of the night or of the day
> Come, as they will; and many a time they come,
> Until this earth he walks on seems not earth,
> This light that strikes his eyeball is not light,
> This air that smites his forehead is not air
> But vision – yea, his very hand and foot –
> In moments when he feels he cannot die,
> And knows himself no vision to himself,
> Nor the high God a vision, nor that One
> Who rose again: ye have seen what ye have seen.'
> (R iii, 490, ll 901–15)

'So spake the King', concludes the narrator, with Browningesque meaningfulness; 'I knew not all he meant.' By the end of the nineteenth-century the intervention of Darwinian theories had undermined hopes that a firm rock for faith might be found by seeking the ground of Being within human consciousness and the Apostles were beginning to turn away from metaphysics altogether. The evidence of McAlister's speech, however, is that even in 1908 they would have recognised a language that was far from unfamiliar.

Notes

1. Coleridge, *Biographia Literaria*, ed. J. Engell and W. J. Bate, *Collected Coleridge* 4 (London and Princeton, NJ, 1983), Ch. X, i, 200.
2. W. Allingham, *Diary*, quoted *Tennyson: Interviews and Recollections*, ed. N. Page (1983), p. 150.
3. Peter Allen, *The Cambridge Apostles: The Early Years* (Cambridge, 1978), hereafter *Allen*; Paul Levy, *Moore: G. E. Moore and the Cambridge Apostles* (Oxford, 1979); Joyce Green, 'The Development of the Poetic Imagination in Tennyson, with particular reference to the Juvenilia and to the influence of Arthur Hallam', unpublished PhD thesis (1954) in Cambridge University Library. Richard Deacon's *The Cambridge Apostles* (1985), although a more coarse-grained account, contains some useful information not otherwise available and includes a glossary of Apostolic terminology. Frances Brookfield, *The Cambridge Apostles* (1906) may also be consulted.
4. Paul Levy, op. cit., quoting *Letters of Roger Fry*, ed. D. Sutton (1972), i, 108.
5. Marginal note by Kemble in a copy of Connop Thirlwall, *Letter to the Rev. Thomas Turton*, (1834) now in the London Library, quoted *Allen*, p. 8.
6. *Allen*, p. 8, quoting Arthur Helps, *Realmah* (1868), Ch. 12.
7. *Allen*, p. 6, quoting A. and E. M. Sidgwick, *Henry Sidgwick: A Memoir* (1906), pp. 34–5.
8. James Pope-Hennessy, *Monckton Milnes: The Years of Promise, 1809–1851* (1949), p. 17, quoting such expressions of romantic affection as 'Sir Jacob and I are inseparable, he is one of the dearest creatures I have ever seen. You would I am sure approve of our friendship, it is so unlike the routine of Cambridge arm-in-arms'; 'Garden and Monteith have not cooled at all' and 'Cavendish's brother is a charming creature and so well fitted for Fitzroy.' On Fitzroy's departure from Trinity in 1831, several of his friends were so affected that they burst into tears. See *Unquiet Heart*, p. 95, for further instances.
9. See *The Writings of Arthur Henry Hallam*, ed. T. H. Vail Motter (New York and London, 1943), hereafter *Hallam Writings*, Preface, pp. v–vii and Appendix B, pp. 317–21.
10. See Christopher Ricks's headnote to *In Memoriam*, R ii, 313–14, and refs.
11. *Allen*, pp. 1, 38, 143, and cf. F. Brookfield, op. cit., p. 10. The 'Ark' refers, of course, to the biblical ark of the covenant in which the tables of the law and other sacred relics were kept. (See Exodus 16, etc. and Hebrews 9: 4.)
12. R. Deacon, op. cit., p. 6; cf F. Brookfield, op. cit., p. 6.
13. Ibid. Deacon states that 'illumers' appears to have gone out of circulation after the 1840s. It is no doubt cognate with the favourite word 'illuminati' of the period. After the visit to Oxford the Apostles reported the Oxonians to be 'a very wise gentlemanly set, about a hundred years behind the iluminati' (Wyndham Farr, letter to Gladstone, 1 January 1830, quoted Joyce Green, op. cit., p. 217).

14. Ibid.; *Allen*, pp. 3, 8. McTaggart, a later nineteenth-century member, reported on one occasion that a fellow-Apostle had 'taken unto himself a phenomenal wife'. See R. Deacon, op. cit., p. 6.

15. See, for example, letters in 1829–30 concerning both his son Derwent and Shelley: Coleridge, *Collected Letters*, ed. E. L. Griggs (Oxford, 1956–71), pp. vi, 797, 849.

16. *Allen*, p. 81.

17. *Paradise Lost*, ii, 147, iii, 374.

18. Coleridge, *Collected Letters*, ed. cit., i, 397.

19. Wordsworth, 'It is a beauteous evening . . . ' l.6; 'Ode: Intimations of Immortality . . . ' ll. 125–6. At first, and up to 1815, the words 'Of heaven-born Freedom,' read 'Of untamed pleasures,'. I hope to take the discussion of Wordsworth further in a later study.

20. Coleridge, *Biographia Literaria*, op. cit., Ch. XIII, i, 304.

21. Sir John Frederick Maurice, *Life of F. D. Maurice* (1884), i, 165; 'To the Rev. F. D. Maurice', R ii, 497–500.

22. Carlyle, *Life of John Sterling* (1851), Ch. VIII, p. 72.

23. John Sterling, Preface to *Essays and Tales* (1848), i, xxv. Sterling goes on to declare Coleridge's conversation superior to Johnson's.

24. *The London Magazine*, as cited in *Athenaeum*, 3 September 1828, pp. 716–17.

25. R. C. Trench, *Letters and Memorials* (1888), i, 10, cited Joyce Green, op. cit., p. 182.

26. *Athenaeum*, 30 April 1828, p. 423. Coleridge's name was spelt out when this was reprinted in Sterling's *Essays and Tales* (1848), ii, 9.

27. Letter to W. E. Gladstone, 26 August 1828: *Letters*, ed. J. Kolb (Columbus, Ohio, 1981), p. 233 (hereafter *Hallam Letters*).

28. Joyce Green, op. cit., p. 134.

29. Letter to J. Frere, 23 December 1828, ibid., pp. 260–1.

30. A brief account may be found in *Hallam Letters*, pp. 346–7. Tennant married and went as English Chaplain to Florence, where he died of consumption in 1842.

31. Letter to Gladstone, 8 November 1828, *Hallam Letters*, p. 244.

32. *Allen*, p. 152, citing letter from J. W. Blakesley to W. H. Thompson, 16 April 1833, Blakesley MSS, Trinity College, Cambridge.

33. Letter to Jack Kemble, 18 October 1832, *Hallam Letters*, p. 667.

34. T. W. Reid, *The Life, Letters and Friendships of Richard Monckton Milnes*, (1890), ii, 432.

35. *Hallam Writings*, pp. 42–3.

36. Lines 160–71, *ibid.*

37. See his half-ironic self-description as 'Heraclitus redivivus' in a letter of September 1817, *Collected Letters*, ed. cit., iv, 775, and flattering references elsewhere.

38. *Allen*, p. 49, citing a letter to his father (pmk 19 February 1829) in the Houghton MSS at Trinity College, Cambridge.

39. F. D. Maurice, *The Kingdom of Christ* (2nd edn, 1842), Dedication, p. xxiv.

40. In 1827 Coleridge took communion for the first time since his first year in Cambridge: see his MS notebook 36 ff. 32v–33, quoted J. R. Barth, *Coleridge and Christian Doctrine* (Cambridge, Mass., 1969), pp. 178–9nn.

41. *Life of Sterling* (1851), Ch. VIII, p. 69.
42. See his letters to Milnes of 21 July and 1 September 1829, *Hallam Letters*, pp. 301, 312.
43. *On the Constitution of the Church and State (Collected Coleridge* 10), ed. J. Colmer (Princeton, NJ and London, 1976), p. 182; *Hallam Writings*, p. 204.
44. *Aids to Reflection* (1825), p. 328. (The spelling 'θηλημα' is as printed.)
45. *Hallam Writings*, pp. 210–11.
46. See, e.g. William Beveridge, *Exposition of the XXXIX Articles of the Church of England* (1710), p. 2.
47. *Hallam Writings*, p. 199.
48. *Ibid.*, pp. 213–79 passim; see also, for instance, P. J. Toynbee, *Dante in English Literature* (1909), ii, 416–24.
49. *Hallam Writings*, p. 203.
50. *Hallam Letters*, p. 360.
51. Coleridge, *Aids to Reflection* (1825), pp. 352–3.
52. 'How is't for every glance of thine . . .?' *Hallam Writings*, p. 83.
53. Ibid., p. 154.
54. *Excursion*, iv, 10–17; *Hallam Letters*, 317–18.
55. He had been fined at the Eton Society on 19 May 1827 for annotating the line from 'Ruth', 'The breezes their own languor lent' with the words 'By Jove they did! at three per cent!!!' See H. N. Coleridge in *The Etonian* i, 103, cited *Hallam Letters*, p. 303n.
56. See 'Wordsworth at Glenarbach', ll. 73–9, *Hallam Writings*, p. 72 and letter to Milnes, 21 July 1829, *Hallam Letters*, p. 301.
57. Letter to Blakesley, 25 November 1829, Blakesley MSS, loc. cit., cited *Allen*, pp. 90–1.
58. For accounts of the enterprise and its failure, see Carlyle, *Life of Sterling* (1851), Chapters IX–XIII, and *Allen*, Chapter VII.
59. *Hallam Letters*, pp. 387–91.
60. See, e.g. letter to W. B. Donne, 29 January 1832, *Hallam Letters*, p. 512, and 'The influence of Italian upon English Literature' (1831–2), *Hallam Writings*, p. 233.
61. *Hallam Letters*, p. 438.
62. *Tennyson: The Critical Heritage*, ed. J. D. Jump (1967), p. 42.
63. *Hallam Letters*, pp. 453, 570.
64. See his letters to Derwent Coleridge and to Edward Coleridge of 11 January and 27 July 1826, *Collected Letters*, ed. cit., vi, 537, 600. The latter was worked up as an appendix to *On the Constitution of the Church and State* (1829) and so directly available to contemporary readers.
65. See above, p. 13.
66. St John, i. 18. Tennyson's immediate turning to the will ('Our wills are ours, we know not how,/Our wills are ours, to make them thine'), which is later echoed in the opening to the last-but-one section, 'O living will that shall endure . . . ', squares interestingly with a similar movement of mind in Coleridge (see, for example, *Aids to Reflection* (1825), pp. 67–71, 131–9; given the centrality of the will in Christian doctrine, however, this may well be coincidence).

67. Letter to B. P. Blood, 7 May 1874, Houghton Library, quoted *Unquiet Heart*, pp. 28–9.

68. *Unquiet Heart*, p. 84, quoting a record of Tennyson's conversation from an unpublished notebook of Audrey Tennyson's in the Tennyson Research Centre.

69. See my *Wordsworth and the Human Heart* (1978), esp. pp. 71–8.

70. Blake, 'There is No Natural Religion', ('1st series') (c. 1788), *Writings*, ed. G. Keynes (1957), p. 97.

71. Milnes, letter to his father, pmk 19 February 1829, Houghton MSS, cited *Allen*, pp. 47–8. He also states that Blakesley 'gave a most eloquent commentary' on the poem.

72. See Joyce Green, op. cit., p. 160, citing Milnes, letter to his father 13 March 1830, T. W. Reid, *Richard Monckton Milnes* (1890) i, 92; R. C. Trench, letter to Blakesley, 24 January 1830, *Letters and Memorials* (1888), i, 50.

73. This anecdote is given, without source, both in *Alfred Tennyson*, p. 70, and *Unquiet Heart*, p. 116.

74. R ii, 403–4; *In Memoriam*, lxxxvii, 21–40. Ricks (ii, 404n) draws attention to a striking parallel in the 'bar, ridge-like, above the eyebrows' of the truly wise in Coleridge's 'Allegoric Vision', printed in his 1817 *Lay Sermon* (ed. R. J. White, *Collected Coleridge 6* (London and Princeton, NJ, 1972), p. 135), and included in his *Poetical Works* from 1829 onwards.

75. Edward Young, *Conjectures on Original Composition* (1759), pp. 30–1. In Young's formulation, 'Genius' was judiciously balanced against 'Conscience', but the exuberance of his imagery for genius was likely to point readers further in that direction. The book was immediately translated in Germany and widely influential there.

76. Coleridge, *Collected Letters*, ed. cit., i, 470.

77. R ii, 366–7; l, 1–4. Ricks notes a parallel to the mood of a 'Meditative Fragment' of Hallam's, *Hallam Works*, pp. 73–4, and Shelleyan uses of 'prick and tingle' (with 'sickness') and of 'wheels of being': cf. *The Cenci*, IV i 163–5, and *Queen Mab*, ix, 151–2 (noted by J. D. Jump). Tennyson is transferring to a torpid mood what is hectic in Shelley, however.

78. De Quincey, 'The Affliction of Childhood', *Collected Writings*, ed. D. Masson (Edinburgh, 1889–90), i, 41n. The importance of the word for him emerges in the fact that he devoted an entire essay to it, 'On the Supposed Scriptural Expression for Eternity': *De Quincey and his Friends*, ed. J. Hogg (1895), pp. 295–313.

79. De Quincey, 'System of the Heavens', *Collected Writings*, ed. cit., viii, 17.

80. See, for instance, his *Poems* (1867), p. 109: 'Heaven's aeonian day'.

81. R ii, 412–13; xcv, 21–44 (1850–70 text here cited). Tennyson's other use of the word in *In Memoriam* is in sect. xxxv, 10–11: 'The sound of streams that swift or slow/Draw down Æonian hills . . . ', where any sense of 'Æonian music' comes rather from the 'moanings of the homeless sea' and the sound of the streams rather than from the erosion of the hills themselves.

82. R ii, 399; lxxxv, 42–4. The term 'Footsteps', at one time Apostolic slang for those who had made their way in the world (see R. Deacon, op. cit., p. 7), may have left a distant echo here in the wake of 'being'.
83. See Ricks's headnotes to each poem and *Mem*, ii, 372.
84. A. and E. M. Sidgwick, *Henry Sidgwick: A Memoir* (1906), cited *Allen*, p. 9.
85. See my discussion in *The Achievement of E. M. Forster* (1962), pp. 77–83. When I wrote this I had not seen its relationship to Apostolic thinking.
86. See her account in *Virginia Woolf: Moments of Being. Unpublished Autobiographical Writings of Virginia Woolf*, ed. J. Schulkind (1976), esp. pp. 70–9. This may profitably be compared with Wordsworth's 'spots of time' as characterised in *The Prelude* (1805), xi, 257–78 (= 1850, xii, 208–25).
87. *Allen*, p. 218, quoting the text enclosed in a missive from Donald MacAlister to William Everett, 24 June 1908, William Everett MSS, Massachusetts Historical Society, Boston.

2

Tennyson's Idle Tears

ERIC GRIFFITHS

Tennyson said that 'if Arthur Hallam had lived he would have been "one of the foremost men of his time, *but not as a poet*"' (*Mem*, l, 299). We cannot know the force of emphasis suggested by the *Memoir*'s italics; Tennyson may have meant that Hallam would have been more or less than a poet. *In Memoriam* imagines him, had he survived, as doubtless 'A potent voice of Parliament' (cxiii, R ii, 434). Maybe it is a cynicism of our day, when we less admire, or have less to admire in, parliamentary speech, that makes us wonder whether the compliment paid Hallam there has an edge to it, the edge of Tennyson's private reservations about his friend's poetic gifts. That is not the only reason for wondering. A friend to both Hallam and Tennyson and one of the most vocal powers in Victorian politics, Gladstone, said, on the occasion in 1883 when he and Tennyson were together granted the freedom of Kirkwall: 'Mr Tennyson's life and labours correspond in point of time as nearly as possible to my own, but Mr Tennyson's exertions have been on a higher plane of human action than my own. He has worked in a higher field, and his work will be more durable' (*Mem*, ii, 280). It is greatly to Gladstone's credit to have said that, and even more to his credit to have meant it. Questions about the respective value and reciprocal bearing of political and poetic speech are Victorian as well as current. Indeed, they are age-old; both Ovid and Mandelstam wrote *Tristia*. Just as we do not know the exact edge of Tennyson's '*but not as a poet*', we do not know how Hallam would have taken the remark, had he lived to hear it. For it is also not quite clear what Hallam thought about poets, though the power which in his sense of the matter most competes with poetry is not politics but philosophy.

It is fair to Hallam to begin by asking whether Tennyson was right to say that had he lived he would not have gained preeminence as a poet. He died young, but his death may not have been a loss to poetry as those of Keats and Shelley are thought to have been. Hallam wrote a sonnet about Shelley's early death which picks up from something like the last half-line of Shelley's unfinished *The Triumph of Life*. It reads:

> 'Then what is Life, I cried.' From his rent deeps
>   Of soul the Poet cast that burning word;
>   And it should seem as though his prayer was heard,
>   For he died soon; and now his rest he keeps
> Somewhere with the great Spirit who never sleeps!
>   He has left us to murmur on awhile
>   And question still most fruitlessly this pile
>   Of natural shews: What life is? Why man weeps?
> Why sins? – and whither when the awful veil
>   Floats on to him he sinks from earthly sight?
>   Some are who never grow a whit more pale
> For thinking on the general mystery,
>   Ground of all being; yet may I rather be
>   Of those who know and feel that it is Night.[1]

Tennyson seems to have had a point. The sonnet begins from something only *like* Shelley's last half-line. In the *Posthumous Poems of Percy Bysshe Shelley* (1824), the text Hallam is mostly likely to have read, that half-line runs '"Then, what is life? I cried." –' Hallam has added a capital to 'life' and removed a comma between 'Then' and 'what';[2] he has also changed the speaker of the words, for in *The Triumph of Life* this question does not belong to a poet but, probably, to the *philosophe* Rousseau (who may or may not be speaking for Shelley).[3] Rousseau's words – 'Then, what is life?' – have an ambiguity which disappears in the sonnet. Coming where they do in Shelley's story, the 'then' may be either chronological ('the next thing that happened was that I cried') or logical ('And because of all these things, I cried' or 'And I cried, "If these things are so, then what is life?"'). With no narrative setting, Hallam's 'cry' more simply launches his poem into ruminations cut loose from time, experienced or imagined, and so leaves it without anchorage in that 'life' which is in question. Hallam loses Shelley's 'life' in order to gain his own 'Life'. Nor is the cry content to remain just a cry, a sharp, uttered instant. In the next line, it swells into a 'burning word'; it very quickly becomes a 'prayer'. Its dimensions grow but its contours and location do not grow any clearer. The prayer is heard by a 'great Spirit' but we know little about this 'great Spirit' except that it lives 'Somewhere' (the capital there is an accident of lineation, but looks, in this company,

loomingly meaningful) and that it 'never sleeps' – which raises the
question how much 'rest' 'the Poet' will get with such an insomniac
divinity.

Shelley drowned in the Gulf of Lerici before completing *The Triumph of Life*. The knowledge of this presses in on Hallam's reflections
but to no more effect than to produce infelicities of phrase: 'rent
deeps/Of soul' tries to imagine Shelley as a volcanic landscape with
fissures down which we see elemental passions at white heat, but
the deeps of the Gulf of Lerici are colder than that. The veil which
'floats' on to abstract 'man', the circumlocution for death – 'sinks
from mortal sight', – both acquire an incongruous particularity in
the circumstances of Shelley's death, as does 'the general mystery/
Ground of all being' when faced with Shelley's unbeing all at sea.
Hallam's sonnet claims to be doubly occasioned – by the words of
Shelley's poem and by the circumstances of those words at the end
of Shelley's life – but it escapes its occasions, occasions which then
inform against its enigmas and ambition of conceptual grandeur.

In the 1830 edition of his poems, Hallam quoted with approval
some remarks by Landor about Shelley: 'Innocent and careless as a
boy, he possessed all the discrimination of the scholar, and united in
just degrees the ardour of the poet with the patience and forbearance
of the philosopher'.[4] (This in a note to one of the two 'Sonnets,
Purporting to be Written in the Protestant Burial Ground at Rome by
Moonlight' – a candidly pseudo-occasional title.) Whatever Hallam's
practical troubles in his sonnet as he tried to unite philosophical
meditation with poetic form, his prose writings constantly show the
appeal such a union had for him, while at other times they argue that
the poet and the philosopher are essentially distinct types of being.
The strains for thought here are not Hallam's alone. In the first half
of the nineteenth century, English itself is unsure where poetry and
philosophy overlap and where diverge, what kin the poet is to the
philosopher. The OED shows that just as 'literature' begins around
1810 to narrow its range from 'humane learning' to 'writing which
has a claim to consideration on the ground of beauty of form or
emotional effect', so too 'philosophy' acquires about 1794 its present-
day sense of the investigation of concepts and starts shedding the
more diffuse meanings of 'love of wisdom', 'empirical science'. The
terms for Hallam's discussions of poetry and philosophy are shifting
even as he discusses; the repercussions of those shifts are widespread, from Coleridge's plan that Wordsworth should write a philosophical poem, a plan announced and encouraged with the urgency

of a need newly-felt, to Byron's vexed and jocular suggestion that Coleridge had defected from poetry to the numinous enemy, 'Explaining metaphysics to the nation – /I wish he would explain his Explanation'.[5]

Keats felt both sides of the quarrel:

> Even here though I myself am pursueing the same instinctive course as the veriest human animal you can think of – I am however young writing at random – straining at particles of light in the midst of a great darkness – without knowing the bearing of any one assertion of any one opinion. Yet may I not in this be free from sin? May there not be superior beings amused with any graceful, though instinctive attitude my mind m[a]y fall into, as I am entertained with the alertness of a Stoat or the anxiety of a Deer? Though a quarrel in the streets is a thing to be hated, the energies displayed in it are fine; the commonest Man shows a grace in his quarrel – By a superior being our reasoning[s] may take the same tone – though erroneous they may be fine – This is the very thing in which consists poetry; and if so it is not so fine a thing as philosophy – For the same reason that an eagle is not so fine a thing as a truth – Give me this credit – Do you not think I strive – to know myself?[6]

If we admire the agility of mind in Keats's letter, his resilience through all his self-checkings – 'Even here though', 'however', 'Yet', 'though', 'Though', 'though', 'and if so', 'For the same reason' – do we admire mental athleticism for its own sake or the sheer pursuit of truth? It is hard to say; we might be with Keats in trying to weigh assertions and opinions, 'straining at particles of light' or, above him, superior connoisseurs of the momentary grace of attitudes into which he involuntarily falls as he struggles to think straight. Certainly, though, as the letter shows, Keats himself has both a superior vantage-point on his own thought-processes and the pained experience of being at a disadvantage in the process of thinking. Just because he is in these two places at once, his letter defies classification as either poetry or philosophy according to his definitions. He writes as 'the veriest human animal': 'veriest' – with a passion for truth; 'animal' – at the mercy of conditions not governable by thought; 'human' – a midway being conscious of its own entanglements. The effort to clarify a distinction between poetry and philosophy grinds itself to a halt. If poetry consists in the appreciation of the charm of reasonings, however erroneous, then it must include at least as much philosophy as is needed to tell whether or not arguments are mistaken (and note the flicker of rhyme across the distinction: 'tone – though erroneous'). Philosophically speaking, to say that poetry is not 'so fine a thing as philosophy – For the same reason that an eagle is not so fine a thing as a truth' is to talk slackly because eagles are not the same sort of thing as truths, if truths are things at all. In the moment he gives philosophy the palm, Keats fails to live up to its standards. But what matters is the evident difficulty which Keats had in trying to state and understand what it is to 'speak philosophically'.

Hallam's sonnet 'Then what is Life . . . ' also contains a hint of a distance, if not a distinction, between poetry and philosophy; the concluding lines read: 'yet may I rather be/Of those who know and feel that it is Night'. In an effort to say what this line actually means, you have to say it in the manner of Hopkins's 'AND the fire that breaks from thee then',[7] with a deliberate risking of ungainliness for the sake of right emphasis. It should go: ' . . . those who know AND feel that it is Night' because the line is built on something like Keats's claim that the axioms of philosophy need to be tried on our pulses before they are truths, even though the line itself fails to have the sort of pulse on which an axiom could be tried.

The distinction between knowing something to be so and feeling something to be so is a Romantic and post-Romantic commonplace, commonplace in the sense of something important which has nonetheless widely lent itself to vulgarisation. In his 1831 essay on the philosophical writings of Cicero, Hallam made explicit what is couched in the 'know and feel' of his sonnet:

> Poetry, indeed, is seductive by exciting in us that mood of feeling which conjoins all mental states that pass in review before it, according to congruity of sentiment, not agreement of conceptions; and it is with justice, therefore, that the Muses are condemned by the genius of a profound philosophy.[8]

The essay shows some trouble in finding a language for philosophical discussion. What, for example, is a 'mood of feeling' and to what would such a mood be contrasted – a 'mood of thought'? It is not wrong to wish, reading such passages, that Hallam had been able to conceive of a philosophy which might have been less 'profound' but more precise. For all its flounderings, this sentence contains a notion which Hallam developed in his seminal essay reviewing Tennyson's *Poems, Chiefly Lyrical* (1830).[9] This notion concerns a difference in the kinds of thinking which Hallam believes go on in poetry and in philosophy, and it lurks in the words 'conjoins all mental states that pass in review before it, *according to congruity of sentiment, not agreement of conceptions*' (my emphasis). This probably means that a poet is apt to join together, for instance, the mention of a woman called Lucy and a memory of a violet seen half-hidden by a mossy stone because the responses they call up in him have something to do with each other though Lucy and violets may have no strict connection with each other. The poetic connection is made through remembered and particular experiences whose occurrence was merely contingent. As such, it may have nothing to do with the articulation of essential attributes which is philosophy's task, and so the 'Muses are condemned by the genius of a profound philosophy'.[10]

This distinction burgeons in the review of Tennyson into a doubt about whether the poet can be a philosopher at all, a doubt Hallam held inconsistently together with the sort of conflation of poetry and philosophy which appears in his admiration for Shelley, and in the language of his sonnet:

> Now there is undoubtedly no reason why [the poet] may not find beauty in those moods of emotion, which arise from the combinations of reflective thought; and it is possible that he may delineate these with fidelity, and not be led astray by any suggestions of an unpoetical mood. But though possible, it is hardly probable; for a man whose reveries take a reasoning turn, and who is accustomed to measure his ideas by their logical relations rather than the congruity of the sentiments to which they refer, will be apt to mistake the pleasure he has in knowing a thing to be true, for the pleasure he would have in knowing it to be beautiful. . . .[11]

'The congruity of the sentiments to which they refer' obviously picks up from 'the congruity of sentiment' in the Cicero essay, and so 'logical relations' helps gloss for us the phrase 'agreement of conceptions'. The polarity is the same in both pieces, though here Hallam has begun to push poetry and philosophy further apart on the grounds that they are two different habits of thought and that one or the other is bound to predominate in any individual. This consideration of poetry and philosophy as habits of thought, and the derived belief that there is a poetical character and a philosophical character is more consequential for literary self-consciousness in the Victorian period than the conceptual distinction between emotion and intellection on which it rests. It testifies to a supposed division of intellectual labour which alienates poetry and philosophy from each other, as the division between manual and intellectual labour is said to alienate the thinker from the worker.

When Hallam comes to characterise Keats and Shelley as precursors of Tennyson, he drives the distinction between sentiment and idea even further:

> They are both poets of sensation rather than reflection. Susceptible of the slightest impulse from external nature, their fine organs trembled into emotion at colours, and sounds, and movements, unperceived or unregarded by duller temperaments. Rich and clear were their perceptions of visible forms; full and deep their feelings of music. So vivid was the delight attending the simple exertions of eye and ear, that it became mingled more and more with their trains of active thought, and tended to absorb their whole being into the energy of sense. . . . They are not smooth and *negatively* harmonious; they are full of deep and varied melodies.[12]

Hallam's admiration shines through his prose. Keats and Shelley overcome the divided intellect which elsewhere must choose between 'congruity of sentiment' and 'agreement of conception' because their delight in their own perceptions was so keen that it absorbed 'their *whole* being into the energy of sense' (my emphasis). They did not know and feel by turns; 'their whole being' was concentrated in sensation. This praise looks forward to a celebrated passage in Eliot's essay on 'The Metaphysical Poets' where he characterises the failure of nineteenth-century English poetry as exactly a failure to do what Hallam says Keats and Shelley did (and what he also thought Tennyson did). Indeed, the concept of 'dissociation of sensibility' which has been used by others than Eliot to identify a malaise in Victorian poetry is itself a very nineteenth-century concept, in some ways *the* distinctively nineteenth-century concept, of a crisis in the intellect which poetry is supposed to resolve or at least abate. The relevant sentences in Eliot read:

> Tennyson and Browning are poets, and they think; but they do not feel their thought as immediately as the odour of a rose. A thought to Donne was an experience; it modified his sensibility.[13]

Eliot is concerned with the way in which intellection may become an experience; Hallam with the way sensations become 'mingled more and more with . . . trains of active thought'. Though they cross the frontier in different directions, it is clearly the same frontier which each crosses.

Immanuel Kant guards that frontier. The terms, the conception of mental activity implied in the terms, come to Hallam from Kant, more generally from that Kantianism diffused in England princi-pally by Coleridge. A key element in the Kantian metaphysic is the distinction between what can roughly be called 'sensation' and 'thought', though Kant's words for these things are now normally translated 'intuition' (*Anschauung*) and 'concept' (*Begriff*).[14] Kant had two main purposes in the *Critique of Pure Reason*: first, to defend the discoveries of the natural sciences against the scepticism of philo-sophers such as Hume; secondly, to curb the pretensions of rational-ist philosophers by subjecting them to a version of the scepticism of Hume. The basic claim which carried out both purposes was that reason cannot operate outside the sphere of what is perceptible to man through his senses but that man's senses inevitably operate under the sway of certain concepts inherent to the human mind. Hence the Kantian maxim 'Thoughts without content are empty, intuitions without concepts are blind'.[15] If no perceptual experience can be found to correspond to a concept which someone is employ-ing, then that concept has no application and is empty – such, for example, is alleged to be the case with respect to the concept of a 'First Cause'. This aspect of Kant's metaphysic entitles him to the title of 'father of logical positivism'. Yet, on the other hand, it is not possible for human beings to have sense-experiences unmediated by certain categories of thought, so that sceptical arguments to the effect that all our terms for the world might systematically distort our experiences of the world must be invalid – and this aspect of Kant fathers idealism in its many nineteenth-century varieties.

Kant may have wished his distinction between intuition and con-cept to be a contribution to an analysis of the logic of sentences, as some twentieth-century exponents have argued, but his early read-ers soon took it rather as a description of types of mental operation, and from there extended it to refer to types of character in which one mental operation tended to predominate over another. Hence Hallam's contrast between the poet and the 'man whose reveries take a reasoning turn'. That is, the sentences 'My heart leaps up when I behold/A rainbow in the sky' and 'A rainbow results from the prismatic reflection, double refraction and dispersion of the sun's

rays in drops of water' make logically distinct kinds of statement;
they depend for their truth on different kinds of evidence and, more
importantly, they depend on that evidence in different ways. We
need to find only one occasion on which rainbows result from something other than prismatic reflection and double refraction, or one
occasion on which these phenomena fail to produce a rainbow, to
falsify the scientific definition, but if we caught Wordsworth in a
grumpy frame of mind one day, quite unimpressed by a rainbow, it
would not *falsify* the lines from his lyric. There arose an inclination to
take the logical differences and map them on to differences in character, as Keats did in *Lamia*, in a passage where 'philosophy' stands
uncertainly between abstract reasoning and scientific observation:

> Do not all charms fly
> At the mere touch of cold philosophy?
> There was an awful rainbow once in heaven:
> We know her woof, her texture; she is given
> In the dull catalogue of common things.
> Philosophy will clip an Angel's wings. . . . [16]

Lamia herself may then stand for the appeal of 'the energy of sense',
and Apollonius for the 'trains of active thought', and, though Kant
argued that no experience is possible without both intuition and
concept, allegorical contests begin to be waged between a life of
sensations and one of thoughts. What were supposed to be two sides
of a coin become two sides of a battle. It is in this sense that Kant is
also the father of the 'dissociation of sensibility'.

These logomachies between sensation and thought can become
wearisome, and may have less content than their proponents believe, but Hallam also took from Kantianism a notion which was to
be more consequential for Tennyson though it is a less familiar topic
for literary-critical debate. This is Kant's thesis of the transcendental
unity of apperception. Hallam expressed the thesis as follows:

> It is an ultimate fact of consciousness, that the soul exists as one
> subject in various successive states. Our belief in this is the foun-
> dation of all reasoning.[17]

In the first *Critique*, Kant attacks Hume's assertion that the self is no
more than a bundle of impressions, the mere series of its own experiences. Against this, Kant observes that I can normally tell whether

an experience is mine or somebody else's; if I have a pain in my foot or a memory of happiness, I am not usually in doubt that the pain or the memory are mine rather than yours. My ability to ascribe experiences to my self entails the fact that my self is something more than the sum of its own experiences.[18] Hallam may not have been right to think that this continuity of the self through its various states was the foundation of all reasoning, but his statement of the Kantian axiom yields, when examined, a better means for distinguishing between poetry and philosophy than the various accounts of psychological self-alienation produced under the influence of a mis-understanding of the sort of line Kant had drawn between concept and intuition.

Why did Hallam believe that the transcendental unity of apperception, the continuity of the self through experiences, was the foundation of all 'reasoning'? The answer is not clear from his writings, but it can, I think be reconstructed. A prime law of reasoning is the law of non-contradiction, which states that it cannot at the same time be the case that 'X is true' and also that 'X is not true', provided that 'X' is an unambiguous proposition such as 'A triangle is a three-sided plane figure'. This is a law about statements, but we can infer from it an imperative which is incumbent on anybody who wishes to engage in reasoning. That imperative is: 'Do not at the same time assert a proposition and its contrary'. In both the law and the imperative, the phrase 'at the same time' has a crucial role, for there are, of course, some propositions which are true at one time and not true at another, such as, to give a melancholy example, 'I have some money in my bank-account'. Therefore, it may be legitimate at one time to assert a proposition and at another to assert its contrary. Hallam's idea, however, is that in order to understand the relation between such changed propositions, in order for that relation to be one about which we can reason, we must conceive of the person who utters them from time to time as a continuous self. So that, if I say 'I have some money in my bank-account' today, and a week later 'I have no money in my bank-account', my saying these contradictory things is intelligible in terms of facts about bank-accounts, expenditure and the finitude of my financial resources rather than in terms of my believing that 'I' no longer has the same referent. (Hence, the terrible moment in Hamlet's encounter with Ophelia in the 'nunnery'-scene, for there when Hamlet says 'I never gave you aught', the point he's needling Ophelia with is that his sense of what 'I' means with reference to himself has changed, though she doesn't know that.) Different propositions may change their truth-values at different speeds; remarks about how many sides a triangle has change either never or extremely slowly, remarks about my bank-balance change regularly but not rapidly, and the truth-value of 'Now I have my eyes open' can change in less time than it takes to utter the proposition.

'The soul exists as one subject in various successive states': the language and purpose of philosophy, as Hallam would have conceived it, tend to emphasise the continuity of the subject in order to secure the application to that subject's utterances of the law of non-contradiction whereas much poetic practice, as he understood and enjoyed it, stresses – in order to show the occasions in and on which thought occurs – rather the 'successive states' through which the subject passes. The truth of Hallam's sentence 'The soul exists as one subject in various successive states' would be put with a philosophical stress by saying 'THE SOUL EXISTS-AS-ONE-SUBJECT (in various successive states)' and put again lyrically by saying '(The soul exists as) ONE-SUBJECT-IN-VARIOUS-SUCCESSIVE-STATES'. This is not only a matter of nuance.

It might, for instance, matter in reading *In Memoriam* that we correctly gauge the respective weights to be given, on the one hand, to the poem's successive expression of a set of attitudes to death and immortality not all of which are compatible with each other and, on the other, to its ascription of many of these attitudes to a continuing 'I', stressing that 'I' by such symmetries as the fact that the first occurrence of 'I' in the poem is in the self-referring phrase 'since I began' (Prologue, l. 34) and the last occurrence of 'I' in the equally self-referring 'till I retire' (Epilogue, l. 105; R ii, 317 and 456, respectively). Eliot said that *In Memoriam* had the unity 'only of a diary', and if this is true, there may be nothing odd or interesting about the way that one section does not quite chime with an earlier or later section, nothing more odd or interesting than that I have money in my bank-account at one time and not at another. But Eliot felt impelled to go on to add that 'the poem has to be comprehended as a whole' and that 'it is a diary of which we have to read every word'.[19] The unity of a diary is something more persistent, however frail, than Eliot's 'only' at first admitted, and *In Memoriam*'s unity principally stems from a feature which would be surprising if ever found in a diary: it is written throughout in the same stanza. This formal stability carries essentially ambivalent implications. It may reflect a self continuous through succession, or protect, shore up, a self that is repeatedly on the verge of becoming mere series. That is, the poem structurally pivots on the lyrical/philosophical turn at the heart of Hallam's 'ultimate fact of consciousness'. It sounds like that from its first section on:

I held it truth . . .

The simple past next to 'I' immediately sets off the existence of the subject against change of state, and very sharply so, for this opening section of *In Memoriam* records altered convictions about the processes of alteration through which a self passes. It does not tell us what I now hold true. Nor does it say whether the accent falls on the tone of reasonings or their being in error. It implies just that the poem has a 'time before' without saying how long that time was. (One question we can't answer about the 'I' of the poem, as we can guess about the 'I' of most diaries, is: 'how old am I?'.) The implied 'time before' is the period before Hallam's death, the gap between 'I' and 'held' the effect of his death, a loss at once of a person, a truth, and that time.

Hallam himself puzzled over these balances of truth and time:

To know a thing as past, and to know it as similar to something present, is a source of mingled emotions. There is pleasure, in so far as it is a revelation of self; but there is pain, in so far that it is a divided self, a being at once our own and not our own, a portion cut away from what we feel, nevertheless, to be single and indivisible.

I fear these expressions will be thought to border on mysticism. Yet I must believe that if any one, in the least accustomed to analyze his feelings, will take the pains to reflect on it, he may remember moments in which the burden of this mystery has lain heavy on him; in which he has felt it miserable to exist, as it were, piece-meal, and in the continual flux of a stream; in which he has wondered, as at a new thing, how we can be, and have been, and not be that which we have been. But the yearnings of the human soul for the irrecoverable past are checked by a stern knowledge of impossibility.[20]

He describes a graver reason why human beings lack wholeness of being than the philosophising which went into the nineteenth-century prototype of Eliot's 'dissocation of sensibility' provides. This graver reason is that we live in time. The passage is extremely Tennysonian in its timbre and preoccupation, as we can see from considering how well 'to know a thing as past, and to know it as similar to something present' conveys the experience of reading *In Memoriam*, an experience simultaneously of series and of unity. Hallam here discovers that the human possession of 'a divided self, a being at once our own and not our own' is not only constitutive of the human self, but also an essential feature which particularly strikes the unitary self in time, for it is at 'moments' that we realise this fact about our selves, this flowing of thought through time which it is so difficult for thought to grasp while preserving a philosophical consistency, a trans-temporal coherence of propositions. There is a slight conceptual inconsistency in Hallam's metaphors: 'to exist, as it were, piece-meal, and in the continual flux of a stream'. A stream, a continual flux, is not something which exists piece-meal. The metaphorical instability may imply an inconsistency of propositions which might philosophically be censured and which yet is apt to the point at issue here, that leakage of thought through time which spills out over a sharp contrast between reasonings ordered according to 'congruity of sentiment' and reasonings ordered according to 'agreement of conceptions'. In so far as the self stands assured of its own existence as one subject through various successive states, it recognises itself in the image of a stream; in so far as the variety and succession of its own states comes to consciousness, it seems disassembled, 'piece-meal'.

There is a similar instability in Shelley's remark in one of his notebooks:

> thought can with difficulty visit the intricate and winding chambers which it inhabits. It is like a river whose rapid and perpetual stream flows outwards – like one in dread who speeds through the recesses of some haunted pile and dares not look behind. . . . If it were possible to be where we have been, vitally and indeed – if, at the moment of our presence there, we could define the results of our experience – if the passage from sensation to reflection – from a state of passive perception to voluntary contemplation were not so dizzying and so tumultuous, this attempt would be less difficult.[21]

Thought appears first to live in rooms, then to be someone pursued through a 'haunted pile'; it is both the process of motion – flowing, flying – and the scene of that process – the chambers which are themselves tinged with a river's nature, for they are not themselves still but 'winding'. Shelley's metaphors, like Hallam's, radiate out from a nodal, assumed difference between 'sensation' and 'reflection' in which, once again, Kant's claim that concept and intuition are necessarily co-present in any experience drops out of sight and mind. Shelley alights, though, on a word which holds his straining figures together: 'passage', for a passage is an architectural fixture, the corridor between 'chambers', and also the act and fact of transition, both movement and the space through which movement runs. Much the same could be said of Shelley's versification in *The Triumph of Life* with its simultaneous establishment and corrosion of *terza rima*.

At the moment Hallam mentions the momentary quality of realisations about the immersion of thought in time, he introduces into his philosophical prose an allusion to poetry. 'He may remember moments in which the burden of this mystery has lain heavy upon him' picks up some lines from that great poem about dead selves and their relation to the current self, which carries in its title and first lines an insistence on the occasioning time of its thinking, 'Lines Written a Few Miles above Tintern Abbey, on Revisiting the Banks of the Wye during a Tour. July 13, 1798':

>   . . . that blessed mood,
> In which the burthen of the mystery,
> In which the heavy and the weary weight
> Of all this unintelligible world
> Is lighten'd . . .[22]

Hallam was partial to the topographical lyric; his 1830 collection bristles with 'Stanzas written in a Steam-boat', 'Sonnet written in the Pass at Glencoe', 'Stanzas written in Dejection at Tunbridge Wells', and many more. (By contrast, no poem in Tennyson's first three books has such a location, though many are dramatically 'situated'.) None of these poems bears the impress of placed and timed experience as do the Wordsworth lines alluded to in Hallam's prose. The characteristically grave insistence of 'In which . . ./In which . . . ', the courted awkwardness in the repeated definite articles – Wordsworth composes these features to witness the contingent actualities through which the lines arise to their sensed reflections. That is all gone from Hallam. In its stead, he provides an airy, oratorical

pattern of alliteration ('may ... moments ... mystery', 'has ... heavy
... him'; contrast the spacious delicacy of 'blessed mood ... burthen
... mystery'). Though Hallam speaks of weighty matters, his sentence is much lighter than Wordsworth's terms of gratitude for
lightening. Hallam's mood reverses the blessedness of Wordsworth's
lines, but still owes much to them, owes them the right words for a
mood, for the moodiness which is a condition of thought in time.

He was also in debt to Tennyson's poetry for at times giving him
a sense of the way in which the yearnings of the human soul for the
irrecoverable past might be met by something less obdurately for-
bidding than 'a stern knowledge of impossibility'. He admired the
'Recollections of the Arabian Nights' which Tennyson published in
his 1830 collection; indeed, it was Hallam's favourite in a collection
which also contained poems such as 'Mariana' and 'A spirit haunts
the year's last hours'. He phrased his admiration like this:

> That happy ductility of childhood returns for the moment; ... and
> yet there is a latent knowledge, which heightens the pleasure, that
> to our change from really childish thought we owe the capacities
> by which we enjoy the recollection.[23]

This is brilliant criticism, however questionable his taste in prefer-
ring this poem to others in the collection; it understands exactly the
complex working of time which Tennyson's genius permitted him
and grants his readers. Hallam describes a set of, in a sense, contradictory attitudes: we read the poem, and we are charmed to be again
impressionable in the way we were when as children we read the
'Arabian Nights' but our pleasure in this recovery of childhood also
contains an acknowledgement that we are no longer children, and it
is because we know we are not children any more that we like to feel
as if we now were children: 'and yet there is a latent knowledge,
which heightens the pleasure, that to our change from really childish
thought we owe the capacities by which we enjoy the recollection'
(my emphasis). If you try to account for this kind of pleasure in
terms of the propositions which a person in such a pleased attitude
must believe, you produce strained logic, though the experience of
being pleased by the poem is not an experience of strain. A crucial
element in the pleasure is its self-conscious transience, something
Hallam points to when he remarks that 'That happy ductility of
childhood returns for the moment'. (The preposition 'for' is rich at
this point; it measures time – 'returns only during a moment' – and

gives a reason – 'returns on account of the moment'.) To the timed quality of the lyric utterance corresponds the conscious timing of the experience of that utterance, the reader knowing that it is only for a time that the poem can work this way, only for a time that he can take up the attitudes it weaves together. Nobody could feel for five years that the happy ductility of childhood had returned and yet preserve all that time a latent knowledge that to his change from really childish thought he owed the capacity for enjoying such recollection.

Empson often makes a critical point like Hallam's, as when he writes of Marvell: 'The poetry does say . . . that the human creature in the world is inherently puzzled or betrayed; but a reader of the poetry is granted, for the time, a more lofty viewpoint.'[24] The patterned stringency of the lyric imagination is such as to make Hallam's 'for the moment' and Empson's 'for the time' both a responsible caution within the verse which holds the poetry back from fantasy or confusion and a focus of our pleasure in the lyric. I mean by 'patterned stringency' something complex but palpable: the formal patterning of the lyric poem, its stanzas, rhythm and rhyme. Such formal patterns make of the poem a thought deliberately etched on time because they are all methods of drawing attention to its work of lapsing and duration.

A lyric poem may signal its dwelling in time by such explicit devices as the past tense of 'I held it truth . . . ' or the 'Five years have passed; five summers, with the length/Of five long winters!' which marks the start of the 'Lines written a few miles above Tintern Abbey . . . ', but the lyric may equally not employ any signposts to its residence in time, and yet be in its composed rhythms a consciously timed utterance. As in the case of 'Tears, Idle Tears' which Tennyson wrote at Tintern Abbey: 'The passion of the past, the abiding in the transient, was expressed in "Tears, idle tears", which was written in the yellowing autumn-tide at Tintern Abbey, full for me of its bygone memories. Few know that it is a blank verse lyric' (*Mem*, i, 253). Tennyson does not say 'passion for the past' but 'passion of the past'; he is writing not about nostalgia, but about what Hallam had described as the knowledge of pastness within one's self and its passions, 'a being at once our own and not our own':

> Then she, 'Let some one sing to us : lightlier move
>   The minutes fledged with music:' and a maid,
>   Of those beside her, smote her harp, and sang.

'Tears, idle tears, I know not what they mean,
Tears from the depth of some divine despair
Rise in the heart, and gather to the eyes,
In looking on the happy Autumn-fields,
And thinking of the days that are no more.

'Fresh as the first beam glittering on a sail,
That brings our friends up from the underworld,
Sad as the last which reddens over one
That sinks with all we love below the verge;
So sad, so fresh, the days that are no more.

'Ah, sad and strange as in dark summer dawns
The earliest pipe of half-awakened birds
To dying ears, when unto dying eyes
The casement slowly grows a glimmering square;
So sad, so strange, the days that are no more.

'Dear as remembered kisses after death,
And sweet as those by hopeless fancy feigned
On lips that are for others; deep as love,
Deep as first love, and wild with all regret;
O Death in Life, the days that are no more.'

She ended with such passion that the tear,
She sang of, shook and fell, an erring pearl
Lost in her bosom . . .
                                    (R ii, 232–3; *The Princess*, IV, 18–43)

If few know, as Tennyson said, that this is a blank verse lyric, that is
because the terminal cadence at the end of each line falls so securely
on the voice, and the refrain of 'the days that are no more' at the end
of each stanza comes so solidly. Cadence and refrain combine to give
a sense of formal stability which we have in the past found with
rhyming stanzas, and which leads us now to imagine rhymes where
there are rhymes no more. The sound of 'Tears, idle tears' is the
sound of prosodic days that are no more. This technical invention
also makes the verse seem as if it had been composed on syllabic
principles, and it is a feature of syllabic verse that the *duration* of its
lines takes more emphasis than in accentual–syllabic verse. Certainly, in 'Tears, Idle Tears' the voice dwells consciously on the units

of time in which the lines are composed. *In* which they are composed, as Tennyson said that the poem was composed 'in the yellowing autumn-tide at Tintern Abbey', as if the season were its material as well as its climate.

F. R. Leavis misunderstood this interpolated lyric in *The Princess* enough to misquote it without noticing he had done so. In '"Thought" and Emotional Quality', he complained that the particularity of the piece was specious, because it had 'nothing that gives the effect of an object, or substantial independent existence', and cited as instances of specious particularity '"the happy Autumn-fields", "the first beam glittering on a sail", and the casement that "slowly fades a glimmering square"'. But Tennyson wrote 'slowly grows a glimmering square', not 'slowly fades'. The misquotation lacks a sense of the substantial existence of the lyric independently of what Leavis wished to make of it. His ear could have alerted him to 'slowly grows' as one of the important, internal rhymes in the poem, something lost in his version, and his understanding could have told him that, because the third stanza of the poem explicitly takes place 'in dark summer dawns', to the tune of 'half-awakened birds', the casement could not be fading but has to be growing lighter. The persistent misquotation in the course of his commentary is the more remarkable as he cites the text correctly when he gives it at the beginning of his discussion.[25] Leavis does not hear or understand the line because to do so would contradict his view of the poem. The stanza in which the line occurs speaks plainly of the independent existence of the world from the person depicted in the stanza, because it concerns the experience of someone who is dying just as the world begins its daily activity of reviving; what is fading is the light in the 'dying eyes' but they see clearly that the light is growing outside the sick-room. At the moment of death, the world stands firm in its independence of the subject.

Leavis nowhere acknowledges that the piece forms part of *The Princess*; he ignores the possible bearing of its context on its cadences. Thus abstracted from its fictive occasion, the poem's tune is changed. As he hears it, it goes like this: 'It moves simply forward with a sweetly plangent flow, without check, cross-tension or any qualifying element.' But it doesn't go like that at all. No lyric with a refrain can move 'simply forward' because refrains are always throwbacks. In the setting Tennyson gave it, Ida checks this lyric as soon as it finishes; she denounces it as a siren's song against which the audience should stop its ears, doing better to concentrate on the social prospects for the future than on the sweetness of the past. (The allusions to the *Odyssey* continue in the subsequent narrative. Odysseus's story figures here because it resolves the conflict between Ida's progressivism and the lyric's harking-back, for his is the story of a homecoming which is also an achievement, a step forward. As such, it stands for the poise between reformism and restoration of old norms which *The Princess* seeks.)[26] Many details of 'Tears, idle tears' are revalued in the tirade it provokes from Ida: she scorns 'idle' as merely 'silken-folded idleness'; the melancholy of the 'first beam glittering on a sail' is dispersed by a curt resolve – 'trim our sails'; the sweetness of past days amounts only to 'So sweet a voice and vague'; the knowledge that 'all things serve their time' sets aside all the wildness of regret. Even the 'half-awakened birds' are anticipated and retrospectively commented on, for the audience listens to this song lounging on pillows of 'broidered down' and Ida had commanded the singing because 'lightlier move/The minutes fledged with music' though after hearing it she dismisses such 'fancies hatched/In silken-folded idleness'. 'Tears, idle tears', in fact, is intricately occasioned, checked, qualified, and, in one of Leavis's favourite words, 'placed'.

Indeed, Tennyson works so carefully around this song that a suspicious mind might think he is supplying it not with a context but with a *cordon sanitaire*, as if he realised that it might be 'on grounds of emotional and spiritual hygiene . . . something to deplore'.[27] Were that so, Leavis's charge against the poem, but not his implied charge against the poet, would stand. The relation of the lyric to its surroundings, though, is more intimate and reciprocal than such an image of containment suggests, for the sound of 'Tears, idle tears' is filtered through its environing verse even as that sound infiltrates that verse. It is, after all, a blank-verse lyric set in a blank-verse narrative; the song and Ida's denunciation of the song are in the same verse-form, though Tennyson deploys rhythmic variation of extreme subtlety to distinguish them even as they are affiliated. That is, *The Princess*, IV, 18–69 conducts a debate *in rhythm* about the relations of poetry and philosophy, the relations between what the unnamed girl sings and what Ida proposes. (Technically, the modulation from blank-verse narrative to blank-verse lyric and back again to narrative is achieved by the dominance of trochaic substitutions in the first foot of the lines in 'Tears, idle tears' when these substitutions are kept scarce in the surround, by frequent adoption of four-stress decasyllabics for the interpolation but not for its frame, and by heavy end-stopping in the lyric where elsewhere the verse runs on freely.)

That debate for this period centres on a supposed gap between 'sensation' and 'reflection' or, as this song calls it in its first stanza, between 'looking' and 'thinking'. Part of the piece's intellectual distinction lies in the way it simply overrides that gap as if it were not there, being rhythmically both continuous and piecemeal with *The Princess.*

Even within itself, irrespective of context and occasion, 'Tears, idle tears' is a profound philosophical lyric and an extreme lyrical surfacing of philosophy's depths. Its philosophical profundity consists in finding a rhythmical shape which simultaneously speaks of the soul's existence-as-one-subject (in various successive states) and of the soul's existence as one-subject-in-various-successive-states. It thinks rhythmically of what it is to exist piecemeal in the flux of a stream, as each line at once preserves its own integrity and is shaded and absorbed into the whole. A similar double being, at once its own and not its own, affects the individual stanzas and their relations one to another.

Consider, for example, the progress of stanzas 2–4. The second stanza compares the freshness of the days that are no more to the 'first beam glittering on a sail,/That brings our friends up from the underworld' and their sadness to the 'last [beam] which reddens over one [sail]/That sinks with all we love below the verge'. The suggested resurrection in the opening lines of this stanza looks at first as if it might be set to contradict the despair at the end of the first stanza which ends convinced that these days 'are no more', because now the days and their inhabitants come back, but come back only as part of a pivotal moment in the stanza to go away again. There is no shock of reversal in the complete shift of direction in the story the verse tells, because the verse is phrased so as to parallel the two motions of approach and loss: 'Fresh as the first . . . ', 'Sad as the last . . . '. At this point, we might wish to say of this lyric: it is about the fact that people we have known are dead; we think of the irrecoverable nature of the past (stanza 1), then the very thinking of the past brings it back to us in memory (stanza 2, lines 1–2) but we are conscious that it is only in memory that it returns and, as in Hallam's comment on the 'Recollections of the Arabian Nights', we acknowledge that it is to the pastness of what we remember that we owe the pleasure of remembering it, and so these recovered dead fade from us again (stanza 2, lines 3–5).

The third stanza compares the days that are no more to the ways that sound and light appear to someone who is dying. This alters our perspective on the subject of the poem. It had seemed before that the poem was, as it were, fully alive itself and just remembering others who had died, but now it expresses the state of a person who is dying, not the state of someone we watch dying. We are in the place of the moribund, not just spectators. Retrospectively then, 'That sinks with all we love below the verge' includes more than had been thought; 'all we love' includes our selves (it now seems obvious) and the death in the lyric touches the lyrical self. The lines come close to Eliot's in *Little Gidding*: 'We die with the dying:/See, they depart, and we go with them./We are born with the dead:/See, they return, and bring us with them.'

Yet once more, the change in sense of the poem is muted and questioned by formal stability. It is as if we keep discovering anew what the lyric is saying, but its form returns on us the fact that it has not changed the subject at all, that it was saying this all along if only we had listened to it. The last stanza takes us from the deaths of our friends, and the dying involved in anything we feel, to a state after death: 'Dear as remembered kisses after death'. The line means primarily 'Dear as the kisses we have given to those we love are to us after those we love have died', but, coming after a stanza about dying, it secondarily suggests 'Dear as the kisses we have been given by those we love are to us after we have died', as if we lay in our graves, remembering those touches of the lip. Then, the most astonishing change of tack: 'And sweet as those by hopeless fancy feigned/ On lips that are for others'. This has become a piece about frustrated desire; the decorum of language should not prevent us from realising that Tennyson refers here to a desperate imagination, the imagining of someone you love, and who has not returned your love, in the arms of someone else. The change of tack makes an implicit comparison: the longing for the past is like unfulfilled erotic longing, particularly so in two respects – it is intimately present, and it is 'sweet'. The implicit comparison is a touch of genius, especially in the calmly tormented admission that the kisses hopeless fancy feigns are 'sweet', by which Tennyson does not mean only that someone erotically or temporally bereaved thinks 'Oh, how sweet it would be if I could kiss those lips' but also 'Oh, how sweet it must be for those lips to be kissed, how much they enjoy those kisses from lips other than mine', for it is of the nature of passionately unsatisfied love to imagine the pleasures the beloved finds elsewhere with a vividness at once self-lacerating and vicariously gladdened, rather as in the jaunty and pained old song, 'I wonder who's kissing her now'. The implicit comparison is not a side-issue but the point of the lyric, because it makes clear to us that this song is about 'living death' in the full sense of those words. It is about an absence at the heart of the heart, a loss in desire and not just a loss of the objects of desire. 'Deep as first love, and wild with all regret' – *'and* wild with all regret' not *'but* wild with all regret' – even first love in this lyric does not have a first, fine, careless rapture but carries a desolating ache because love, as Proust said, is space and time made palpable to the heart. When time is made palpable, it takes away at every instant what every instant brings, the condition of such delight as is here recalled being constantly that of Indian-giving. Hence the 'Death *in* Life' (my emphasis), hence these idle tears.

The greatness of 'Tears, idle tears', the completeness of its poetic achievement, consists in a special kind of hollowness which can be mistaken for vacuity. It exceptionally realises a 'central hollowness' in lyricism,[28] its willed elapsing of managed time, without believing that anything can stop the gap, heal this wound imagination makes in even the most ardently longing of words. To convey what Tennyson called 'the abiding in the transient' calls for a careful sense of the weight of words but calls also for an ability to dissolve the solidities of language, to sound out the inconsistencies time builds into human thinking. So it is as necessary to say that 'Tears, idle tears' is a philosophically superficial poem as to insist on its profundity; the difficulty is to realise how philosophy may inhabit the surface of words as well as lurk in their 'rent deeps'. That is the difficulty of coping with what Wittgenstein called the illusion of depth, an illusion which philosophy may at times foster and which at other times it may assist to dispel. When, in *Philosophical Investigations*, II, xi, he discusses the various phenomena of aspect-perception, he is in part engaged in a criticism of the Kantian metaphysic with its distinction between sensation and thought, between concept and intuition. To see an aspect – as when I see a face in a crowd and then recognise that it is the face of a friend, or as when I see that a Gestalt drawing is ambiguous and may represent a black cross on a white background or a white cross on a black background, or as when I come to hear 'Tears, idle tears' in an acoustic, part of which consists of the philosophical quandaries about the status of poetry amidst which Tennyson grew up – to see an aspect seems, as Wittgenstein writes, 'half visual experience, half thought'.[29] Being such, being both concept and intuition, it questions those shaky lines between sensation and reflection, between the poetic and the philosophic character which Kantians such as Hallam illicitly developed from what they misunderstood of Kant's theses. And Tennyson's lyric does so too; its existence has the force of an antinomy which requires us to think things out again.

'Tears, idle tears' creates a pleasure in aspect-shift, tunes the antinomies as they dawn on us. As Wittgenstein wrote:

> It is almost as if 'seeing the sign in this context' were an echo of a thought.
> 'The echo of a thought in sight' – one would like to say.[30]

One would like to say that 'Tears, idle tears' is an echo of a thought in sound. But one would like to say it only because one is used to a certain philosophical interpretation of human practices in which primacy is accorded to thoughts, and it is on just such a philosophical interpretation that 'Tears, idle tears' induces a new aspect to dawn. This is why it is both profound and superficial at once. The poem is indeed a hollow sound, but then it is also the sound of the hollowness of some philosophical longings for depth. It is perfectly superficial; there is nothing 'behind' or 'beneath' it, though that does not prove that there may not be times when we talk, and need to talk, as if we had been behind the poem, and found something there.

Notes

1. Reprinted in T. H. Vail Motter (ed.), *The Writings of Arthur Hallam* (New York, 1943), p. 92; this edition is hereafter referred to as Hallam.
2. The vagaries of practice at this period with regard to capitalisation mean the point should not be pressed hard, but it probably holds. Consider also the effect of translating Shelley's *terza rima* with its inherent, narrative propulsion into Hallam's equally Italianate but stilled sonnet, a form regularly 'all in war with Time'.
3. In the 1824 text, the identity of the speaker of the lines is less clear than it becomes in later texts, but even in 1824 the speaker is clearly not the 'I' of the poem.
4. Hallam, p. 7.
5. *Don Juan*, Dedication, ll. 15–16; I quote from Jerome McGann's edition (Oxford, 1986).
6. Letter to the George Keatses, February–April, 1819, in *The Letters of John Keats, 1814–1821*, ed. H. E. Rollins (Cambridge, 1958), II, 80.
7. G. M. Hopkins, 'The Windhover'; I quote from Catherine Phillips's *Gerard Manley Hopkins* (Oxford, 1986).
8. Hallam, ibid., p. 150.

9. First published in *The Englishman's Magazine*, August 1831.
10. Hallam was probably wrong to think that such alogical connections are specially 'poetical'. Consider, for instance, Newman's account of 'connatural senses' and 'credences' in ordinary speech; see *An Essay in Aid of a Grammar of Assent* (1870; edited by Ian Ker, Oxford, 1985), pp. 41–4 and 174–5.
11. Hallam, pp. 184–5.
12. Ibid., p. 186.
13. 'The Metaphysical Poets' (1921), in *Selected Essays* (1932; 3rd, enlarged edn, 1951), p. 287.
14. See *Kritik der reinen Vernunft* (1781; 2nd edn, 1787), trans. N. Kemp Smith (1929; corrected edn, 1933), p. 65; hereafter referred to as KRV. Although, as Kolb notes, 'There is no evidence that AHH attempted to read Kant in the original German' (*The Letters of Arthur Hallam*, ed. J. Kolb, Columbus, Ohio, 1981, p. 327), from 1829 on there are several references to his plans to learn the language to do so. He could have absorbed the Kantian ethos, though not the precise terms, from his readings in Coleridge and Schiller. I know of no reference to Kant by Tennyson, but his 1833 work plan (*Mem*, I, 124) shows the intensity with which he studied German.
15. KRV, p.93.
16. *Lamia*, ii, 229–234. I quote from *The Poems of John Keats*, ed. M. Allott (1970; rev. edn, 1975), pp. 645–6.
17. Hallam, p. 137.
18. See KRV, especially pp. 141–9. I am indebted to P. F. Strawson's exposition of these matters in *The Bounds of Sense* (1966), pp. 85–117.
19. 'In Memoriam' (1936), in *Selected Essays*, pp. 334–5.
20. Hallam, p. 138.
21. Notebook of 1815. I quote from *Shelley's Prose*, ed. D. L. Clark (New Mexico, 1966), p. 186.
22. Title and text of *Lyrical Ballads* (1798), as given in *Wordsworth and Coleridge: Lyrical Ballads*, ed. R. L. Brett and A. R. Jones (1963, rev. 1965).
23. Hallam, p. 193.
24. 'Other People's Views', in *Using Biography* (1984), p. 39.
25. The misquotation appeared first in '"Thought" and Emotional Quality', *Scrutiny* (1945); it is repeated in *Selections from 'Scrutiny'*, Vol. 1 (1968) and in *The Living Principle: 'English' as a Discipline of Thought* (1977).
26. Consider also the allusions to *Samson Agonistes*, Dante and Byron which occur in the poem around the phrase 'Fresh as the first beam'. Tennyson's remarkable letter to his aunt, Mary Ann Fytche, cites the passages all in the same context; see *The Letters of Alfred Lord Tennyson*, ed. Cecil Y. Lang and Edgar F. Shannon, Jr, Vol. 1 (Oxford, 1982), pp. 1–2.
27. Leavis, *Selections from 'Scrutiny'*, I, p. 218.
28. The phrase is R. C. Trench's. In the letter to W. B. Donne from which it comes it refers to literature more generally and expresses a dissatisfaction similar to Ida's about 'Tears, idle tears': 'Literature will not do

for me . . . there is always the central hollowness, the cold black speck at the heart, which is spreading and darkening, and which must be met by other arms than those which Letters supply: we are now moreover on the eve of the mightiest change, which the world has ever known – all forms and institutions, which however little we recognized it, supported mightily our moral being, all these must give way . . . '. I quote the letter (11 December 1831) from P. Allen, *The Cambridge Apostles: The Early Years* (Cambridge, 1978).

29. Ludwig Wittgenstein, *Philosophische Untersuchungen* (1953, trans. G. E. M. Anscombe, repr. 1968), II, xi, p. 197.

30. Ibid., p. 212e.

3

Tennyson: The Lyric in the Distance

JEROME H. BUCKLEY

In his ode on Queen Victoria's Golden Jubilee, celebrated in June 1887, Tennyson asked ominously, but apparently with the Queen's assent, 'Are there thunders moaning in the distance?' (R iii, 162, l. 66). Both the sentiment and the image, odd intrusions on the jubilation, echo the epilogue to *Idylls of the King*, written fifteen years earlier, where the poet fearfully trusted that 'Heaven/Will blow the tempest in the distance back' (R iii, 563, ll. 46–7). Elsewhere in Tennyson the 'distance' as social or political future could hold promise rather than menace. In the first 'Locksley Hall', especially, though the distant vision of a war-free world and a peaceful 'Parliament of man' might seem utopian, the immediate presence of the steamship and the railway and 'the thoughts that shake mankind' were real enough to justify a shout for progress:

Not in vain the distance beacons. Forward, forward let us range,
Let the great world spin for ever down the ringing grooves of change.
(R ii, 130, ll. 181–2)

'Distance', the word and the concept, in its various connotations, whether of space or time, fact or metaphor, was from the beginning a necessary component of Tennyson's thought and language, his yearning and his quasi-mystical predisposition. The faint music that accompanies the nun's glimpse of the Holy Grail in the *Idylls* as 'from a distance beyond distance' (R iii, 467, l. 112) is close to the 'weird soul phrase' that haunted the child at Somersby, as described in the late lyric 'Far——Far——Away', and akin to the whisper remembered in 'The Ancient Sage', some 'Desolate sweetness – far and far away', and perhaps even to the bodiless voices 'in the distance calling' in 'The Lover's Tale'.

In discussing the lyric in the distance, I shall construe lyric as song but also as expression of personal emotion, especially that seeming to convey the characteristic voice or signature of the poet, though often reaching us only with some obliquity. And the distance, then, will be not only the remote source of inspiration, past or future or supersensory, but also the self-protective barriers that Tennyson frequently set up between himself and his readers, the sensitive evasions, the 'feints' at objectivity. A few of the most memorable lyrics, of course, are direct, as naked cry or invocation: 'Break, Break, Break', for instance, or 'Crossing the Bar' or 'A Farewell' ('Flow down, cold rivulet, to the sea'). But many others are set in more or less ambiguous contexts, 'distanced', as it were, or hedged off, from an immediate subjective interpretation.

Tennyson employs a number of strategies to distance apparently personal feeling. The lyric 'Far——Far——Away' recedes, appropriately to its subject matter, as we examine manuscript revisions moving from a first-person statement ('That strange world-whisper came to me, a boy,/A haunting notice, neither grief, nor joy') to a second-person question and finally, as published, to the third person:

> What vague world-whisper, mystic pain or joy,
> Through those three words would haunt him when a boy,
>   Far——far——away?[1]

And a similar shift in person, from 'my' to 'thy', along with an evasive new title, 'On a Mourner', prepares an elegiac lyric, one of the first occasioned by the news of Hallam's death,[2] for its appearance years later as a remote descriptive piece with no obvious personal reference whatever. The subject of 'The Dead Prophet', written in the 1880s – to cite yet another example of disowning distance – seems to have been the late Thomas Carlyle, and the occasion, the poet's angry revulsion from J. A. Froude's too-candid *Life of Carlyle*, prompted no doubt by Tennyson's dread that an irreverent biographer would one day desecrate his own memory. But the addition of a misleading date as subtitle, '182–', obscured the allusions, and a blank denial was intended further to depersonalise the spleen: 'It may be as well to state', Tennyson insisted, 'that the allegory is not in any way personal. The speaker in it is as imaginary as the prophet.'[3]

Whether or not we still accept T. S. Eliot's view of *In Memoriam* as 'the concentrated diary of a man confessing himself',[4] the elegy remains for most of us an intensely personal lyric sequence. At the same time we are constantly aware of the extent to which the poet self-consciously mediates or distances even here his relatively direct emotion – by his free use of poetic artifice, by his bold adaptation of motifs from the ancient pastoral convention, by his modern aware- ness of the possible imprecision of language itself. Moreover, we have Tennyson's own gloss on the ambiguous first-person pronoun: the 'I' is 'not always the author speaking of himself, but the voice of the human race speaking through him' (*Mem*, i, 305). Terry Eagleton has recently complained that it is ludicrous for 'a particular Vic- torian middle-class conservative'[5] to claim the role as spokesman for the human race. I grant that the phrasing here may be unfortunately grandiloquent, but I submit that Tennyson rather than making a class statement is merely suggesting that the 'I' of the poem fre- quently reflects current intellectual opinion, general rather than pri- vate, as it confronts traditional, and by no means ludicrous, beliefs concerning life, death and immortality. Even the primary or per- sonal 'I' of *In Memoriam*, however, stands somewhat aside from its deepest subjective experience. Section XCV brings the elegist closest to a personal sublime, as it describes the mystical coming upon 'that which is' and catching 'The deep pulsations of the world'. But this last climactic line, we discover, though no doubt experientially valid, was itself 'literary' in origin, in so far as it was lifted without change from 'An Idle Rhyme', written about 1837 and unpublished, where it appeared in a relaxed colloquial context as a bit of half-ironic rhetorical inflation:

> However, you have spoken well,
>   But, now the summer sun descends,
> Unbroach that flask of cool Moselle
>   And let us drink to all our friends. . . .
>
> As stretched beside the river clear
>   That's round this glassy foreland curled,
> I cool my face in flowers, and hear
>   The deep pulsations of the world.
>   (R ii, 92, ll. 29–32, 37–40)

Tennyson was well aware both of the impersonal artifice involved in the writing of *In Memoriam* and also of the expectation of his readers that they might find in the poem an undistanced revelation of private emotion – and the sense of the latter was surely a principal reason for the long delay in publication. But late in life – and clearly for the record – he told his son that 'Ulysses' gave his 'feeling about the need of going forward and braving the struggle of life perhaps more simply than anything in *In Memoriam*' (*Mem*, i, 196). The point here may be that the diffuse elegy presented other and more subtly mixed attitudes. But even so, comparison of the monologue with the 'diary' seems odd, for 'Ulysses' is far more obviously distanced from the poet – in space, time and situation, and especially in age and identity of speaker. And, what is more, to many latter-day readers, searching for a contrary subtext, 'Ulysses' conveys not a will to go forward at all but a determined retreat, a yearning, behind allegedly tired rhythms, to join the great Achilles (or possibly Arthur Hallam) in an Elysian retreat from life's vexations. New questions now assail us, questions that seem scarcely to have occurred at all to Victorian critics. Is the wily Greek deluded? Is he talking only to the dead? Is desertion of an aged wife a considerate or heroic act? Is abdication of political responsibility in Ithaca admirable polity? In short, does Tennyson mean us to believe that the old man has really found the way to brave life's struggle? The monologue form of the poem does indeed make for some ambiguity, though I for one am not convinced that the declared emotion is really so suspect as it often now appears. But, even if we accept the feeling as directly heroic, we can still see the poet almost immediately exploring its contrary in 'Tithonus', which was written at about the same time explicitly, Tennyson tells us, as 'a pendant' to 'Ulysses',[6] or rather a counter-cry, an incontestably overt death-wish.

From first to last the monologue form proved Tennyson's favourite device for distancing himself from his subject, as it may well have been the dominant mode of other Victorian poets – not only Browning, with whom we first of all associate the type – but also of Clough, Swinburne, Morris, and Meredith. Linda K. Hughes in a recent, detailed study, *The Manyfacèd Glass: Tennyson's Dramatic Monologues*, includes a great deal of the Tennyson canon under the rubric and patiently describes many variations on the poet's practice.[7] Alan Sinfield's earlier and more general essay on the monologue (1977), however, suggests approaches to the form more immediately relevant to my argument. The dramatic monologue, Dr Sinfield believes, must necessarily involve some degree of 'feint', the pretence that the speaker of the poem is not to be directly identified with the poet, though we may sense the presence of the poet behind the persona, and since we recognise the function of the feint, 'we are obliged to posit simultaneously the speaking "I" and the poet's "I".'[8]

Tennyson's classical monologues, often among his best poems, such as 'Ulysses' and 'Tithonus', adapt a persona from established myth or legend – for example, Tiresias, Oenone or Demeter – with whose dominant emotion the poet may feel some lyric sympathy. A similar personal need or self-conscious parallel prompts lesser monologues, like 'Columbus' and 'Romney's Remorse', in both of which the real historical protagonists wince with a Tennysonian fear of public defection.[9] Other pieces with well-defined speakers, on the other hand, are more clearly detached from the poet's personal concern or compulsion and his private demand for obliquity; the mordant 'St Simeon Stylites', for example, Browningesque before Browning in its dramatic energy, or the numerous forays into Lincolnshire dialect, seem first of all objective exercises in satiric or humorous characterisation.

But the monologues that interest me most at the moment are more lyrical and less like Browning's than any of these detached pieces; that is, the feint is less consistently obvious; the speaker is less defined in his distinction from the poet; and the two 'I's', the first persons we must deduce, merge as well as diverge in our perception. The protagonists of 'Locksley Hall' and *Maud* are both entangled in webs of off-stage melodrama, events that have driven them to the emotional breaking-point or beyond it altogether. But neither, despite bizarre circumstance, is a distinct individual identity; both indeed are much alike, both anonymous children of the nineteenth century, typical Byronic heroes, or, more accurately, post-Byronic sensibilities, injured like Tennyson himself by their own insights and the crass materialism of their time, contemptuous of their societies, yet eager in the end to reach some sort of *modus vivendi* with their peers. Both are aware of their maladies and malaise – 'foolish passion', 'palsied heart', lonely 'raging', violence of response and heated overstatement, incipient madness – and Tennyson expects their confessions of instability to distance them from himself and to set our judgement as readers on guard. (In a recently published letter he insists that the hero of *Maud* 'was intended to have an hereditary vein of insanity' and that, as 'a man constitutionally diseased', he was accordingly not to be regarded as an equable analyst of his own inner turmoil or as a trustworthy advocate of the impending war without.)[10] Yet Tennyson also achieves what I might call an 'owning by disowning', in so far as he makes the troubled context of each poem the vehicle of an acceptable lyric meditation. In 'Locksley Hall' the evocation of young love before its betrayal counter-balances the ranting narrative, and a naive confidence in the idea of progress, the

early-Victorian 'march of mind', overcomes the fear of the speaker
(and the poet) of being misunderstood or summarily rejected by his
society. In *Maud*, where the operatic plot swirls around in the wings
of a mental theatre, the alternate rage and reflection of the hero, in a
varied recitative, accommodate the great arias, some of which
Tennyson was eager to 'own' as 'songs of the deeper kind',[11] but all
of which he virtually 'disowns' by placement in a melodramatic
setting, the distorted imagination of an unreliable witness. The most
intense of these, 'Oh! that 'twere possible', the germ of *Maud*, originally had strong personal resonance in apparent reference to
Hallam's recent death; now, in the monodrama some twenty years
later, it acquires new relevance and pathos as the reminiscence of the
Byronic lover, who is and is not Tennyson but is clearly overwhelmed
by the loss of Maud. The subjective cry accordingly receives the
protection of a new contextual distance. We are no longer asked to
speculate on the half-hidden private meaning of the lyric as published reluctantly, without such support, in the 1837 *Tribute*.[12]

In a few monologues, notably 'Supposed Confessions', 'The Two
Voices' and 'The Ancient Sage', all less distracted than *Maud* by
peripheral action, the feint, if any, scarcely extends beyond the titles,
for the personae seem to differ in no conspicuous way from the
composing poet. 'Supposed Confessions of a Second-Rate Sensitive
Mind Not in Unity with Itself', as it was when published in 1830,
alludes to the piety of the speaker's dead mother (Elizabeth Tennyson
was still very much alive) but otherwise seems best read as an
account of the young Tennyson's religious doubts and his regret that
he cannot hold fast to the conviction of his childhood, tormented as
he now is by both hunger for belief and morbid dread of decay and
annihilation:

> Ay me! I fear
> All may not doubt, but everywhere
> Some must clasp Idols. Yet, my God,
> Whom call I Idol? Let Thy dove
> Shadow me over, and my sins
> Be unremembered, and Thy love
> Enlighten me. Oh teach me yet
> Somewhat before the heavy clod
> Weighs on me, and the busy fret
> Of that sharp-headed worm begins
> In the gross blackness underneath.

O weary life! O weary death!
O spirit and heart made desolate!
O damnèd vacillating state!
(R i, 222, ll. 177–90)

The disarming apologetic title, however, is not enough to establish
the required distance or to impose form on the ambivalent rambling
confession. Accordingly the poet, not to be embarrassed by what
must have seemed little more than a personal complaint of irresolu-
tion, suppressed the piece for some fifty years till it could be safely
assigned with abridged title to his 'Juvenilia'.

Nonetheless, essentially formless though it is, 'Supposed Confessions' prepared the way for the much finer monologue, 'The Two
Voices', where the vacillating state is absorbed by the discipline of
debate. Written partly before and finished soon after Hallam's death,
'Thoughts of a Suicide', as it was called in manuscript, avowedly a
product of personal melancholia, obtains its strength from the fact
that the poet, whether or not his own emotion were ever proximately
suicidal, for the better part of the poem waveringly endorses both
sides of the argument, the seductive voice of negation and the ego's
attempt to reassert its bruised but never wholly vanquished idealism. The bitter voice begins with an echo of Hamlet's 'To be or not to
be' and proceeds with a devastating cosmic irony:

A still small voice spake unto me,
'Thou art so full of misery,
Were it not better not to be? . . .

'Self-blinded are you by your pride:
Look up through night: the world is wide.

'This truth within thy mind rehearse,
That in a boundless universe
Is boundless better, boundless worse. . . .

'Forerun thy peers, thy time, and let
Thy feet, milleniums hence, be set
In midst of knowledge, dreamed not yet.

'Thou hast not gained a real height,
Nor art thou nearer to the light,
Because the scale is infinite.'
(R i, 571–6, ll. 1–3, 23–8, 88–93)

But the ego eventually counters with a faith beyond sense and reason, a life-affirming intuition:

> 'Who forged that other influence,
> That heat of inward evidence,
> By which he doubts against the sense? . . .
>
> 'The end and the beginning vex
> His reason: many things perplex,
> With motions, checks, and counterchecks. . . .
>
> 'Heaven opens inward, chasms yawn,
> Vast images in glimmering dawn,
> Half shown, are broken and withdrawn.'
>   (R i, 585–6, ll. 282–5, 298–300, 304–6)

The lyric potential in both directions is not so much held at a distance as checked by the alternating currents of the intellectual logic,
which destroy and restore both the despairing and the assertive
strains of feeling. Eventually the second voice, an almost inaudible
murmur at the end, is hardly necessary, and certainly no match for
the Mephistophelean tempter, who is the vigorous first voice; the
second rises simply as a confirmation of the ego's resilience and
offers a sanction for the sentimental domestic vignette of the chapel-
bound family and the final exuberant Wordsworthian resort, after
the dark night, to the refreshed morning fields.

Some fifty years after 'The Two Voices', 'The Ancient Sage' continues – and on one level resolves – the debate. The title announces
an obvious feint, and the brief narrative introduction establishes a
great distance in place and time from nineteenth-century England:
an Asian terrain, 'A thousand summers ere the time of Christ'. But
the sage's monologue makes clear that the ideas are more
Tennysonian than oriental, and the reader soon suspects that the
composing poet in venerated old age is quite prepared to play the
speaker's role, without much disguise, and, with a welcome freedom
from orthodox Christian restraints, is ready to defend a 'Faith beyond the forms of Faith'. The counter-voice now is that of the sage's
companion, a disillusioned young poet who does not address us
directly but whose verses the sage reads aloud from a scroll. The
lyrics are by no means nugatory, or to be easily shrugged off by the
sage's wiser experience; they offer a bitter but honest view of this-

worldly betrayal and defeat, the mockeries of evanescence and senil-
ity, in rhymes somewhat reminiscent in tone and imagery of
FitzGerald's *Rubáiyát* (which indeed Tennyson admiringly saluted
elsewhere in the same 1885 volume):

> 'The statesman's brain that swayed the past
>   Is feebler than his knees;
> The passive sailor wrecks at last
>   In ever-silent seas. . . .
> The plowman passes, bent with pain,
>   To mix with what he plowed;
> The poet whom his Age would quote
>   As heir of endless fame –
> He knows not even the book he wrote,
>   Nor even his own name.
> For man has overlived his day,
>   And, darkening in the light,
> Scarce feels the senses break away
>   To mix with ancient Night. . . .
>
> 'Yet wine and laughter friends! and set
>   The lamps alight, and call
> For golden music, and forget
>   The darkness of the pall.'
>   (R iii, 142–4, ll. 134–53, 195–9)

The negations here are real enough, but to the sage they represent
only one side of the picture, perhaps little more than a function of
language, implying their positive contraries; the sage comments:

> Some say, the Light was father of the Night,
> And some, the Night was father of the Light.
> No night no day! – I touch thy world again –
> No ill no good! such counter-terms, my son,
> Are border-races, holding, each its own
> By endless war: but night enough is there
> In yon dark city. . . .
>   (R iii, 145–6, ll. 247–53)

On one level, the sage is himself a radical sceptic, convinced that
'nothing worthy proving can be proven,/Nor yet disproven'. Yet his

own escape from an endless dialectic is a private intuition of meaning, or simply a yearning for something stable, 'lost and gone', distant and unattainable, a longing comparable perhaps to the *Sehnsucht* of the German Romantics. 'The whole poem', Tennyson said, 'is very personal. The passages about "Faith" and the "Passion of the Past" were more especially my own personal feelings. This "Passion of the Past" I used to feel when a boy' (*Mem*, ii, 319). And beyond the boyhood yearnings, which still invite lyrical description, are more elusive moments of complete 'loss of Self' gained through intense self-contemplation, a variety of mystical transcendence, ultimately inarticulate, wordless, 'unshadowable in words,/Themselves but shadows of a shadow-world' (ll. 238–9). 'The Ancient Sage', in effect Tennyson's last will and testament, thus proves highly subjective, modern, and even 'confessional', aware of life's mundane anomalies, yet independently visionary up to the strained limits of language itself, revealing a reticent sensibility rather than an indiscreet autobiography – a 'very personal' monologue held within a dialogical form.

Other poems, less starkly 'mystical' but still lyrical in shape or sentiment, achieve distance through a protective – or is it ambiguous? – framing by narrative rather than monologue. With characteristic naiveté Tennyson told his friend James Knowles that he had done nothing he could think nearly perfect, 'only fragments of things . . . such as "Come down, O Maid" . . . and "Tears, Idle Tears."'[13] Though composed as serious self-subsistent units, both of these lyrics appeared embedded in the mock-serious *Princess*, from which they have since been frequently disengaged like memorable arias from some half-forgotten opera.

Restored to its context, 'Tears, Idle Tears' must endure the disdain of Princess Ida, who scorns every concession to the past, prefers 'A trumpet in the distance pealing news/Of better,' and requests a song that moans not 'about the retrospect/But deals with the other distance and the hues/Of promise' (R ii, 234, iv. 63–4, 67–9). Some recent critics are inclined to assent to Princess Ida's judgement; James Kincaid, for one, argues that the song 'offers a kind of luxuriance that is regressive and imprisoning'.[14] I should accept such a reading as at best a half-truth, but one that ignores the integrity of the lyric itself, as well as Tennyson's declared sympathy with its 'mystic, *dämonisch* feeling' (*Mem*, i, 253). Impressed by the near-perfection of 'Tears, Idle Tears' in texture and imagery, I should find it strengthened rather than weakened by its sceptical context, an example of the more complete 'owning' by a vigorous 'disowning'.

Reviewing the 1842 volume, Leigh Hunt complained about the not-dissimilar framing of the 'Morte d'Arthur' and 'Godiva', the heroic narrative of each introduced by colloquial banter, with an air, he said, 'of literary dandyism, or fine gentlemanism, or fastidiousness, or whatever [the poet] may *not* be pleased to call it.' 'We suspect', Hunt continued, 'that these poems of *Morte d'Arthur* and Godiva are among those which Mr Tennyson thinks his best, and is most anxious that others should regard as he does, and therefore it is that he would make trifles of them.'[15] Whatever he thought of 'Godiva', Tennyson surely did value the 'Morte d'Arthur',[16] with which he would eventually conclude *Idylls of the King*, but 'The Epic', the 1842 domestic idyll that encased it, was not designed simply to pass it off as a trifle and so by indirection to establish its worth. Though the frame self-consciously mocks the poet Everard Hall, who, after 'some prelude of disparagement', reads the manuscript aloud, with a Tennysonian sonority, 'mouthing out his hollow oes and aes,/Deep-chested music' (R ii, 3, ll. 49–51), it raises – with some irony, of course – the serious question of how acceptable medieval legend may be to an early-Victorian public; Hall himself, sensitive to 'the fashion of the day', asks,

> 'Why take the style of those heroic times?
> For nature brings not back the Mastodon,
> Nor we those times; and why should any man
> Remodel models? these twelve books of mine
> Were faint Homeric echoes, nothing-worth. . . . '
>
> (R ii, 2, ll. 35–9)

After the reading the first-person narrator, who has observed Hall with some amusement, modulates the facetious note of the frame to assure us that the auditors were indeed respectful of the story, perhaps because it was redeemed by 'some modern touches here and there' (R ii, 19, l. 278). The apology, I suggest, is not just a product of 'literary dandyism', for the composing poet, as distinguished from Everard Hall, sees not only the strength of the narrative, which engages much of his own deepest emotion, but also a partial validity in the modern frame and in his own sense that he might perhaps better have chosen a modern subject and setting.

Over 'The Epic', as over much of Tennyson, plays a Romantic irony, inviting open-ended participatory judgement and what might now be called a varied 'reader-response'.

In view of some of the distancing I have been describing, it may not be too fanciful to set Tennyson at least briefly in this ironic perspective, from which he has seldom been appraised. Best exemplified in English by the Byron of *Don Juan*, 'the authentic romantic ironist', as Anne K. Mellor has recently defined him, 'is as filled with enthusiasm as with skepticism. He is as much a romantic as an ironist. Having ironically acknowledged the fictiveness of his own patternings of human experience, he romantically engages in the creative process of life by eagerly constructing new forms, new myths.' Romantic irony shows an 'inevitable and all-important consciousness of the limitations of human knowledge and of human language. . . . It criticizes and thus negates one's excessive commitment to the fictions of one's own mind,' and in the process it recognises the place and necessity of 'self-parody'. Byron in particular, according to Miss Mellor, practised 'a heroic balancing between enthusiastic commitment and sophisticated skepticism', in both of which he might believe, however sharply the one challenged the other.[17]

Tennyson, of course, was much less the persistent Romantic ironist than the sardonic Byron, but he was also, as I have tried to show, frequently aware of conflicting claims and eager then to seek a reasonable balance. His deeper 'commitment' was surely to his *lyric* impulse, his assurance of high poetic endowment, and his delight in verbal mastery; ideally he too would be, like the Virgil he saluted, an acknowledged 'lord of language'. But in his scepticism he questioned the stability of his medium and his own complete adequacy as dedicated artist. Though he would have resisted current notions of linguistic indeterminacy and final lack of referentiality, he was nonetheless troubled, as he confesses in *In Memoriam*, by a real sense that his words only half-revealed his thoughts and that the 'matter-moulded forms of speech' could scarcely encompass his vision. He rightly considered each of his longer poems, *The Princess, Maud*, the *Idylls*, as a new experiment designed to accommodate diverse tones and shifting points of view. And his irony often led, especially in his early work to self-parody, or at least to half-humorous deflation of his too-anxious poetic pride. 'Will Waterproof's Lyrical Monologue . . . made at the Cock', the most amusing and best-sustained of his self-satires, places the poet's role, his illusions of fame, and even his habitual melancholy in a vinous haze at the self-saving distance of the Romantic ironist:

> High over roaring Temple-bar,
>   And set in Heaven's third story,
> I look at all things as they are,
>   But through a kind of glory.
> (R ii, 99, ll. 69–72)

Finally, the failure to maintain a measure of disengagement like Will Waterproof's, a proper distance of the artist and the art work, is the burden of 'The Vision of Sin', which we may regard as Tennyson's most exemplary self-admonition. Here the sinner is a richly endowed sensuous poet destroyed by self-indulgent abandon to the life of sensations, and his last cry is a bitter lyric of disenchantment, in the tempo of a desperate *danse macabre*. A stronger man, we must assume from the allegory, would have attained the reverence of detachment, not the proud isolation from humanity condemned in 'The Palace of Art' but an aesthetic release from selfish delusion; he might have tried, we could say, to emulate the disciplined objectivity of the ideal artist in Joyce's *Portrait*, the artist who, 'like the God of the creation, remains within or behind or beyond or above his handiwork, invisible, refined out of existence, indifferent, paring his fingernails'. Tennyson himself did not always aspire to this ideal. But in 'The Vision of Sin', while the poet–sinner remains to be understood rather than to be judged, the ultimate archetypal Artist silently fashions the perfect lyric artifact, at the appropriate enigmatic distance:

> And on the glimmering limit far withdrawn
> God made Himself an awful rose of dawn.
> (R ii, 164, ll. 223–4)

Notes

1. I borrow from my own discussion of 'Far——Far——Away', drawing on the Harvard Notebooks 54, 55, in *Tennyson: the Growth of a Poet* (Cambridge, Mass.: Harvard University Press, 1960), pp. 1–2. Ricks prints some of the variants, iii, 197–8.
2. 'On a Mourner', see Ricks's headnote, i, 610.

3.   Tennyson, quoted by Ricks from a manuscript, iii,112.
4.   T. S. Eliot, *Essays Ancient and Modern* (London: Faber & Faber, 1936),
      p. 183.
5.   Terry Eagleton, 'Editor's Preface' to Alan Sinfield, *Alfred Tennyson*
      (Oxford: Blackwell, 1986), p. x.
6.   Tennyson, letter to George Smith, 26 December 1859, Cecil Y. Lang
      and Edgar F. Shannon, Jr (eds), *The Letters of Alfred Lord Tennyson*
      (Oxford: Clarendon Press; Cambridge, Mass.: Harvard University Press,
      1981, 1987), II, 248.
7.   Linda K. Hughes, *The Manyfacèd Glass: Tennyson's Dramatic Mono-
      logues* (Athens, Ohio: Ohio University Press, 1987): 'Almost a fifth of
      his poems, and some of his finest, are written in the dramatic mono-
      logue form' (p. 1).
8.   Alan Sinfield, *Dramatic Monologue* (London: Methuen, 1977), pp. 29,
      32.
9.   Columbus, once idolised, now repudiated, meditates on the cruelties
      of fame ('Columbus', 1880, R iii, 49–57). Romney as artist – though his
      life was surely more irregular than Tennyson's – speaks vehemently
      for the poet of the instability of reputation:

> . . . The painter's fame? but mine, that grew
> Blown into glittering by the popular breath,
> May float awhile beneath the sun, may roll
> The rainbow hues of heaven about it –
>   There!
> The coloured bubble bursts above the abyss
> Of Darkness, utter Lethe. . . .
>
> Then, in the loud world's bastard judgment-day,
> One truth will damn me with the mindless mob,
> Who feel no touch of my temptation, more
> Than all the myriad lies, that blacken round
> The corpse of every man that gains a name.
>   (R iii, 212, 214–15, ll. 47–52, 114–18)

10.   Tennyson, letter to Archer Thompson Gurney, 6 December 1855,
      Letters, II, 137–8.
11.   Late in his life (1890) Tennyson spoke of his 'songs of a deeper kind'
      (*Mem*, ii, 377). Thomas J. Assad analyses ten such songs in his
      Tennysonian Lyric (New Orleans: Tulane Studies in English, XXIV,
      1983).
12.   Susan Shatto (ed.), *Tennyson's Maud* (London: Athlone Press; Norman,
      Oklahoma: University of Oklahoma Press, 1986), supplies a detailed
      history of the evolution of *Maud*, pp. 1–35.
13.   Knowles, reporting conversation of October 1872, in Hallam Lord
      Tennyson (ed.), *Tennyson and his Friends* (London: Macmillan, 1911),
      p. 252n.
14.   James R. Kincaid, *Tennyson's Major Poems* (New Haven, Yale Univer-
      sity Press: 1975), p. 67; also quoted by Henry Kozicki, who effectively

reviews the problem and diverse interpretations in his 'Tennyson's "Tears, Idle Tears": The Case for Violet', *Victorian Poetry*, XXIV (1986), 99–113.

15. Hunt, quoted by Ricks (ii, 172) from *Church of England Quarterly*, XII (1842), 361–76. The review is reprinted at length in J. D. Jump (ed.), *Tennyson: the Critical Heritage* (London: Routledge & Kegan Paul, 1967), pp. 126–36. Tennyson thought Hunt's review 'very unhappy in its want of insight': see letter to Edward Moxon, 11 October 1842, *Letters*, I, 212.

16. See letter to James Spedding, October 1834: 'Mort d'Arthur (which I myself think the best thing I have managed lately)', *Letters*, I, 125.

17. Anne K. Mellor, *English Romantic Irony* (Cambridge, Mass.: Harvard University Press, 1980), pp. 5, 11, 13, 31. See also D. J. Enright, who draws briefly on Mellor but with a good deal of scepticism about the validity of 'Romantic irony', *The Alluring Problem: An Essay on Irony* (London: Oxford University Press, 1986), p. 13. Neither Mellor nor Enright discusses Tennyson as Romantic ironist.

4

The Archetype that Waits: *The Lover's Tale, In Memoriam* and *Maud*

AIDAN DAY

Difficulty, obscurity, are not conditions characteristically associated with Tennyson's poetry. And up to a point there is good reason for this. W. W. Robson, commenting on the mimetic precision which seems to some a typical excellence in Tennyson's verse, has observed that Tennyson's lines from *In Memoriam* on the sunflower that will, '. . . shining fair,/Ray round with flames her disk of seed' (R ii, 422; ci, 5–6), would help the police to an identification better than Blake's: 'Ah Sunflower, weary of time,/Who countest the steps of the sun . . .'[1] The same might be said – begging the constabulary's indulgence – of the *In Memoriam* speaker's description of the prominent frontal bone over Arthur Hallam's eyes: 'over those ethereal eyes/ The bar of Michael Angelo' (R ii, 404; lxxxvii, 39–40). But one of the peculiarities of Tennyson's verse is that a special branch of difficulty might arise if one were to fill out, say, a missing person's file in the terms of *In Memoriam* xcvii:

> My love has talked with rocks and trees;
> He finds on misty mountain-ground
> His own vast shadow glory-crowned;
> He sees himself in all he sees.
> (R ii, 415; xcvii, 1–4)

As W. W. Robson notes, 'Tennyson is by no means always as sweetly pellucid as he is commonly held to be'.[2]

In this chapter I want to look at the root in Tennyson's own work of some of the less transparent features of *In Memoriam*. I want to suggest that behind these features – as behind some of the more obscure configurations of *Maud* – lies an imaginative paradigm which

Tennyson was working with from a very early stage in his poetic career. I begin with a detailed consideration of the paradigm as it appears in what Tennyson once agreed were his most 'touching' lines (*Mem*, ii. 466) and which the *Edinburgh Review* in October 1837 called a 'somewhat mysterious' piece, the lyric 'Oh! that 'twere possible', before going on to suggest the senses in which the paradigm may be seen to be at work in *The Lover's Tale*, *In Memoriam*, and *Maud*.

I

'Oh! that 'twere possible . . .'. Such is the opening lament of the lyric which Tennyson first wrote in 1833–4 and then contributed in an expanded form under the title 'Stanzas' to Lord Northampton's 1837 anthology *The Tribute*:

> Oh! that 'twere possible,
>   After long grief and pain,
> To find the arms of my true-love
>   Round me once again!
>   (R ii, 21, ll. 1–4)

But it is not possible: in so far as a literal story is ever engraved in this lyric, the loved one is dead. Her arms can neither reach nor her 'hand', her 'lips', her 'eyes' be reached: 'Alas for her that met me,/ That heard me softly call' (R ii, 21–2, ll. 25, 49–50). And yet her ghost haunts the speaker in the present of the lyric. Perhaps it should more properly be said, her ghosts: since she comes, on the one hand, as ominous 'shadow' and, on the other, as 'phantom fair and good' (R ii, 21, 23, ll. 11, 91). Thus it is that George Marshall can speak of the way in which the 'mourner' of 'Oh! that 'twere possible' is 'governed by the dual aspect of the spiritual presence of the dead loved one'.[3] But the problem is that while a mode of possession *is* recounted by the speaker of the lyric, we do not have here merely a Gothic tale which endorses the possibility of the literal presence of an unearthly exhalation. In the closing stages of the poem it is true that the speaker identifies the 'good' spirit of the lyric as the 'phantom' of 'the maiden, that I lost' (R ii, 23, l. 79). 'Fair and kind' and 'lovely by my side' is this phantom (R ii, 23, ll. 86, 88). But lovely as it may be, it is not claimed as a spiritual phenomenon touching the speaker, as it were, from the outside. This apparition is confessedly a construction of the speaker's own mind, an image drawn from memory, and it explicitly stands in lieu of that which it images. 'Would' that 'the happy Spirit' *would* 'descend/In the chamber or the street' declares the speaker –

> But she tarries in her place,
> And I paint the beauteous face
> Of the maiden, that I lost,
>   In my inner eyes again . . .
>
> I can shadow forth my bride
> As I knew her fair and kind . . .
>   In the silence of my life –
> 'Tis a phantom of the mind.
>   (R ii, 23, ll. 71–2, 77–80, 85–6, 89–90)

These lines explore not so much some kind of supernatural presence as the way in which the speaker's representation of the loved one is haunted by her absence. It is the emptiness of the mind's images – its *re*presentations – that is phantasmal here. What the inner eye possesses – what it beholds and holds in its picturing – defines only an embracing dispossession. To be haunted thus in 'Oh! that 'twere possible' is to be possessed by nothing.

A similar sort of thing may be said of the alternative manifestation of the lost beloved: the disturbing 'shadow' or 'abiding phantom cold' (R ii, 22, l. 35) which the speaker describes as 'ghastly sister' (R ii, 23, l. 94) of the 'phantom fair'. This first 'flits before' the speaker in the third stanza (R ii, 21, l. 11) and in the fourth it

> . . . leads me forth at Evening,
> It lightly winds and steals
> In a cold white robe before me . . .
>   (R ii, 21, ll. 17–19)

We might take this as a stock property of paranormal romance, a dramatisation of the 'visible but impalpable form of a dead person' (*OED*). But the lyric undermines clear distinctions between speaker and shadow. The nightly emaciations of the speaker in the fifth stanza, for example, 'Half the night I waste in sighs' (R ii, 21, l. 23), prelude a progressive reduction of the speaker to a wraith of himself, a blurring of contrast between him and the condition of the shadow.

Thus, the 'abiding phantom cold' which in the sixth stanza attends the speaker at dawn and wakefulness is followed in the seventh by the speaker rising only to be lost within a city scene that is itself phantasmal, characterised by images of the erasure of substance and form:

> Then I rise: the eave-drops fall
>   And the yellow-vapours choke
>   The great city sounding wide;
> The day comes – a dull red ball,
>   Wrapt in drifts of lurid smoke,
>   On the misty river-tide.
>   (R ii, 22, ll. 36–41)

And where, in the fourth stanza, we had heard that the shadow 'winds and steals', in the eighth the speaker himself moves through the unreal city with the elusive insubstantiality of the shadow that accompanies him:

> Through the hubbub of the market
>   I steal, a wasted frame;
> It crosseth here, it crosseth there –
> Through all that crowd, confused and loud,
>   The shadow still the same. . . .
>   (R ii, 22, ll. 42–6)

In stanza three we had heard that the shadow 'flits' before the speaker. In the tenth stanza the confusions of speaker and shadow are intensified as the 'eye' which 'flits' in the second line of that stanza reads simultaneously as the eye of the speaker and of the shadow. The point of view of the depleted and depressed psyche is punningly elided here – through the homonym 'eye'/'I' – with the look of the shadow itself:

> Then the broad light glares and beats,
>   And the sunk eye flits and fleets,
>   And will not let me be.
>   (R ii, 22, ll. 55–7)

As *sister* of that construction of the speaker's mind which is cast as the 'phantom fair', it is perhaps only to be expected that the loved one's 'shadow' should be cast as haunting the speaker as an individual may be haunted by his or her own shadow; or as an individual possesses and is possessed by the reflections of his or her own mind. In the eleventh stanza, connotations of the shadow are indeed not merely confused with but assimilated to a manifestation of the bereft speaker's brain:

> Get thee hence, nor come again,
> > Pass and cease to move about . . .
> 'Tis the blot upon the brain
> That *will* show itself without.
> > > (R ii, 23, ll. 65–6, 69–70)

Like the 'phantom fair', the 'shadow' is a sign of the loved one's absence and its first manifestation is as of a negative impression of her: '*Not* thou', says the speaker in the second line of the third verse, 'but *like* to thee' (R ii, 21, l. 12; my emphases). And, as in the case of the mind's eye painting of the 'beauteous face', that 'Not' and that 'like'-ness locate a vacancy in the speaker's figurings of the beloved. As projections of the mind both fair and foul ghosts ascribe to the motif of the lost loved one a self-referential dimension in respect of the speaker that exceeds the terms of literal reference to a dead lover. The figure of the lost loved one in 'Oh! that 'twere possible' functions critically as a figure of the speaker's own identity.

The narcissistic value of the figure of the beloved in 'Oh! that 'twere possible' is manifest in the tenth stanza where the speaker as shadow, the 'sunk eye', expresses a desire to escape definition in a public world: a world in which the speaker experiences himself as alienated, unable to find in the interplay of gazes from which social identities are formed the kind of complementation or filling-out of self which he identifies in terms of love. 'I loathe the squares and streets', he admits, 'And the faces that one meets,/Hearts with no love for me' (R ii, 22, ll. 58–60). Unwilling to prepare a face to meet the faces that he meets and recoiling from the blankness of being gazed through – like a shadow – by such faces, the speaker turns, in a solipsistic appeal, towards the figure of the loved one. But this is itself a turning towards an evanescence. It is a turning inwards that is at the same time a turning out of self. For the impulse is towards a type of infantile dependence that would define a freedom from self-responsibility, a freedom from self. It is an impulse towards a condition free of individuation and all its separations and divisions.

It is an impulse towards a condition free of individuation and all its separations and divisions. It is an impulse towards an imaginary state outside or anterior to that loss of wholeness and fulness which is the inevitable access of self-consciousness. The loved one is addressed as the object of a psychic regression that would fulfil the speaker by stripping him of himself. The closing four lines of stanza ten image an orgiastic dissolution of the pains of that bereavement which is the gain of individual identity:

> Always I long to creep
> To some still cavern deep,
> And to weep, and weep and weep
> My whole soul out to thee.
> (R ii, 22, ll. 61–4)

For the 'sunk eye' so to dissolve would be to sink entirely out of sight. And not only out of sight – and out of memory and mind – but also out of language. The fair 'phantom of the mind' of 'Oh! that 'twere possible' inhabits, according to the speaker, 'the silence of my life'. As an absolute Other, a figure by whom and in whom the sole self of the speaker might be completed through the suspension of his solitude, through an absolution from himself, the fair spirit is necessarily posited as moving beneath or beyond language. For union with this Other – patriarchally stereotyped in terms of the feminine – would be to be redeemed of the self-consciousness, the selfhood, that is co-extensive with language. A comparable emphasis haunts the speaker's projection – as he imagines perfect union in the past with the beloved – of a primordial state of full and complete being. For all that the beginnings of present life are in one sense the subject of the second stanza, the verse deals expressly in an ideal construction of the past. Positing an intact, unitary origin here is to posit an imaginary space removed from temporal sequence, a space characterised in terms of an unearthly suspension of consciousness, a space typified by its muteness:

> In the silent woody places
> Of the land that gave me birth,
> We stood tranced in long embraces,
> Mixt with kisses sweeter, sweeter,
> Than any thing on earth.
> (R ii, 21, ll. 6–10)

As it is, the speaker remains defined within the self-consciousness and representation of language and in so being remains, like the poem which constitutes his voice, outside or dispossessed of the unitary condition which is reflected upon and represented. The speaker's trauma in 'Oh! that 'twere possible' turns on the sense in which his self-consciousness distances him from himself. The lyric's 'I' – as sign and re-presentation – stands always outside its own 'true' self, as empty and spectral as the shadow with which it is ambiguously exchanged in the poem. Hence the special connotation of lack in those lines of the eleventh stanza which both convey the speaker's recognition of the shadowiness, the second-handedness, of his own self and imply the emptiness of the poetic writing or shadowing – the lyric 'Oh! that 'twere possible' – which *is* that self: "Tis the blot upon the brain/That *will* show itself without'. An exteriorisation of self in words that spell the want of that to which they refer. Likewise, lyric and lyric-speaker, bearing only the status of a shadow, a copy, an unreal appearance, an emptiness, an effacement, a blot, endlessly pursue a sacramental presence as a shadow may be pursued – forever at hand, forever out of reach. Articulating the fantasy of a wholeness and self-possession to-be-regained, the speaker of the lyric is split by his very articulation from the object of his desire. That potency of the speaker which recognises the shadowy insubstantiality of his own self-consciousness causes him to question the veracity of the images he simultaneously draws of an actual past state of fulness. In the eleventh stanza, one self of the speaker would cast an injunction against the self which insinuates the spectral nature of his own history:

> Get thee hence, nor come again,
>   Pass and cease to move about –
> Pass, thou death-like type of pain,
>   Mix not memory with doubt.
>   (R ii, 23, ll. 65–8)

Losing the certainty of a complete and pure origin, the speaker is haunted as by a nightmare. Like the self-reprobation which possesses the speaker of *In Memoriam* in response to the absence of Hallam ('like a guilty thing I creep . . .', R ii, 326; vii, 7), the speaker of 'Oh! that 'twere possible' is possessed by a sense of his own unreality as by a conviction of transgression. The mind as narcissistic shadow modulates into its own incubus:

> It crosseth here, it crosseth there –
> Through all that crowd, confused and loud,
>   The shadow still the same;
> And on my heavy eyelids
>   My anguish hangs like shame.
>   (R ii, 22, ll. 44–8)

But the deepest shame associated with the figure of the loved one as shadow resides in the fact that desire for the beloved, desire for union with the Other that lies beyond contingency, division, and language, touches at root a death-wish. The ideal Other – possession of whom would relieve self-consciousness of perpetual displacement from itself – is to be gained only at the self-contradictory cost of dying out of self and out of the language in which that self is constituted. To fulfil the paradoxical logic of its own desire for absolute peace and completion the self as shadow must turn shade, must embrace utter annihilation, become a blank. The self's compulsion to unself itself, to unwrite or blot out its own existence – its 'suicidal wish for oblivion', as Christopher Ricks puts it[4] – is granted the power of an unconscious drive. In stanza fourteen the 'ghastly sister' glides and is 'moved around me still/With the moving of the blood,/That is moved not of the will' (R ii, 23, ll. 94–7). But shame at this compulsion is lodged in the conscious self's and language's resistance to that which they are compulsively bound to pursue. Contemplating his own shadowy nature and inclination the speaker in the thirteenth stanza expresses a fear –

> Lest my heart be overborne
> By the thing I hold in scorn,
>   By a dull mechanic ghost
>   And a juggle of the brain.
>   (R ii, 23, ll. 81–4)

Against his own darkest proclivity the speaker of the lyric constructs a countermanding position in the figure of the beloved as 'phantom fair': 'I paint the beauteous face/In my inner eyes again,/Lest my heart be overborne' (R ii, 23, ll. 78, 81–2). In the fourteenth stanza:

> 'Tis a phantom fair and good;
>   I can call it to my side,
>   So to guard my life from ill,
>   Though its ghastly sister glide. . . .
>   (R ii, 23, ll. 91–4)

Yet the 'phantom fair' is no less a 'phantom of the mind', no less a substanceless image, than the self as shadow which seeks fulfilment through final confirmation of its own nothingness. What, then, may be an accounting for the 'dual aspect' of the beloved Other in 'Oh! that 'twere possible'? Not least, that the mind's image that is the 'fair' spirit articulates a wish for fulfilment not in terms of negation and absence but in terms of positive presence. The fair phantom is taken as the mark of an original, transcendent guarantor of the content of the self. In the closing vision of the lyric, the 'phantom fair' –

>   like a star,
>   Through the channel windeth far
>   Till it fade and fail and die,
>   To its Archetype that waits,
>   Clad in light by golden gates –
>   Clad in light the Spirit waits
>   To embrace me in the sky.
>   (R ii, 24, ll. 104–10)

Even the mind's dearest image must give up the ghost. Formulated in this way, however, desire for an object outside time and space involves a transvaluation of death-wish into legitimate spiritual aspiration.

But the would-be transubstantiation between phantom of the mind and Archetype remains a rhetorical twist: the real presence of the Archetype is no more sealed by the word which speaks it than the fair phantom of mind clasps the substance of what it substitutes for. The difference between the two phantoms remains drawn within language and the lyric, registering a genetic link between the two sisters, fears and acknowledges the possibility of the illusoriness of the distinction it would insist upon. For all that it seeks at one level to make an absolute contrast between them, traces of the one sister are continually surfacing in the other. Throughout, the poem witnesses the two spirits collapsing lexically into each other. The Archetype of the 'phantom fair' is 'Clad in light' but the shadow *'lightly winds'* its 'white' winding-sheet. The 'phantom fair and good' would represent a different principle from that signalled by the 'shadow' but, in the making, the two phantoms fall surreptitiously together: 'I can *shadow* forth my bride/As I knew her fair . . .' confesses the speaker. And while, in stanza fourteen, the 'ghastly' shadow may be distinguished from the deliberate imaginative projection of its sister by the fact that the shadow's appearance 'is moved not of the will', nevertheless, in the eleventh stanza: 'Tis the blot upon the brain/ That *will* show itself without'. And when we take it that the long-wished-for rest of the tenth stanza is to be provided by the *fair* spirit, 'Always I long to creep/To some *still* cavern deep', we should at the same time recall the grave stasis that in the eighth verse typifies 'The shadow *still* the same'. 'Oh! that 'twere possible' does not conform to a simply sequential narrative convention, so that there are numerous abrupt shifts and transitions between its stanzas. One such dislocation works to great effect in dissolving certainties of separation between the two phantoms of the lyric. When the eleventh stanza opens, 'Get thee hence, nor come again,/Pass and cease to move about – /Pass, thou death-like type of pain', we can read *in* a connection with the 'shadow' that flits. But we might equally read the lines as referring to the impulse just recounted at the end of the tenth stanza, 'Always I long . . ./. . . to weep . . . /My whole soul out to thee'; and that 'thee' may address a loved one as shadowy as she is fair.

Against its surface avowals and disavowals, 'Oh! that 'twere possible' betrays an anxiety that there may be no transcendental authority for its dualities of dark and light, voidness and content, negative and positive. An anxiety that these are differences without absolute status, perceptible only within and relevant only to a mortal realm of difference and division. An anxiety that it may not be possible to credit a value system and a pattern for living that projects Heaven from one term of a relative opposition. A fear that it may never be possible to grasp – of the souls we loved – what and where they be. Tension remains high at the end of the lyric. Questions posed in respect of the shadow are juxtaposed, not exorcised, by the affirmation of an Archetype that itself delays and postpones belief as much as it incites it:

Let it pass, the dreary brow,
  Let the dismal face go by.
Will it lead me to the grave?
  Then I lose it: it will fly:
Can it overlast the nerves?
  Can it overlive the eye?
But the other, like a star,
Through the channel windeth far
  Till it fade and fail and die,
To its Archetype that waits. . . .
       (R ii, 23–4, ll. 98–107)

II

It is a commonplace that 'Oh! that 'twere possible' is the 'germ' of *Maud*[5]: several sections of the lyric were incorporated verbatim into the 1855 poem (II. iv; R ii, 571–6). It is also well-known that, as Christopher Ricks summarises, 'Oh! that 'twere possible' has 'many links with *In Memoriam*' (R ii, 20). With these links in mind, Ricks observes that 'Oh! that 'twere possible' as originally conceived 'is plainly precipitated by the death of Hallam' (R ii, 20). But just how plain is this connection? For while the lyric as constituted in 1833–34 and 1837 does indeed look forward to both *In Memoriam* and *Maud*, it seems to me that the work at once looks backwards through the 'chill . . ./Day' (*In Memoriam* lxxii, 17–18; R ii, 387) of 15 September 1833 to a poem substantially written, though not completed, before Hallam's death.

    The Lover's Tale, the earliest of Tennyson's long poetic disquisitions upon love, was first published in four parts in 1879. But Tennyson had begun composing it at least as early as 1828 and by 1832 had completed versions of the first three parts of the work: the fourth and concluding part was not composed until the late 1860s.[6] It is not my purpose here to get tangled up in the complex recensions of *The Lover's Tale*. What I do want to suggest is that 'Oh! that 'twere possible' reads in certain senses less like a precipitate from Tennyson's experience of Hallam's death than as a distillation of some of the fundamental elements of *The Lover's Tale* as it stood in 1832.

    The plot of the 1832 *Lover's Tale* – and, for the sake of some local textual variations between 1832 and 1879, I shall be taking the 1832 version as my text[7] – is simple enough. In part I, we come upon the speaker – the lover–protagonist – of the poem as he relates the story of his past life to a group of unspecified companions. He tells how he was brought up with his foster-sister Cadrilla and of how his childhood closeness to her extended into a youthful love for her. We hear of his pain upon discovering that Cadrilla was in love with another man – Lionel. The second part of the poem tells of the speaker's withdrawal into solitude and of the unsettling of his mind following Cadrilla's revelation. The third part continues with a further account of his disturbed state of mind.

Whatever the melodrama of the literal story, there moves beneath the surface of the narrative a psychological drama whose terms Edmund Gosse was quick to identify in the 1879 version of the poem, where the broad scheme of the first three parts remains the same as in 1832. Reviewing *The Lover's Tale* upon its publication in 1879 – and apparently quite unaware that the poem had first taken shape within the charged Shelleyan atmosphere of Tennyson's undergraduate career – Gosse discerned in the work the influence of a 'recent reading of *Epipsychidion*'.[8] The point, in brief, is that lover and loved one in *The Lover's Tale* masquerade upon a self-referential stage. As Emily is 'soul out of my soul' to the protagonist of *Epipsychidion*, so within the literal action of *The Lover's Tale* there is a Cadrilla who functions as a potency of the speaker's own identity. This dimension to the lovers' story is patent in a passage of 1832 where the speaker remembers times when he and Cadrilla would gaze – lover-like – into each other's eyes. The passage enacts a series of duplicitous transactions between lover and loved one in which the possibility of maintaining a literal distinction between them is suspended. On the one hand the protagonist speaks of his contemplation of the ideal object of his love in terms of an exercise in self-contemplation. On the other, he speaks as if entirely capitulating himself to the object of his love. The two perspectives are not held in stable and clearly contrasting frames of reference, but throughout the passage modulate indeterminately into each other. These large modulations are reinforced by the way in which difference between lover and loved one is undercut as the possessives that locate the speaker and the pronouns that designate the loved one give way at cardinal points to a definite article that subsumes the two: '*the* soul'; '*the* deep soul'. As lover and loved one interfuse in this passage, the identity that is asserted between them is the identity that comes of losing to the Other, the soul, that separation which delimits the estate of the conscious self:

Eye feeding upon eye with deep intent;
And mine with love too high to be exprest,
Arrested in its sphere, and ceasing from
All contemplation of all forms, did pause
To worship mine own image, laved in light,
The centre of the splendours . . .
                          mine image in her eyes . . .
Moved with their motions, as those eyes were moved
With motions of the soul . . .
                          She was darkhaired, darkeyed:
Oh, such dark eyes! . . .
                                     look at them,
You lose yourself in utter ignorance;
You cannot find their depth; for they go back,
And farther back, and still withdraw themselves
Quite into the deep soul . . .
                          Trust me, long ago
I should have died, if it were possible
To die in gazing on that perfectness
Which I do bear within me . . .
            (I. 62–88. R i, 331–3; I. 61–85*)

The implication of lover in loved one and vice-versa, and the
referral of the fulness and unity that is so figured to an absolute,
quasi-metaphysical principle defined by the capitalised abstraction
'Love', recur throughout *The Lover's Tale*. In the following passage,
for example, the protagonist, asked to recall the beginnings of his
experience of love, insists on the untraceableness of such beginnings.
It is simply not an appropriate question to ask of something drawing
from the deep soul (or Soul), drawing from without memory and
self-consciousness. 'Love,/Warm in the heart' cannot 'remember',

            Love in the womb, but resteth satisfied,
            Looking on her that brought him to the light . . .
            So know I not when I began to love.
            This is my sum of knowledge – that my love
            Grew with myself. . . .
                        (I. 154–62. R i, 336; I.152–60)

In its immediate sense specifying the speaker's own capacities of
love, the possessive formulation here – 'my love/Grew with myself'

– elides a few lines later with the same construction used in reference to Cadrilla:

> As Love and I do number equal years,
> So she, my love, is of an age with me.
> (I. 191–2. R i, 337; I. 189–90)

The elision is part of a broader identification of lover with loved one manifested at even the literal surface of the narrative. For, as the story would have it, Cadrilla – the foster-sister – indeed grew with the speaker. Born on the 'same morning', under 'the selfsame aspect of the stars' (I. 194–5. R i, 337; I.192–3), the two children shared the same mother and 'ever drew from thence/The stream of life, one stream, one life, one blood' (I.234–5. R i, 338; I.232–3). Echoing some of the features of what Carlos Baker has termed Shelley's 'psyche-epipsyche strategy',[9] the stylised symmetrical patterning of the histories of the protagonist and Cadrilla in *The Lover's Tale* forms part of a fable of lost psychic integrity. Like the construction of an ideal past condition of unity and harmony in 'Oh! that 'twere possible', *The Lover's Tale* projects the speaker's past with his loved one as a condition exceeding at once finite stricture and language. Of his happiest, most lovingly replete, 'hour' with Cadrilla the protagonist enthusiastically reminds his listeners that he is, after all, recounting the unrecountable:

> Sooner Earth
> Might go round Heaven . . .
> Than language grasp the infinite of Love.
> Oh day, which did enwomb that happy hour,
> Thou art blessèd in the years, divinest day!
> (I. 472–7. R i, 347; I. 471–6)

'Love in the womb'; 'she, my love, is of an age with me': in the plot of *The Lover's Tale* the complete reciprocation of being – the unbroken continuity of inner and outer, self and imago – pictured in the speaker's early experience and relationship with Cadrilla is subjected to a violation. With the interposition of a third term, Lionel, between speaker and Cadrilla, the plot of the poem articulates the shattering – as in some displaced Oedipal trauma – of the lover's uninterrupted communion with himself, his own soul, the object of his love. The rupturing of the imaginary wholeness that is emblematised by the word 'Love' and represented in the fable of the speaker's original relationship with Cadrilla initiates the speaker into the world of time and contingency – the realm of 'Change and Chance', as it is put at the end of the first part of *The Lover's Tale* (I.847. R i, 361; I.794).

Towards the beginning of part II the speaker recalls asking himself, after the failure of his union with Cadrilla:

> Was this the end?
> Why grew we then together i'the same plot? . . .
> Why were we one in all things . . .
> if that same nearness
> Were father to this distance, and that *one*
> 'Vauntcourier to this *double*?
>   (II. 21–9. R i, 362–3; II. 21–9)

Estranged from Cadrilla – ejected from the 'glad newyear/Of Being' (I. 277–8. R, i, 339; I. 275–6) – the speaker of *The Lover's Tale* finds himself subjected to the law of distance and doubling, exiled in a realm defined by the divisions, the iterations and duplexities of self-consciousness. Like the bereft speaker of 'Oh! that 'twere possible' the grieving and alienated lover of *The Lover's Tale* is constituted in a process of figuring fulness and completeness where the figuring itself defines the lack of fulness and completeness. Finding himself constituted in an order of simulation and representation – 'The precious jewel of my honoured life,/Erewhile close couched in golden happiness,/Now provèd counterfeit' (II. 77–9. R i, 364; II. 67*) – the speaker's sense of the vacuity of his own reality takes on the force of a dementia. In the closing stages of part II the lover is haunted by a dream of the loved one in her most positive aspect:

> her eloquent eyes . . .
> Filled all with pure clear fire, thro' mine down rained
> Their spiritsearching splendours . . .
> those fair eyes
> Shone on my darkness, forms which ever stood
> Within the magic cirque of memory . . .
>   (II. 149–64. R i, 366–7; II. 142–57)

But the representations of memory fail to guarantee the presence of the splendours they name. In a prefiguring of the 'dual aspect' of the

ghost of the lost loved one in 'Oh! that 'twere possible' – in a pre-
monition of the exchange between 'phantom fair' and 'shadow' or
'phantom cold' in the later lyric – the 'fair' form of the speaker's
vision at the conclusion to part II of *The Lover's Tale* darkly betrays its
own insubstantiality:

> I wound my arms
> About her . . .
> I clasped her without fear: her weight
> Shrank in my grasp, and over my dim eyes,
> And parted lips which drank her breath, downhung
> The jaws of Death: I, screaming, from me flung
> The empty phantom . . .
> and I
> Down weltered thro' the dark ever and ever.
> (II. 204–12. R i, 368–9; II. 197–205)

Nor is the situation redeemed in the third part of the poem. The
hollowness of the mind's images of a perfect spiritual Other is explored in different terms in this section. Dreaming a vision of the
loved one's death, the lover envisages also her rebirth. But it is a
vision of merely naturalistic rebirth – of the loved one 'Studded with
one rich Provence rose' (R i, 371; III. 45) rising 'from out her death-
like chrysalis' (R i, 370; III. 41) amid 'wild Bacchanals' (R i, 370;
III. 25). The vision comprises a parodic image of resurrection and the
speaker is left rooted in an unleavened natural world – 'the phantom, Nature', a 'hollow form with empty hands' (*In Memoriam*, iii, 9,
12; R ii, 321) – as isolated and spiritually blank as at the end of part
II: 'And I stood sole beside the vacant bier' (R i, 371; III. 58).

The fable of a primordial state of unity in *The Lover's Tale* is
founded on the contradiction that what is fabled is excluded by the
fabling. The narrative of a space 'shut in from Time', as the lover's
early experience is described (I. 430. R i, 345; I. 428), rehearses in its
very status as narrative the lack of that space. For it is the self-
conscious self – with its memory of things lost and its fantasies of
future *dénouements* – that moves and has its relative being in narrative. And the self-consciousness of narrative turns on an alienation
from the unselfconscious unity of the soul. The 'Being limitless'
(I. 510. R i, 348; I. 504/5) posited in the lover's original union with
loved one is known only by virtue of a narrative reflection that is
sundered from the condition of which it speaks. In a passage at the

end of part I that has implications for the narrative that is *The Lover's Tale* itself, the lover tells of the way in which his reviewing of the story of his loss impotently re-enacts the grievous splitting of which that story was born:

> . . . Love mourned long, and sorrowed after Hope;
> At last she sought out Memory, and they trod
> The same old paths where Love had walked with Hope,
> And Memory fed the soul of Love with tears.
>
> (I. 862–5. R i, 362; I. 807–10)

The impulse to recount a condition of integrity – to tread the same old paths where Love had walked with Hope – may manifest desire for a regaining of that lost condition. But it is a desire doomed to the tears of frustration as the recounting endorses the banishment it would rescind.

No doubt it could be taken as symptomatic of the essential uncloseableness of the narrative Tennyson set himself in *The Lover's Tale* that the poem remained formally incomplete for so many years. But even in the conclusion somewhat arbitrarily imposed in the text of 1879 – a concluding fourth movement that seeks awkwardly to suppress the psychological nuances characterising the first three parts of the work – Tennyson does not insist on showing his protagonist returned from exile and closing with all he loved.[10] 'He past for ever from his native land', we are told (R i, 381; IV. 384); forever displaced, we must infer, from his love and the perfectness within him.

Such an ending may seem unsatisfying. But the speaker's finally unsatisfied desire to close with all he loved is a desire for an unselving, a desire for a space outside narrative itself, outside time, memory and mind. That desire may ground the story that articulates it but fulfilment of the desire cannot be delivered by the story. Such a story may be brought formally to an end – even an end which claims repossession of 'Being limitless' – but any such formal ending is bound in its temporal fixture to fail to satiate a motivating desire for something that cannot be told, something that lies outside discourse and narrative. The story of *The Lover's Tale*, with its image of a lost psychic Eden and its recurrent projection of a return to that Eden, can never really be finished. And that is why the paradigmatic fable of *The Lover's Tale* comes to be told again in Tennyson, with whatever different emphases and accretions. Not only in 'Oh! that 'twere possible' but also in *In Memoriam* and *Maud*.

III

'We seem to hear of a person unlike ourselves in failings and virtues. . . . Instead of a memorial we have a myth. . . . The lost friend stalks along a giant of 11 feet, or moves a spiritual being, with an Eden-halo . . .'. Thus the reviewer of *In Memoriam* in *The Times* for 28 November 1851, reacting to a dimension of Tennyson's projection of the figure of Arthur Hallam in the poem. It is this dimension of Hallam in *In Memoriam* that is descended from the representation of the lost loved one in the 1832 *Lover's Tale* and in 'Oh! that 'twere possible'. There are other Hallams in *In Memoriam*: some of them more obviously memorial, more obviously adjusted to a biographical plane of reference, than others. *In Memoriam* weaves together a variety of Hallams, just as it weaves together a plurality of speakers, a plurality of voices all enunciating the word 'I'. But one of the dominant stitches in the fabric of the poem takes up the question of the divisions and alienations upon which self-consciousness is founded. Perhaps the most familiarly cited of *In Memoriam*'s engagements with this matter is that in section xlv, a lyric which, as Terry Eagleton observes, 'unquestionably proves' that Tennyson 'had read Lacan's *Ecrits*':[11]

> . . . as [the baby] grows he gathers much,
> And learns the use of 'I', and 'me',
> And finds 'I am not what I see,
> And other than the things I touch'.
> (R ii, 362–3; xlv, 5–8)

It is in relation to this kind of preoccupation in *In Memoriam* that the Hallam of biographical reference is co-opted to the paradigm of the lost loved one that Tennyson had first exploited before his friend had died. It is in relation to this kind of preoccupation that there is in *In Memoriam* a figure of Hallam projected as an ideal Other, a figure of the poet's own soul.

The reviewer of *In Memoriam* in *The Times* was disconcerted not only by the 'Eden-halo' of the lost friend, but disliked also 'the tone of – may we say so! – amatory tenderness' pervading the poem: 'Very sweet and plaintive these verses are; but who would not give them a feminine application.' It is not merely that in the sometimes 'feminine' application of the figure of Hallam in the poem we may trace vestiges of the feminine stereotyping of the lost loved one in *The Lover's Tale* and 'Oh! that 'twere possible'. It is that as a projection of an ideal Other, the figure of Hallam, like the nominally feminine loved ones in the earlier poems, is a token of a space outside narrative and language; and, accordingly, eluding the gender divisions and specificities of language. The energies of a 'space underlying the written', 'indifferent to language', 'anterior to judgement', as Julia Kristeva puts it,[12] are energies that ever subvert and destabilise syntactic coherence, pronominal fixture, and the subject and gender positions that are constituted in language. The 'bafflingly complex series of slippages'[13] in the gender applications of the loved one in *In Memoriam* are in significant part an effect of the unwritten and unwriteable dimension which that loved one betokens in the poem. If *The Lover's Tale* and 'Oh! that 'twere possible' subscribe too easily to a monolithically feminine characterisation of that which lies outside discourse, *In Memoriam* treats a comparable area with greater sophistication in its casting of Hallam as a type of the Other.

The Hallam of the Eden-halo, the Hallam of myth rather than of memorial, forms one of the principal elements in *In Memoriam*'s pervasive and variously-defined fable of a vanished state of psychic integrity. The appropriation of the biographical to the mythic Hallam starts early in the poem. As, for example, in the speaker's ultimately un-ironised construction of the literal past with the friend in terms of a 'pastoral', pre-lapsarian innocence: 'round us all the thicket rang/ To many a flute of Arcady' (R ii, 343; xxiii, 23–4); ' . . . this was Life' (R ii, 343; xxv, 1). It is at the psychologically mythopoeic level of the poem that, as Eagleton says, 'Hallam's death has dislodged the poet from 'an "imaginary" narcissistic plenitude of identity and left him dolefully stranded in the "symbolic" order, marooned in that ceaseless play of difference, loss, absence and exclusion which is part of the very linguistic form of the text'.[14]

Against the troubled play of the conscious, linguistically defined, volitional self *In Memoriam* sets – like a redeeming phantom of the mind – the countenance of the loved one:

> . . . all at once beyond the will
> I hear a wizard music roll,
> And through a lattice on the soul
> Looks thy fair face and makes it still.
> (R ii, 385; lxx, 13–16)

Elsewhere the speaker asserts that 'the face will shine/Upon me' (R ii, 437; cxvi, 9–10), filling out the desolating distances of time and

memory, resolving the doublings of selves past and a self conscious
of past selves. And if the apparition of this 'face' refuses easy cat-
egorisation as a literal ghostly haunting, if it eludes classification
either as something generated from within the mind or as something
issuing from some supernatural 'outside', then the construction in
the first stanza of section xcvii directly accommodates reference to
the loved one within a self-reflexive frame. In these lines Tennyson
invokes the 'spectre of the Brocken'[15] – as Coleridge had invoked it
in his poem 'Constancy To An Ideal Object' – to figure a communion
between self and Other. It is a figure that projects a recovery of
imaginary union between subjective and objective realms:

> My love has talked with rocks and trees;
> He finds on misty mountain-ground
> His own vast shadow glory-crowned;
> He sees himself in all he sees.

In the closing stages of *In Memoriam* the loved one is again a
vehicle for speaking of an absolute dissolution of contrast and opposition. 'Thou standest in the rising sun,/And in the setting thou
art fair'; 'Mixed with God and Nature thou'; 'Far off thou art, but
ever nigh' (R ii, 450–1; cxxx, 3–4, 11, 13); 'Known and unknown;
human, divine'; 'Mine, mine, for ever, ever mine' (R ii, 449; cxxix, 5,
8). But to speak in such terms of possession of the Other, to speak of
identity with a Hallam apotheosised in an universal principle of
'Love' (R ii, 445; cxxvi, 1), a Hallam who is everywhere and nowhere,
is to speak of a transcendence of the separations and alienations
belonging to the self-conscious self. It is to speak of a plenitude that
comes of losing the self, of capitulating the self to all that is not itself.
To speak of Hallam as a potency of the speaker here would be to say
the same of rocks, trees, stars and flowers. Speaker and Hallam
would be united in these sections of *In Memoriam* as the speaker
would be One with the rising and setting sun. The paradox being, of
course, that the speaking voice is engaged in affirming its own
dissolution, affirming a loss of the difference that constitutes its
speaking.

There are instances even in the later stages of *In Memoriam* where
the self-contradiction that the speaking 'I' is caught in – as it posits
communion with a dimension beyond time and language – leads it
to envisage the Other not in terms of presence but in terms of
spectral illusion: 'What find I in the highest place', we hear in section

cviii, 'But mine own phantom chanting hymns?' (R ii, 430; 9–10). Yet the speaking voice in the penultimate moments of the poem seeks to exorcise all shadows, to fill out all empty phantoms, and to insist that settling to One-ness, settling to non-existence, would be to assume the 'diffusive power' (R ii, 450; cxxx, 7) and positive countenance of the loved-one who is 'fair' in the setting sun. Of the dual aspect of the lost loved-one, *In Memoriam* in its closing stages privileges the 'phantom fair'. In the very last resort it rests upon an economy that, deferring final consummation beyond the bounds of the poem itself, nevertheless insists upon the real presence of an Archetype that waits: the 'one far-off divine event,/To which the whole creation moves' (*'Epilogue'*, 143–4; R ii, 459).

Not so in *Maud*. Ward Hellstrom has spoken of the figure of Maud in this poem as 'the Beatrice of the piece' who 'plays . . . a role similar to that played by Hallam in *In Memoriam*'.[16] This, up to a point, is apt enough. In the early sections of *Maud* the protagonist offers a picture of both inner and outer worlds as fractured and torn, racked with unregenerate forces, devoid of saving spiritual content. The suicide of the protagonist's father is presented as an effect and an evidence of such worlds. Contemplating that suicide in the opening lines of the poem the protagonist introduces an image that, as it recurs in a multiplicity of guises throughout the work, comes to figure the spiritual void that was the condition of the father's self-destruction: 'Echo there, whatever is asked her, answers "Death"' (R ii, 519; I. i. 4). Figures of vacancy circumscribe and define the psychological dissociation of the speaker himself:

> Living alone in an empty house . . .
> Where I hear the dead at midday moan . . .
> And my own sad name in corners cried,
> When the shiver of dancing leaves is thrown
> About its echoing chambers wide . . .
>   (R ii, 536; I. vi. 257–63)

It is as a symptom of a despairing vision of the 'nothingness' (R ii, 555; I. xviii. 638) of the human situation that the speaker also betrays not only a destructive but a self-destructive drive: 'Must *I* too creep to the hollow and dash myself down and die . . .?' (R ii, 523; I. i. 54). And it is against this drive that he comes to affirm, in his celebration of a reciprocated love for Maud in I. xviii, the discovery of a principle of love which redeems at once the void and negative self and the void and negative cosmos:

what care I,
Who in this stormy gulf have found a pearl
The countercharm of space and hollow sky . . .
(R ii, 555; I. xviii. 639–41)

But the countering fulness and purity which the protagonist lays claim to has indeed only the questionable status of a charm, a doubtful magic, a temporary stabilisation. The precariousness of his fantasy of regeneration, the continuing force of despairing compulsions within the self, is acknowledged if not admitted in the vertiginous, foreboding menace touched on in the closing lines of I. xviii:

Beat, happy stars, timing with things below,
Beat with my heart more blest than heart can tell,
Blest, *but for some dark undercurrent woe*
That seems to draw – but it shall not be so:
Let all be well, be well.
(R ii, 557; I. xviii. 679–83; my emphasis)

The pressure that is sublimated in these lines is at once regressive, pointing back to the nightmarish obsessions and suicidal proclivities of the past, and prophetic, pointing forwards to the failure of the fantasy. Whatever the speaker asserts, negative forces have been neither accommodated nor exorcised. The 'holy power of Love'[17] is vitiated by an unholy undercurrent; a current re-emphasised in the imagery of the protagonist's projection of resurrection in the concluding stanza of part I, where the powers of revived life congenitally fuse with the powers of blood that might be thought to have brought about death in the first place:

She is coming, my own, my sweet;
Were it ever so airy a tread . . .
My dust would hear her and beat,
Had I lain for a century dead;
Would start and tremble under her feet,
And blossom in purple and red.
(R ii, 565; I. xxii. 916–23)

It is not surprising, then, when baleful powers break out again and the speaker forfeits, in violence against Maud's brother, his never truly 'thornless' (R ii, 554; I. xviii. 625) garden of love: 'a million horrible bellowing echoes broke/From the red-ribbed hollow be-

hind the wood' (R ii, 566; II. i. 24–5). Nor is it surprising when the
third and concluding part of the poem refuses to sustain a clear
separation between the two 'ghosts' of the lost Maud. Ghosts that,
drawing on the model of 'Oh! that 'twere possible', haunt the speaker
as valencies of his own psychological state. Part II of *Maud*, incor-
porating 'Oh! that 'twere possible', had witnessed the speaker con-
ceiving the lost loved-one as 'happy spirit' (R ii, 575; II. iv. 221), on
the one hand, and as 'shadow still the same' or 'abiding phantom
cold' (R ii, 574, 575; II. iv. 212, 195), on the other. And in the concluding part of the work the loved-one again appears, under one aspect,
as blessed spirit articulating an impulse towards war as a positive
virtue:

> She seemed to divide in a dream from a band of the blest,
> And spoke of a hope for the world in the coming wars –
> 'And in that hope, dear soul, let trouble have rest,
> Knowing I tarry for thee', and pointed to Mars . . .
> > (R ii, 582; III. vi. 10–13)

But at the same time it is Maud as 'abiding phantom cold', as shadowy inclination towards suicide, 'a juggle born of the brain' (R ii,
569; II. ii. 90), who appears as the presiding spirit of the Northern
theatre of war:

> . . . . I saw the dreary phantom arise and fly
> Far into the North, and battle, and seas of death.
> > (R ii, 583; III. vi. 36–7)

No simple equation is made in the concluding part of *Maud* between
an autonomous spiritual virtue and the impulse towards war. Fair
and foul phantoms collapse into each other as both lead in the
direction of war, whether the killing is set by the Baltic or the Black
Sea. The notionally positive presence of the self reflected in the
blessed spirit calling for war is evacuated by the 'dreary phantom'
that simultaneously defines 'battle, and seas of death'. The pull
towards annihilation as a symptom of the self's spiritual destitution,
the 'dark undercurrent woe' running through the early sections of
the poem, still apparent in the sequence of supposed fulfilment in
love, and remanifest in the 'shadow' that haunts like a 'blot upon the
brain' (R ii, 574; II. iv. 200), is again evident in the speaker's glori-
fication of war in the closing moments of the poem. The difference in

the protagonist's position between the opening and the closing of the poem is the difference between a death-wish that cannot be justified and the same instinct dressed up in a respectable, publicly-sanctioned form. As Christopher Ricks observes, the 'honourable suicide of a soldier may redeem the dishonourable suicide'[18]. But it is not merely that *Maud* carries thus a critique of war fever. It is that its conclusion presents the protagonist's impulse towards war as a confirmation of his inability to resolve upon a vision of his own and the world's spiritual plenitude. The glossing of the 'shadow still the same', the 'dreary phantom', with the spirit that in a dream seems to divide from a band of the blest is a glossing that, unlike 'Oh! that 'twere possible', contains no projection of an Archetype that waits beyond the spectral forms of identity. 'I tarry for thee,' the blessed spirit had said. But she waits in the same space as the 'dreary phantom'. Reunion with the lost loved-one here is not fulfilling consummation but erasure only. J. R. Lowell called *Maud* the 'antiphonal voice to *In Memoriam*' (*Mem*, i. 394). If *In Memoriam* privileged the 'phantom fair', then *Maud*, refusing to allow the same, ends by privileging nothing. The peculiar passion of *Maud* is the passion of a profound regret, the passion of a desperate lament over the absence of the spiritual absolutes, the transcendent presences, which the poem itself has insisted relentlessly on emptying out. Yet the desperation, the alarm at being cast without a sufficient system of belief, does not qualify the intense honesty with which the poem confronts at once the disturbing potential of certain fictions of spirituality and the dangerous stereotyping of the 'masculine' and the 'feminine' that may be implied in such fictions. In section v of part II of *Maud* the speaker's insanity had granted him an insight not available within the approved codes of thought of his culture. As he speaks in this section of the 'keeper' of the 'garden' of love (or Love), an entire tradition of spiritual idealisation is exposed as a form of spiritual pride whose intolerable demands have had grotesque and destructive consequences for both men and women:

> But I know where a garden grows,
> Fairer than aught in the world beside,
> All made up of the lily and rose
> That blow by night, when the season is good,
> To the sound of dancing music and flutes:
> It is only flowers, they had no fruits,
> And I almost fear they are not roses, but blood;

> For the keeper was one, so full of pride,
> He linkt a dead man there to a spectral bride;
> For he, if he had not been a Sultan of brutes,
> Would he have that hole in his side?
>
> (R ii, 580; II. v. 310–20)

Notes

1. 'The Present Value of Tennyson', *Studies in Tennyson*, ed. Hallam Tennyson (1981), p. 51.
2. Ibid.
3. 'Tennyson's "Oh! that 'twere possible": A Link Between *In Memoriam* and *Maud*', *PMLA*, LXXVIII, 3 (June 1963), p. 229.
4. *Tennyson* (London, 1972), p. 143.
5. In a diary entry for 25 June 1865 William Allingham reports Tennyson speaking of 'Oh! that 'twere possible' as the 'germ of the whole' of *Maud*: *William Allingham, A Diary*, ed. H. Allingham and D. Radford (1907), p. 118.
6. For a detailed survey of the textual development of *The Lover's Tale* see Ricks's headnote to the poem, R i, 325–8.
7. Of the first three parts of *The Lover's Tale* completed by 1832, Tennyson had parts I and II set up in the proofs for his 1832 volume of *Poems*. Deciding at the last minute against including *The Lover's Tale* in *Poems*, 1832, he had several copies of these first two parts of the poem privately printed. Quotations below from 1832 parts I and II are taken from a copy of the private-printing (corrected by Tennyson) now in the British Library (Ashley 2075). Line-references to 1832 parts I and II precede reference to the equivalent passages in the 1879 text (where textual variation is considerable an asterisk after a line-reference means 'corresponding to' the lines of the final text). An early 1830s draft of part III of *The Lover's Tale* appears in a manuscript notebook at the Houghton Library, Harvard University (MS. Eng. 952 (12)). Since there are only very slight textual differences between this draft and part III as published in 1879, quotations below from part III are taken from 1879.
8. *The Academy*, XV, 7 June 1879, p. 489. Paul Turner has observed that the 1832 *Lover's Tale* 'is full of Shelleyan echoes' (*Tennyson*, 1976, p. 57). 'Nobody admires Shelley more than I once did. . . . I like his *Epipsychidion* as much as anything by him', Tennyson told Frederick Locker-Lampson in 1869 (*Mem*, ii. 70). In old age, Tennyson – perhaps assuming an elder Victorian's view of the young Romantic as the poet of adolescence – sometimes sought to deny the possibility of a Shelleyan influence on *The Lover's Tale*. But Tennyson's Cambridge circle, in the years when he was first writing the poem up to 1832, was one which placed special value on Shelley's work; see, for example, Peter Allen, *The Cambridge Apostles: The Early Years* (1978) and also *The Writings of Arthur Hallam*, ed. T. H. Vail Motter (1943).

9. *Shelley's Major Poetry: The Fabric of a Vision* (1948), p. 53.

10. Tennyson did at one stage look for a way of concluding the work with a suggestion of the possibility of such a return, as is apparent from a version of *The Lover's Tale* privately printed in 1868 and from a version set up in proof for the 1869 volume *The Holy Grail and Other Poems*. For further details, see R i, 381.

11. 'Tennyson: Politics and Sexuality in *The Princess* and *In Memoriam*', *1848: The Sociology of Literature*, ed. Francis Barker *et al.* (1978), p. 104.

12. *Revolution in Poetic Language* (English trans. by Margaret Waller, 1984), p. 29.

13. Eagleton, op. cit. (note 11 above) p. 105.

14. Ibid., p. 104.

15. Tennyson's note on l. 3 of xcvii: 'Like the spectre of the Brocken', in *The Works of Tennyson. With Notes by the Author*, ed. Hallam, Lord Tennyson (1913), p. 952; hereafter *Works*.

16. *On the Poems of Tennyson* (1972), p. 73.

17. Tennyson's note on the 'central idea' of I. xviii. 651–9, *Works*, p. 958.

18. *Tennyson* (1972) p. 263.

5

Tennyson in the 1850s: From Geology to Pathology – *In Memoriam* (1850) to *Maud* (1855)

ISOBEL ARMSTRONG

The gap between *In Memoriam* and *Maud* seems as decisive as the huge breaks and fractures Lyell sees as constitutive of geological structures in *The Principles of Geology* (1830–3). The two poems belong to different kinds of history. To speak of them together appears to commit what Lyell described as the fundamental intellectual mistake of creating artificial connections between different geological phases by transposing the temporal sequence evident in one area of the world to fill in the break existing at the same time in another. All that they share is the fact of succession in time, and 'will therefore no more enable us to trace the signs of a gradual change in the living creation, than a fragment of Chinese history will fill up a blank in the political annals of Europe'.[1] Lyell's recognition of the culturally specific nature of experience and knowledge here is a reminder that *In Memoriam* and *Maud* were written in radically different historical circumstances. The watershed of the Crimean War, and its consequent reconceptualising of Britain's relation to Europe and of Europe itself, divides them.

Lyell's model of 'gradual change in the living creation' is negotiated in the movement of *In Memoriam* itself, which uses the myth of geology structurally as well as absorbing its language. It is partly the incipient problems of this model which create a fracture which makes possible the new rhetoric of *Maud*. But this way of understanding the change from one mode of writing to another in terms of transition from a Tennysonian 'norm' of *In Memoriam* to an aberrant text, *Maud*, constitutes another kind of misreading. It is much more plausible to think of *In Memoriam* as the exceptional text. For this memorial poem to Arthur Hallam reneges on his principles. On one reading, it abandons the poetry of 'sensation', which is the solvent of habit and the defamiliariser of ideology, and appears to turn towards the poetry of 'reflection' of which Hallam had been so critical. It seems to be abandoning the culturally marginalised status of the poet axiomatic to Hallam and making a bid to be 'universally agreeable', taking for its 'primary subject the *usual* passions of the heart. . . Love, friendship, ambition, religion, etc . . . matters of daily experience', all of which Hallam had deprecated in his review of Tennyson's early poems.[2] It even seems, with consummate duplicity, to be dealing with the 'usual' passions 'in a simple state', using without disruption the existing 'forces of association' which are already 'ready to work in these directions'.[3] Hallam's death seems to have made necessary a memorial poem which would transgress all his propositions by dealing with love, friendship, religion (and perhaps even ambition). *Maud*, on the other hand, returns to the poetry of sensation, to an attack on ideological formations, to Hallam's belief that consciousness is constituted by discontinuous fragments of sensation connected by the 'ligature' of thought, to his belief that sexuality and libido are at the centre of existence, and that the image of the God of love in which man is created must mean that the intensity of love and passion is subsumed into sexuality.[4] And it manages to make all these things work towards a politics scarcely envisaged in *In Memoriam*.

But if *Maud* returns to the concern with consciousness (with its concomitant interest in non-rational conditions and madness) and to the concern with politics evident in the 1830s, it does so in cultural conditions which had fundamentally changed in twenty-five years. For one thing, Hallam's marginalised poet was becoming institutionalised in the vocabulary of madness, as the controversy surrounding the spasmodic poets, Alexander Smith and Sydney Dobell in particular, is witness. 'Rant', 'Bedlam','epilepsy', 'lunatic', were common epithets. 'My brain is whirling like a potter's wheel': *Firmilian*, a parody of spasmodic writing, enunciates the connection between pathology and poetry.[5] At the same time, the clinical categories of the new discipline of psychiatry assimilated the language of literary criticism. Henry Maudsley's *The Physiology and Pathology of Mind* (1867) uses a strangely aesthetic terminology, *Neurosis spasmodica*, for 'the tyranny of bad organisation', and associates linguistic tropes, punning and the double meaning of ambiguous words, with madness.[6] In the discourses surrounding the Crimean War there was a tendency to speak of both peace and war in terms of cultural pathology, and so *Maud* or 'Mad' negotiates political symptoms in terms of clinical psychosis and excess, recognising that there are political stakes in the definition of madness.[7] And, since one of the signs of madness is the madman's belief that his account of things is self-evidently 'true', to claim the truth becomes a problematical act.

The trauma of grief in *In Memoriam* occasions the madness of contradictory states in which 'calm despair and wild unrest' (xvi) are perceived to coexist, but this is diagnosed as a private tragedy. Its public dimensions are generally theorised in metaphysical terms; or else the huge, impersonal movement of geological time is invoked both as analogy for the frightful break in continuity occurring with death and as a mode which provides, literally, residual comfort. For the geological model makes it possible to reconstruct continuities out of rupture itself, as the massive diachronic subsidence and shift of deposits from one era to another creates an 'economy' (Lyell's word) which destroys in one place and repairs with the residues of a former age in another. The poem, or at least the poem requiring a reading which is 'universally agreeable', lyricises the constant flux of displacement which is both undermining and reassuring. The sea's movement will 'Sow the dust' of the great continents of futurity: 'The moanings of the homeless sea,/The sound of streams that, swift or slow,/Draw down Æonian hills, and sow/The dust of continents to be' (xxxv).[8] In organic continuity seas sow dust in which the sown seed grows, the seed both of crops and future races and cultures. Geological process is associated with the marvellous and uncanny and yet assimilated into a seemingly reassuring economic pattern of exchange and transposition. 'There rolls the deep where grew the tree . . . There where the long street roars hath been/ The stillness of the central sea . . .' (cxxiii). Here the equanimity of exchange is satisfying because of its not quite symmetry; sea supersedes tree, city supersedes sea and, though the 'roars' of the street carry a residual sound deposit from the 'roll' of the deep, the tree carried along in s(tree)t is not quite recuperated, and not quite suppressed, by the city. Continuity and displacement achieve an always precarious but just demonstrable equipoise. Thus although the text repudiates the facile economy of loss and gain, refusing to see loss as an investment recuperated in the future, 'the far-off *interest* [my italics] of tears' (i), there is, or seems to be, to use Freud's words, an 'economics of pain' in mourning equivalent to the consolatory redistributions of the earth's matter in geological process.[9] The self's relationship to the world is redistributed as it gives up, at some, though at not all, points in the poem a longing to incorporate the dead.

Lyell's writing, to which I will return, paradoxically encourages a grasp of slow process (though not a teleology of it) by describing the passage of millions of years in a way which makes geological movement rise and fall with great rapidity. 'If we are lost in conjectures when speculating on the ages required to lift up these formations to the height of several thousand feet above the sea, how much more remote must be the era when the same rocks were gradually formed beneath the waters'.[10] It is the extraordinary movement of this rhetoric which *In Memoriam* registers. In *Maud*, on the other hand, geology as fluid process and change has hardened and atrophied. It returns in the local squalor of the hollow, pit or quarry where suicide or murder occurs and stones are human weapons. It is metaphorised as leavings, unassimilated shards, residues and the impacted stone of the nameless narrator's heart. Maud's cold 'clear cut face, icily regular, splendidly null', cut like a jewel, or the 'glassy smile' of her brother take on the inorganic attributes of the geological product worked by human labour. The profiteering father of Maud's suitor bequeathes a coalmining fortune plundered from labour underground: 'And left his coal all turned to gold.' The trope in which coal turns to lumps of gold registers the troping nature of profit itself, in which resources become the subject of economic exchange and imaginary value. The organic world of natural growth is endowed with the imaginary value of inorganic matter 'turned' to jewels in a deranged ecology: 'A million emeralds break from the ruby-budded lime.' This reversal of organic into inorganic in the process of consumption appears in the crucial example of the exploitation of the poor: chalk and alum and plaster are sold to the poor as bread and geological residue, refined to a spirit of murder, 'works' like yeast in the means of life so that a double exploitation and alienation of human labour takes place. The structure of the pathetic fallacy, which had attracted Tennyson because the world answers to moral feeling and emotion, is 'turned' or troped against itself. The world is seen in terms of the artefacts of consumption and the categories projected on to objects become themselves the dead products, the end of a process of manufacture, returned to an inanimate world and seen with a hypersensitive, narcissistic intensity. When the larger movements of the world impinge they do not belong to the

impersonal violence of selection but to a 'sad astrology' and a
Schopenhauerian universe of intentional violence and mutually
antagonistic wills.

> The mayfly is torn by the swallow, the sparrow speared by the
>   shrike,
> And the whole little wood where I sit is a world of plunder and
>   prey. . . .
> We whisper, and hint, and chuckle, and grin at a brother's shame;
> However we brave it out, we men are a little breed.
>
> (R ii, 529–30, I, iv, 124–5, 130–1)

It is tempting to associate *In Memoriam* with 'normal' mourning
and *Maud* with the 'pathological' mourning of melancholia according to Freud's distinction in 'Mourning and Melancholy': this can
lead to some insights but it can also obscure the exceptional nature
of *In Memoriam* as exceptional text in the Tennyson canon by virtue
of its very struggle to normalise itself. Understanding the struggle of
In Memoriam is a prerequisite for understanding that of *Maud*.

The great complexity and incipient collapse of *In Memoriam*, which
is called a 'contradiction on the tongue' (cxxv), emerges in its attempt to negotiate the mourning process through two different and
antagonistic accounts of geological process which are continually
disrupting one another. Each is associated with a theory of language
founded on a politics and a teleology with quite different implications for the love which the poem is so desperate to celebrate and
consolidate. One discourse is represented by the intensely conservative work of Richard Chenevix Trench, whom Tennyson knew as an
undergraduate and Cambridge Apostle, and the other by the more
subtly conservative Charles Lyell's *Principles of Geology* (1830–3). A
'universally agreeable' poem obedient to Trench's principles is fused
with an uncomfortable and transgressive text which opens up the
problematical nature of Lyell. A massive double poem is the result.
I will consider how this double poem works, or rather, begins to pull
apart, and how this creates a movement from the language of geology to the language of madness.

Trench's *The Study of Words* appeared a year after *In Memoriam* in
1851 and was followed up with *English Past and Present* in 1855. The
immediate ideological purpose of these works was to consolidate an
account of the national language which offered a coherent understanding of national consciousness and consequently a rationale for

the approaching Crimean War.[11] In *Maud* these theories disintegrate, but they appear to sustain parts of *In Memoriam*.

Trench's paradigms are responsible for those parts of *In Memoriam* which the reader hurries over with embarrassment. But it is important to see how these embarrassments arise. For Trench language is not the construction of 'arbitrary signs'. He argued that language is Adamic, even though in order to do so it was necessary to resort to a casuistical revision of Adamism: God laid down the fundamental principles of language which were then progressively developed by civilisations, particularly the English. The permanent roots of Indo-European linguistic formations discovered by nineteenth-century philologists enabled Trench to elide the idea of the buried root with the fossil, with a store of underground treasure, and with the buried fragments of bone which are a clue to the essential form of the Cuvierian type, the universal structures which enabled early geologists to believe that missing elements of form could be constructed by extrapolating from the nature of a single bone. Conveniently, such a geological type can be assimilated to the theological type, the universals which are a teleological guarantee of permanence, and enable one experience to be seen in terms of another. Thus the possibility of analogy and symbol also arises from the fixed and universal type.

Leaning heavily on Emerson, Trench argues that our language is not simply 'fossil poetry', but 'fossil history' and 'fossil ethics' as well.[12] Using the idea of geological strata to constitute a hierarchy of change in which the earliest meaning is the truest and essential meaning of a word, he can say that the legitimate or originary meaning is embalmed in history and sanctifies the concept of ancestry. Access to the buried treasure of meaning is only through the past and it is always necessary to return to a fixed and univocal definition in order to keep language pure. The store of language has to be restored and desynonymised to prevent the unfortunate tendency of words to possess a downward social mobility from producing meaning which becomes a degenerate form of the original. But if the social and racial purity of language can be maintained by vigilance, this is also a treasure to be exploited, 'more precious than the mines of California'.[13] Treasure is elided with currency as the circulation of the national incarnation which is language opens up new dominions and empires of meaning through developing its legitimate roots. If a language can degenerate it can conversely conquer. A rationale for profit and colonialism emerges in the rejection of the 'Orang-outang' theory of the growth of language from primitive to more complex forms. The language of the savage is the manifestation of a fallen state. Trench instances the 'brutal poverty' of the language of uncivilised tribes (the Bechuanas have no words for 'God' or 'Thank you').[14] Not to have a language is a sign of debasement and degeneration. To be with 'no language but a cry' (li) is a shameful confession in these terms. The Yew-tree poem configures roots, names, stones, bones, in a painful effort to 'incorporate' death into history and language, and fails (ii). In fact, the poem reverses into a critique of Trench's categories as death or its symbolic representation, the Yew, disperses and rapaciously ('graspest') engorges language and history. Roots trap bones and reach out to dislodge the stone monuments which in their turn ossify the naming processes of language. This calls out an equivalent in the self-murder of suicide which longs to become 'incorporate' or bodiless. The extraordinary pun of 'incorporate' also yields an opposite but reciprocal meaning, the atavistic desire to incorporate the lost object in the darkness of the Yew cannibalistically as part of the self. The Trenchian requirement to repress double meaning actually doubles it and 'incorporates' it in the pun. The brilliance of *In Memoriam* is its capacity to assimilate an investigation of psychogenetic, linguistic and geological movements to one another. To research into what remains of both geological and human 'remains' is the project of the poem. The research into mourning is a research into history and culture.

The investigation of Trench's categories is not always so complex as in the Yew poem though, even at its crudest, the text is always in dialogue with them. Nevertheless, to Trench may be attributed the insistent desire to fix and stabilise in the authority of the type. The typing of language extends to include religious experience, ethics, history. A Christian typology of fossilised universals is ambiguously conflated with the geological type and produces a new kind of bourgeois social typologising. Hierarchies of class and gender are generalised as universal commonplaces. The undebased language which is committed to 'fitting aptest words to things' (lxxv) in desynonymised purity is analogous to the permanent type of Lazarus's sister, whose faith can 'fix itself to form' (xxxiii). The God who can 'type this work of time' (cxviii) creates a progressive, linear history in which degenerate forms can be superseded and 'man' can 'Move upward, working out the beast,/And let the ape and tiger die'. This sanctions a conservative ideology which condemns the destabilising of faith and 'form' in the revolutionary 'red fool-fury of the Seine' (cxxvii). Just as the fixity of the feminine type is associated with the pure form of religious faith, so the immutability of class comes together with the fixed category of the feminine; 'Like some poor girl whose heart is set/On one whose rank exceeds her own' (lx). Conventionalised types reinforce convention, or seem to, such as the waiting woman of section vi, whose colour 'burns' as she awaits the lover who is in fact dead; 'she turns/Once more to set a ringlet right'.

Such quintessential bourgeois sentiment is endemic to parts of *In Memoriam*. Though Tennyson's negotiations with it are arguably, upon closer investigation, much more complex than they seem, the strategy of the text is to present such moments as if they are simple and unproblematic. A moment's thought reveals that section vi is an almost ribald parody of Robert Montgomery's *The Omnipresence of the Deity* (1828); Arthur Hallam had derided Montomery in his review of Tennyson. The shipwrecked sailor is not saved by a God prepared to save the drowning believer; the statement that death is common is uttered by a suspect witness – it derives from Hamlet's Gertrude.[15] Section vi is a double poem, but the expressive idyll masks the satire on domesticity. The text seems to long for the simplicity it betrays. At the time *In Memoriam* was published, Tennyson became interested in the poetry of William Allingham and, if Coventry Patmore can be trusted, enthused over Allingham's *Poems* (1850).[16] Allingham's work is reminiscent of the Apostles' much earlier interest in fairy mythology and the supernatural. 'The Fairies' ('Up the rocky mountain,/Down the rushy glen . . .') appeared in this volume, which also explores a much weakened aesthetics of the poetry of sensation. Allingham is fascinated by the intense image in the mind, by feeling, emotion and memory, but these are assimilated into Wordsworthian commonplaces and didactic 'contemporary' idyll on the modern situation. Class, work, emigration, the poor, the industrial scene, are addressed in poems such as 'The Pilot's Pretty Daughter' (another of the numerous 'daughter-category' poems which seemed to cathect Tennyson and other Victorian poets), 'The Music Master', 'The Emigrant's Dream', 'The Train'. In fact, Allingham had found a way of domesticating the poetry of sensation and contemporary politics by eliding both in the pathetic fallacy, much as Tennyson was tempted to do after 1842, in parts of *In Memoriam*, and well beyond this in later poetry of the sixties. His work must have seemed to ratify those parts of *In Memoriam* which can be associated with conservative readings of language and politics and, more dangerously, to provide a model for the future.

Yet whatever Tennyson's interest in the work of a poet who seemed to be adopting the strategies he was exploring in his own poem, *In Memoriam* does not consolidate the bourgeois idyll or confirm the affective morality of the pathetic fallacy. It does constantly betray its own simplicities, in the first place by subjecting the idea of the pathetic fallacy to a fierce critique and secondly by invoking the non-progressive, non-developmental aspects of the geological model proposed in Lyell's work. I have discussed elsewhere poems such as 'Calm is the morn' (xi) and the Wye poem (xix) as enquiries into the psychological lie of the pathetic fallacy.[17] Here I shall concentrate on the double poem created by the use of Lyell's theorising of change, which is in direct opposition to the conceptualising of the past to be found in the work of Trench. The two epistemologies run counter to each other. Section lvi, 'So careful of the type . . .', is the central poem here. Section xxxvi, following on the Lazarus poems, prepares the way for it. It is at one and the same time a poem about the power of the biblical story to convert both the poor and the non-Christian savage (a thoroughly Trenchian theme), and a poem which self-consciously uses geology as myth to dissolve the Christian legend into Feuerbachian fiction.[18]

The poem carefully debates the failure of philosophy, truth in 'closest words', and even poetry, in comparison with the dissemination made possible by legend, which is not an elite form, and can enter in at 'lowly doors'. With the deceptive equanimity of generalising pastoral so common in *In Memoriam*, it moves to the celebration of abstract types of worker; the reaper, the builder, the gravedigger, without whose labour the processes of life and death would not be supported:

> Which he may read that binds the sheaf,
>   Or builds the house, or digs the grave,
>   And those wild eyes that watch the wave
> In roarings round the coral reef.
>
> (xxxvi, 13–16)

But there is a subliminal shock here, disguised by a seemingly smooth compatibility, as the familiar tasks of native England are juxtaposed

with the action of another 'native', the unconverted primitive tribes-
man in the tropics whose 'wild eyes' gaze on the coral reef in
incomprehension. The coral reef was for Lyell, and for Darwin too,
the only visible instance of continuous development in the world.
All other geological remains are evidence of displacement and cannot be read as continuity. The coral reef, building living matter on
the stepping stones of its dead selves (section i implicitly refers to
this) can be seen as the single, but for this very reason, precarious
example of unbroken continuity in time. Hence Lyell's fascinated
but sceptical response to the formation of coral as a living exception,
a virtual aberrancy of nature.[19] And in Tennyson's poem it is this
precariousness and the erosion of 'the wave' which is uppermost –
so another poem emerges. The savage nature, like the Chinese history wrongly interpolated into European time, cannot be seen in
continuity with the pastoral figures delving the native English soil.
Thus the continuity of the Christian myth breaks down. And along
with it the highly unstable nature of the subjunctive, *'may* read',
comes into prominence. The English builder 'may' read the Christian story, *if* he is literate, or interpret it if he is illiterate, but what the
savage may read in his culture is surely an unknown possibility. The
poem undoes its earlier assurance: truth is 'embodied in a tale', a
legend, a fiction, or a lie. Truth, which is 'darkly' or obscurely appre-
hended is in fact set in opposition to the 'name' of Christ, which is a
fiction which circulates in a culture as money, 'current coin', or a
currency with a fluctuating value, in a state. This is not Trench's
buried treasure of primal meaning but a signifying system in which
language carries fossil history, but not truth. Lyell often thinks of
geological remains as a language created by the 'author' of the
world. But he recognised that there is a gap between the inferences
we make and the empirical reconstruction of geological process, that
the meaning we give to it is arbitrary. This poem proves the greater
sceptic here, seeing the Christian 'tale' as a human fiction constructing language or the 'Word' rather than being determined by it.
Section xxxvi moves to a Feuerbachian account of belief as the projection of human categories, and culturally and historically specific
categories at that, on to the world.

The difference between Trench's fossilising and Lyell's geology is
the difference between a naive search for systematic continuity and
the theorising of change. The same difference is to be seen between
Chambers, the populariser of geological ideas, and Lyell, who is
epistemologically sophisticated.[20] To put Lyell by Trench is incon-

gruous: it is to put an infinitely subtle intellect beside a superficial populariser, and it would not be necessary to make the comparison were it not that the double poem of *In Memoriam* implies the juxtaposition. It establishes continuities only to fracture them by understanding change in terms of breaks and discontinuities, the very opposite of linear progress.

Section lvi, 'So careful of the Type', one of the climactic moments of *In Memoriam*, envisages the obliteration of the human species, the end of its history, as the logical consequence of the fractures of 'scarpèd cliff and quarried stone'. It registers the paradoxical nature of Lyell's geology. For Lyell's charting of the ceaseless subsidence, upheaval, displacement and transfer of the earth's matter turns all geological evidence into material remains, the non-volitional posthumous monuments of past process. It posits a diachronic flux in which we can discover the manifestations of secondary causes, but not origins, an economy which demonstrates a pattern but no meaning and teleology – except the one we choose to give it.

The meaning Lyell chose to give what Tennyson was to call 'the dust of change' was that of the uniformitarian slow continuity of change itself through time. This view of creation is agnostic enough. But in order to demonstrate continuity he had to consider the nature of change and to found his argument on the evidence of *discontinuity*. Simply because of the fact of flux itself it is impossible to see the coherence of geological structure which has itself been formed through the operation of chasms, breaks and gaps in time and space. The like formation has been sundered, the unlike and discrete juxtaposed in the eternity of the past.[21] Add to this that at any one point in space and time, multiple causes acting at different rates and subject to different conditions are the very essence of change, then it must be that though there may be continuity we do not *experience* change like this.[22] Lyell reiterates that we cannot see change at work, cannot be in possession of the subterranean workings which suggest from the 'decomposition of rocks, and the transportation of matter by rivers to the sea', that 'new strata' are being built 'beneath the waters'.[23] 'It should, therefore, be remembered that the task imposed on those who study the earth's history requires no ordinary share of discretion; for we are precluded from collating the corresponding parts of the system of things as it exists now, and as it existed at former periods.[24] We cannot learn 'the living language of nature' by our 'daily intercourse with what passes on the habitable surface'.[25]

Though the principles of Lyell's great work depend on the Kantian *a priori* categories of space and time for their foundation, the epistemological *effect* of his argument is to dislocate these categories from the ordering power of the perceiving consciousness. Because he envisages a world continually in a state of repositioning, a shifting condition of mobility in which areas literally 'move about', the perceiving consciousness is in a corresponding state of repositioning.[26] It cannot fully comprehend what is acting on it and cannot act on the immediate evidence of its perception. It is not simply that it cannot trust its correlation of perception with the world: it is not in *control*. It is in a world of *non sequitur*, constructing and reconstructing phenomena which it cannot know. In a thoroughly Kantian manner it has to presuppose the categories of space and time in order to *represent* the thing in itself which it cannot ever know. *In Memoriam* itself works as a series of discrete repositionings, *non sequiturs* and continual rethinking and new representations of loss.

The radical decentring of the subject inadvertently achieved in Lyell's text is perhaps what causes him to insist so tenaciously on the permanence of the type. He rejects Lamarck's orang-outang hypothesis as emphatically as Trench. The possibility of hybrids, the monstrous births bred out of 'promiscuous' alliances between species, is also discounted. It is *not* the case either, that genera 'are mere arbitrary and artificial signs' invented for the purpose of classification; inventions, in other words, merely of the categories of language.[27] Yet Tennyson's section lvi, using the evidence of Lyell himself, reverses this argument and goes beyond it to the final collapse of language and the 'artificial signs' which designate the human species and which are used by the human species to designate itself.

Section lvi begins by refuting the poem prior to it and challenging its argument. "So careful of the Type?' but no.' It is not concerned with the arbitrariness of natural selection but with the conceptualisation of the 'type', here the biological type, but implicitly the biological type elides with the theological type and the categories of language or a text set up in type (the word allows a multiple pun). Section lv had retrieved comfort from the preservation of the type but lvi abolishes this. Here nature, gendered as female, is in conflict with a masculine God who may have been a fiction of the human species. The point is not that Nature is 'red in tooth and claw' for, the poem asserts, man has always known of this aspect of creation ever since he set up the loving God whose creed contradicts the evidence of the natural world. What is appalling for this poem is that the possible extinction of man as species follows upon the collapse of the idea of the type which had sustained the notion of man as a distinct species. The type is thus one of the 'mere arbitrary and artificial signs' of classification and nothing more. The poem certainly envisages the end of man, physically dispersed as mere material particles, 'blown about the desert dust,/Or seal'ed within the iron hills'. The mourner of Wordsworth's Lucy poem can at least envisage the incorporation of the dead in rocks and stones and trees. The *In Memoriam* mourner sees the lost race both as indistinguishable from dust and hill and yet forever unassimilated, 'blown about', 'seal'd within'. By implication, this is also the fate of the dead Hallam, whose death provoked the enquiries into the death of a species. By implication, too, the process of mourning is blocked by such thoughts and made impossible by the inferences which follow in the final two stanzas. For there is worse to contemplate than the annihilation of the species, as the question, 'No more?', suggests.

> No more? A monster then, a dream,
> A discord. Dragons of the prime,
> That tare each other in their slime,
> Were mellow music, matched with him.
>
> (lvi, 21–4)

Logically, there may be nothing to mourn. The fragmented syntax, in keeping with the disintegration of categories which is envisaged, implies a number of meanings: 'a monster then, a dream,/A discord'. Both man and his God, the syntax allows, are monsters, the hybrids and monstrous births of arbitrary nature, and partake of its violence. They are the constructs of an insane dream which is both nightmare and fiction. They are creatures of discord or violence, like the clashing of musical notes and, the third sense of 'discord' implies, they are the aberrant products of a *grammar* which is itself aberrant. For the collapse of concord implied in the disintegration of the type is the collapse of categories which make thought and the construction of relationships possible. If the type goes, the idea of difference on which language is based also disappears. 'Man' is not only the phantasmal classification of 'artificial signs' but the very arbitrariness of those signs ensures their instability and collapse. The undifferentiated, primeval world of the dinosaur (here classified as 'dragons' with the slippage which would characterise the untyped language) was a world of 'slime' in which attacker could barely be distinguished from what is attacked. The ambiguity of 'their' slime registers an undifferentiated world in which it is not clear what belongs to subject and object, to self and other, or to the environment. The language becomes like slime and collapses subject, object, time, space and gender in the final instability of 'match'. The beings of the primeval world 'Were mellow music matched with him'. In a brilliant indication of what would disappear with linguistic difference, the capacity for making relationships and correspondences, 'matched' means 'compared with'. The primeval world would seem harmonious compared with, if we could compare it, what would now be brought about. But in another equally brilliant pun 'matched' means 'mated', and the syntax brings into being a chain of miscegenation which would be consequent on the disappearance of the type. The dragons would be sexually mated with an unspecified 'him': for a moment the syntax even holds out the miscegenated mating of categories, of music with a biological existence; but it also holds out the mating of monster with the God which would be itself the product of monstrous birth, and a making of the monster with the untyped, post-linguistic 'man' of the future.

Logically, there would be no gender, or only one gender, that of the male. Since elsewhere in *In Memoriam* Tennyson happily uses the language of marriage and sexual love when he is speaking of the loss of a male friend, I do not think that what is shocking here is the 'mating' of men. It is the transformation of sexuality into unknown forms which is at issue. Sexual and linguistic difference seem here to depend on one another. When linguistic difference collapses all difference collapses. The poem has reached the state Nietszche hoped for but envisaged as a remote possibility: God goes when grammar goes.[28] And when for Tennyson God and grammar disappear, man goes too.

The final cry, 'Behind the veil, behind the veil', perhaps restores the poem to a more conventional hope for transcendental existence and revelation. It can certainly be read like this, just as the whole poem can seem to be a comparatively orthodox lament for the disappearance of God. However, for Lyell the 'veil' is the physical world of the earth's surface, which veils further manifestations of the material world from sight. The hidden forms of organic life, 'though now existing, are veiled from sight'.[29] We cannot see *through* the veil, but have to construct possibilities only from what we know of the physical world, out of the veil itself. The veil is not a medium *of* representation. As so often, Lyell sanctions both knowledge and nescience.

The manner in which section lvi veers towards a more dangerous poem than it seems to promise is shared by a number of poems in *In Memoriam*. This is particularly noticeable in two unnoticeable poems on the institution of marriage placed before and after section lvi, 'How many a father have I seen' (section liii) and 'O sorrow, wilt thou live with me' (section lxix). These, along with section ciii, a poem envisaging union with the dead Hallam, will form the last part of my discussion of *In Memoriam*. Before moving to these it has to be made clear what underlies the preoccupation with marriage in the poem. It is not simply that the marriage theme prepares for the attempted resolution of marriage in the final section. Rather, that itself is a sign of deeper concern. Throughout the poem, Tennyson experiments with what he calls the 'double name' (section cxxi) and a double syntax which yields antithetical readings. The poem tests out the extent to which language can be freed from the univocal 'type' of meaning without becoming deranged. His fascination with systematic ambiguity (the first Yew-tree poem is an example already discussed) discloses puns where metaphorical relations are responsible for producing opposite categories of meaning. Pun and metaphor become models of the hybrid, the bringing together of unlike categories. The hybridisation which Lyell took pains to reject turns out to be at the heart of language. For Lyell the impossibility of the biological hybrid confirms the type, but its possibility just as easily confutes it. The sexual model, marriage, the embrace, union in love, that which mixes, as the land can 'mingle' with the 'bounding main' in section xi or as the fields and farms of section cii 'mix in one another's arms/To one pure image [or metaphor] of regret', becomes metaphor for the possibility of metaphor, correspondence and analogy. The hybridising process of metaphor both stabilises and dissolves categories. It legitimises their integrity by making possible the act of comparison between unlike things, but the transformation of metaphor also becomes the miscegenated union of different orders of being. For an anxious text which longs to make the mourning process one which both slowly detaches the consciousness from the lost object *and* also one which needs to see the mourner fused with what is lost, the strange miscegenation of metaphor is as enthrallingly beautiful as it is dangerous. If it holds out the possibility of the union and transformation of categories just as certainly as it marks their difference, its unstable manoeuvres presage the collapse into arbitrary signs which Lyell had worked so hard to avoid.

The authority for seeing the manifestations of language as a model of the union of sexual love may have been Arthur Hallam's understanding of God's love as libido, the most intense experience of passion. The 'word' correspondingly manifests the same pattern as love itself. There was also a more theologically orthodox and more limited sanction for such metaphorical structures in Keble's *Tract 89*. There Keble naturalises and stabilises the theological Type by suggesting that, though natural objects are so 'fraught with historical difficulties' that each person may make symbols out of things permanently existing in the external world, common symbols can exist. A symbolic correspondence and exchange of attributes can arise between a cross and a tree, for example. Common objects produce associations held in common, but at the same time each person will have a poetry of his own, a set of 'associations' peculiar to him.[30] Though *In Memoriam* often works to create a network of common associations around natural objects, however (we can return again to the Yew as an example), it often simultaneously undermines the fixity of the category and the projection of human feeling on to these. Section ci, about the departure from Somersby, envisages a world in which 'fresh associations' supersede and eradicate those of the earlier inhabitants. Indeed, it considers a subjectless world, in which the remains of the humanly cultivated environment – beech, maple, sunflower and carnation – act and react upon themselves 'unwatched'. No agency or cognitive centre exists to read the world as communal memory and (by implication) language, and to die. We are back with the universe of remains, albeit the delicate remnants of pastoral, opened out in Lyell's text.

The permanence of institutions and the language which sustains them, though not often remarked, is a preoccupation of *In Memoriam*. It follows from the enquiries set in motion by the supposition of multiple change and the elimination of human culture which geological theory can support. Since marriage, betrothal and the institution of the family become major concerns in *Maud*, it is important to see what is going on in sections liii and lxix.

Section liii begins with a bourgeois picture: 'How many a father have I seen,/A sober man, among his boys . . . '. But such a family is founded, if not on prostitution, certainly on promiscuity. The poem deals with the social implications of the following sections liv and lv in a typically veiled and tentative way: if 'not a worm is cloven in vain' (liv), and if of fifty scattered seeds only one is brought to fruition (lv), it may be possible to 'dare' to suppose 'That had the wild oat not been sown' the 'hale' patriarchal figure of the first stanza of section liii would have been subjected to an enforced continence. His capacity to reproduce, not only sons, presumably, but the institution of the family, would be endangered. Because the premises of the argument of liii *follow* its conclusions in liv, and because the sexual meaning is encoded in the 'double names' of circumlocution – 'barren' soil, the 'grain' by which 'a man may live' – the implication that sexual health and the survival of the family depends on sexual activity rather than continence is disguised. There are so many outrageous conventional and unconventional assumptions here (nothing is said about the women who make legitimate and illegitimate sexuality possible) that it is arguable that the poem thoroughly disingenuously supports the status quo. But the 'green' manhood of the patriarchal male is itself disingenuous and cannot but question the 'legitimate' family here by bringing its structure into the open. A similarly deconstructive movement ends the poem, which reads two ways at once. The daring thoughts of the poem are not advice to give to the promiscuous. Rational thought, 'divine Philosophy', can overreach itself and become 'Procuress', interestingly gendered as a female pimp, for male evil. This would be a suitably orthodox conclusion were it not that, in Milton's *Comus*, 'divine Philosophy' is not scepticism but the divine reasoning which sanctions chastity.[31] In this reading the strict philosophy of chastity itself becomes the procurer of prostitutes as the ethics of continence lead to their violation by being too strict to bear.

Section lix, partly a pastiche of the famous lyric of Catullus to Lesbia, returns to the idea of marriage, and the question of gender with the same ingenious diction. Here the women's part, largely repressed until now, enters fully into the debate. Like the reckless 'Nature' of sections lv and lvi (which perhaps owes her gender to Hallam's understanding of the sensuous life of women as being outside the restrictions of rational male law), 'Sorrow' is gendered as female. But here she is institutionalised and taken into legitimate wedlock, 'No casual mistress, but a wife'. In recognition of the poet's absolute union with grief, Sorrow becomes 'half of life'. But here the poem takes an unexpected turn, emerging out of the recognition that profound Sorrow is allied to the play of sexuality. The poet is a capricious lover, whose 'blood', or sexuality, and faithfulness – 'If thou wilt have me wise and good' – can only be subject to Sorrow's 'rule' if she is as gentle as a new bride. Despite the guarded and subjunctive syntax, marriage emerges as a play of power-relations which can only be sustained if these are self-consciously *enacted* as 'centred passion' requiring relief: 'But I'll have leave at times to play/As with the creature of my love'. These words bring together both the onanistic nature of sorrow, and the wife's ambiguous status as 'creature', subject, possession, plaything and thus a wife who plays the role of mistress. The ownership confirmed by marriage enables the poet to 'set thee forth', to set up the woman with the status of wife, but also, the strange ambiguities assert, to set up the woman like a kept mistress in perpetuity. As so often, the last lines of the poem read in opposite ways, splitting the nature of marriage into private and public domains. 'Howsoe'er' the poet husband may 'know thee' (and *exactly* how this private knowledge operates is left unstated), the external world can 'hardly tell what name were thine'. If Sorrow is a conventional wife the poet has taken her to himself so intimately that her name is obliterated by his: she now *is* the poet. If Sorrow is a wife-mistress her independent identity is dominant and escapes the patriarchal name which designates appropriation. Language and naming are now brought directly into relation with institutions. Names are not intrinsic but controlled by institutions, which control identity.

The sophisticated virtuosity of this poem with its scene of personification is more complex than section liii. The exuberance of the Catullus poem is re-routed towards an exploration of the passion of loss which becomes libidinal and begins to displace the manifestations of libido. The contradictions of mourning, which require grief to be an end in itself, which envisage grief now as a capricious separate entity, now as fused with the self, which require a self-conscious theatrical drama in order both to sustain itself and to provide the superficial play which makes Sorrow bearable, these are all released in this poem. It is about the impossible psychic condition of the perpetual night of mourning, which can neither be fully assimilated nor fully detached from consciousness. One needs to beware of forgetting this poem about grief when remarking the poem about marriage, and of assuming that the double poem will always be constituted by one sophisticated and one unsophisticated text. Nevertheless, in exploring how the process of mourning is blocked when loss is internalised, the text uses the internal contradictions of marriage to pursue the implications of grief. And in order to consider how identity is transformed by Sorrow, it concludes that names transform identity, but that names are not fixed except by the power of institutions, which are highly artificial forms.

I have looked, of course, at one of the points of greatest turbulence in *In Memoriam*. Though the conclusions reached at all stages of its movement are always provisional and divided, it could be argued that poems such as section xcv and ciii resolve some of the difficulties explored in lv and lix by assuming an ultimate transcendence. Despite the return to 'matter-moulded forms of speech', the materiality of language, in section xcv, the poet achieves a visionary, longed-for union with the dead.[32] In section ciii transformed poet and muses sail into the sunset with the strangely enlarged being of Hallam who is figured as Christ. However, the intrinsic scepticism of *In Memoriam* qualifies such events. And since such scepticism motivates *Maud*, which does not take the way of transcendence – for there the supersedence of the self by the 'higher' needs of the nation in war is implicitly denied – it is necessary to note the agnosticism of *In Memoriam*.

The elaborate allegory of section ciii leaves the 'veiled' statue of Hallam behind in the hall of the earthly muses as they move to the mystical reunion with the dead. But, with the ingenuous cunning which the reader of *In Memoriam* begins to recognise, the memorial statue is hidden by the veil of representation, the mythic being of poetic language which must constitute all we can know of human art and history. Allegory is also such a 'veil', and thus the poem offers itself as a representation of representation, not as an escape into a new form of experience. It is an enquiry into the way representation can re-order experience, fusing the human image with the myth of Christ's love. Like the geological myth of section lvi it envisages the transformation of gender, literally taking the problem on board as the female muses beg for a passage on the departing ship. Interestingly it is they who create the songs of history, and they who are capable of engendering a fruitful androgyny as they become 'lordlier than before'. At this point in the poem the artifice of names and the collapse of categories this makes possible leads to transformation, and to new myths.

But the gap between the transformation of categories and their disintegration is a narrow one. Section lvi threatens the 'dream' or nightmare of insanity. Madness enters the poem earlier in sections xv and xvi and recurs in section lxx. Insanity occasions and is occasioned by the disintegration of language. Just as in Lyell's text the geological formation returns and revisits the same place in a different context and another time, madness revisits the text of *Maud*, bringing with it the derangement of language. In a famous comment Keble envisaged madness as a consequence of the poet's failure to give expression to feeling. His solution was the attachment of feeling to objects in the world, as we have seen. It is as if *Maud* is a study of the expressive theory of self as madness itself, where everything reflects the narcissistic desires of the speaker in a delusory way. The pathological disjunction of the unnamed protagonist's 'will', a recurrent word, and the exploration of sexuality and marriage, however, now take place in a different ideological context and another politics. The speaker's narcissistic desire for appropriation, for Maud to be to him 'lovely like a bride', to use the words of *In Memoriam* (lix), occur in the feverish overwrought period of the Crimean War. It is as if the mourning process of *In Memoriam* has been arrested at its early stage and turned morbid. In *Maud* the object of love is simultaneously loved and lost and the speaker's grief and aggression prey upon the loved object and itself, projecting its condition on to a similarly destructive universe possessed of that cannibalistic movement Freud noted in the mourning which has gone wrong. So both erotic passion and war are brought together in feverish aggression.

The shift from geology to pathology could occur for several reasons. The unfixing of the type which we have seen at work in both Lyell's and Tennyson's texts produced the condition for the disordered conjugations of a deranged language, as has been seen. Following from this the permanence of truth collapses, so that it becomes a function of solipsism to 'hold it truth', and paradoxically a feature of mania to believe fixedly in the absolute reality of a particular proposition. The psychiatrist, Henry Maudsley, points out that this is often a 'proof' of madness. (In *Maud* the asylum contains people who believe unshakeably that they are princes or politicians.) Furthermore, the structure of geological process could be given an analogy in the structure of mind, and this psychological structure could be extended to the organisation of a whole culture. Lyell's account of geological change in terms of discontinuous fracture, where the formations of earlier and later periods millions of years apart coexist on the earth's surface, bears an uncanny resemblance to Freud's model of psychic formation as a city in which primitive remains coexist with highly developed buildings of a later period.[33] Lyell's epistemology can sanction a discontinuous consciousness, fractured into moments of being, constituted by gaps. Just as important to psychiatry was the geological idea of concealed process, the energy at work *underground*. Concealed, irrational energies, not apparent to the rational surface but continually threatening to disrupt it, work like the 'vitriol madness' which 'flushes up in the ruffian's head' (Part I, i, 37). This parallels and can be sanctioned by Lyell's understanding of the hidden processes of the earth's movement which cannot be known. Such a model radically undermines the idea of the integrated, rational identity, though as we shall see, one of the drives of psychiatry is to make that hidden energy overt and rational; when transferred to the social and political sphere it produces an account of repression in which the hidden energies of the oppressed classes threaten to disorganise and overwhelm the state. In fact, the self and society are always in a condition of potential anarchy. The anonymous 'hero', driven underground in fantasy, imagining himself pounded by the traffic above a shallow grave (Part II, v, 244) continually attempting to 'bury' his melancholy (Part I, i, 75), is aligned with the violence of the poor, 'hovelled and hustled together, each sex, like swine' (Part I, i, 34) and the underground miners exploited by the father of his rival. He drags even Maud – mad, mud, and 'mine', as he asserts, the woman who belongs to him – and also, tropingly, of the depths – to his subterranean world. At several points in *The Principles of Geology* Lyell considers what the world would look like to a creature living underground in order to defamiliarise accepted propositions about the nature of the earth's structure.[34] *Maud* sees what the social and political world of British upper-class life looks like from underground. It defamiliarises this society, and its assumptions about property, privilege and sexuality. Ownership of the 'ground' itself becomes a contestable matter, a contest not only relevant to class privilege but to the nature of war, which is a struggle for ground.

The dangerous energies of *Maud* have always been difficult to place ideologically. The reactionary violence of the attacks on the peace party and the xenophobic celebration of war in Part III are particularly vicious. It all looks like a conservative writing wildly out of control. *Anti-Maud* (1855), by a 'Poet of the People', a satirical pastiche of *Maud*, assumes that Tennyson (who as Laureate after 1850 had a prominent public position) is to be identified with the speaker of the poem.[35] It sees the war as a ruthless attempt to repress social protest by deflecting attention overseas: 'Drown the clamour with drums and fife'. The starving poor are used as cannon-fodder and resources are directed away from improving their plight into a war economy. It sees the war as straightforward ideological and material exploitation and oppression. Addressing stanzas 10–13 of the first section of the poem, it attacks their picture of the degenerate poor:

There in the by-lane foul, where the air and the water is bad
And fever is never away, – women and children are crying for
  food, –
Drown the clamour with drums and fife! The sinews of war must
  be had –
Money and men, money and men; the poor man's earnings, the
  poor man's blood!

The Laureate, who is not 'ready to fight', but 'merely intends to write' (stanza 21), is incapable of understanding the real politics of the war, in which Russian wheat is wantonly burned instead of supplying desperately-needed bread (stanza 16). The poem attacks the irrationality of a position which advocates war simply because peace does not produce ideal socio-economic conditions. It charts the blessings of peace – homes, schools, churches (stanza 14), the spread of science, art and education to the poor – 'millions of minds were fed' (stanza 16). Its analyses are magnificently lucid, for it sees above all that the war-hysteria of *Maud* is a condition of *disease*. It is bred of an irrational fear of being absorbed into the filthy degeneracy of the classes it fantasises as 'swine'. That is why the first stanza begins with the bathos of 'I hate the murky pool at the back of the stable yard' and ends with the complaint of Echo, 'I feel very unwell'.

Maud probably ought always to be read alongside this anti-poem because it is deeply ambiguous. But it is itself a form of parody and this complicates its status. Gerald Massey's *War Waits*, a volume of orgiastically patriotic war poems, appeared in 1855, the same year as *Maud*, though some similar poems had been published earlier in *The Ballad of Babe Christabel, with other Lyrical Poems* (1854). Massey had begun life as a radical but he turned to a violently hysterical celebration of the war.[36] There is an uncanny parallel between the rhythms of these poems, and their blood-drenched, pulsating, sado-masochistic imagery, and those of *Maud*. Where Massey assimilates the discourse of sexuality and uses it in the service of the discourse of war, *Maud* reverses this and fuses the language of erotic passion with aggression and violence. Whether or not Tennyson had direct knowledge of Massey's work is not the point at issue here. He could not have seen the poems published in the same year as his own. What is important is that there is an intuitive recognition in the text that the privacy of sexual experience and its powerfully affective language is linked with aggression just as aggression is linked with sexuality. The effect of these elisions is to politicise sexuality and to sexualise war, questioning the roots of violence which they share. Such language implicitly investigates the psychopathology of war, and simultaneously asserts that passion and sexuality cannot be free and exist independently of cultural and ideological forms.

Tennyson's poem works as if it is reconfiguring the elements of Massey's war poems – the blood, the flush of battle, the fire and rage and wine of war, the rose of England, the lilies of France, the sanctification of English soil, the print of battle, the garden of the nation, and above all the energising throb, pulse and beat of heart and drum; all these find a place in the supremely erotic language of *Maud*. The derangement of categories made possible by Lyell's epistemology enters disturbingly in to the love lyrics as they absorb the rhythms of violence.

> Maud has a garden of roses
> And lilies fair on a lawn;
> There she walks in her state . . .
> (Part I, xiv, 489–91)

The speaker's dawn visit to the garden gate – 'A lion ramps at the top,/He is claspt by a passion-flower' – picks up the movement and some of the iconography of Massey's 'A Battle Charge', adding the British lion to it. Beside the Massey poem the lion and the picture of Maud walking 'in her state', seem less innocent. Maud's 'state' is a garden, a patch of ground. Massey envisages the garden as a battlefield, a symbolic patch of ground disputed by warring states.

> We have chosen a goodly garden,
>   Where our old Red Rose may blow!
> With bloody hands, eyes red and burning,
>   There the living our dead laid low!
> Shall the foe keep his Bacchanal triumph
>   Blood-drunken, and dance on the sod
> That is quick with the Flower of our nation,
>   In the name of the most high God?

Maud's 'feet have touched the meadows/And left the daisies rosy' (Part I, xii, 434–5). Tennyson writes of the blushing world of erotic feeling conjured by Maud's footprints: Massey writes of England's 'footprints red with blood' ('The Battle-March'). The speaker's heart is 'Ready to burst in a coloured flame' (Part I, vi, 208), he experiences 'the new strong wine of love' (vi, 271), 'his heart beat stronger/And thicker' (viii, 308–9), his 'pulses play' (xviii, l. 664) and in the climactic garden tryst of section xxii, 'Come into the garden Maud', 'the soul of the rose went into my blood', and 'My dust would hear her and beat . . . And blossom in purple and red' (ll. 882, 920, 923). To name only one poem among many by Massey, 'The Fifth of November at Inkerman' is saturated in the same language. The 'fiery tide of war' reaches 'to the red roots of the heart'. England is a Bride wedded to the Bridgeroom of War, a rampant lion on ground where wheels grind and feet trample, drums throb to the 'red-mouthed cannon's fiery tongues'. Men fight in the 'gory red' and 'fervent heat' 'With a throbbing in the pulse that beat voluptuous blood'. 'O but it is a gallant show, and a merry march, as thus/We run into the glorious goal with shouts victorious!'

Massey's poems suggest that war is a gallant show in more senses than one. It is the theatre of the territorial imperative of imperialism. It requires representations or 'shows' which stir deeply irrational impulses. The erotic violence which plays around the hysteria of imperialistic feeling registers a new phase of British expansion. Here the rush toward the goal of victory is the assertion of sexual power. It is fascinating that in *Maud* the Tsar is seen as a violent father-figure subduing an 'infant civilisation' with 'rod or with knout' (I, iv, 148) who has to be encountered with violence. He is the parallel of the rival father-figure at home who subdued the protagonist's own father and made compacts over the infant bodies of Maud and her lover.

Maud's alliance with Massey, the voluptuary of war, may be read, of course, as a form of collusion rather than critique which does not by any means redeem the poem from the attacks of *Anti-Maud*. But in another reading the poem does turn the language of madness towards a critique of the politics which actually engender war and madness. It is common to avoid the discomfort of *Maud*, as the Victorians did, by pointing to its dramatic nature as monodrama. It is seen as the dramatic exploration of a diseased subjectivity. But this is to turn the poem into a restricted case-history and to eradicate or minimise the politics of the poem by seeing them as the excrescence of madness. The double poem of *Maud* is not quite like this. Rather the critique is of a structural kind, turning on the definition of madness itself. The speaker of *Maud*, looking at the world from the underground of madness, is excluded and oppressed, or believes himself to be. He is the alienated other of the privileged world he longs to join. This enables the poem to look at privilege from the outside but, more importantly, the society of the Hall, its land, possessions, politics, power, entertainments, are defamiliarised, and alienated in their turn, other to the speaker. By making the speaker a madman, or at least a highly disturbed figure, the arrangements of privilege come to seem no longer natural or inevitable. They begin to seem the products of madness. This is particularly the case as the speaker constantly argues that he is the *same* and as *sane* as the people of privilege. But for the accident of a financial collapse he would be like them. So irrational and rational come to be elided. We are back with the obliteration of difference and the collapse of categories explored so persistently in *In Memoriam*.

The definition of madness disclosed in the text assumes the elision of the irrational and rational, as did contemporary psychiatry. Matthew Allen, whom, of course, Tennyson knew, bases his work on the premise that the madman is *not* irrational. He is like rational people. His writing substantiates Foucault's claim, in *Madness and Civilisation*, that advanced, benevolent theory in the nineteenth-century presupposed the rationality of the madman.[37] His treatment consisted of kindness, persuasion, training, discipline and self-control, and the lure of returning to 'normal' life in the privileged house which marked the achievement of rational behaviour. In fact, his *Essay on The Classification of the Insane* (1837), is not so much a taxonomy of madness as an account of the spaces the insane should belong to according to their degrees of rationality.[38] Madness is a space rather than a condition, and certainly not a criminal condition as it was in the eighteenth century. He describes civilised conversation worthy of the most respectable gathering taking place in his asylum, which is for him truly the 'home' or place of refuge of its etymological origin. But this normalising of madness sends insanity underground, refusing to recognise it as a category, at the same time as it makes the madman morally and rationally responsible for controlling his disease – a disease, however, which is deemed not to exist. It is a form of degeneracy rather than a mental condition. Foucault is quick to see the contradictions in such coercive kindness. The madman becomes unbearably responsible for his condition. He is forced to normalise himself because other people are like him and he is like them.[39] His illness is either repressed or forced upon him as the result of biological or hereditary determinism, which in fact reinstates madness as a condition outside the control of rational discipline altogether.

Allen adds a further deterministic element to his definition of madness which has the effect of dissolving it into a larger cultural situation. Madness is a social condition, an 'over-excitation, arising from our mad desires after wealth, fame, and distinction', with its consequent disastrous social failure, the 'overwhelming miseries of misfortune, poverty.' Sensitive persons become 'victims' to the 'modes and amusements of fashionable life.'

> Still we have reason to fear that we pursue the important duties of civil life, whether it be the weighty matters of legislation, or the scarcely less responsible exercise of the learned professions, or what ought to be the binding and sweet influence of faithful dealings in trade, and our common intercourse with each other, in an improper spirit, and from improper motives, and not with that singleness and simplicity of heart for each other's good, which alone is useful and safe; which we could not fail to do, were we sufficiently aware, that in as far as we depart from this purity of spirit, our views of truth must be perverted, and our healthy vital energies, causing fever, paralysis, or some morbid state, and all our sympathies poisoned and deranged.[40]

This elementary but in many ways admirably liberal attempt at socio-economic diagnosis nevertheless has the effect of pathologising the arrangements of everyday life – madness can be explained rationally from cultural derangement and malaise. The effect is to pass on the responsibility for madness to an ever-widening circle of agencies and to undermine, or open up, the definition of madness. If madness is a morbid form of the norm, the norm itself is always potentially morbid. Madmen are disorganised rational people, or society is regulated derangement. Such a collapse of terms means that Maud's brother can be called a 'madman' when he perpetrates a duel because his rage forces him to violate the law, just as the ruffian wife-batterer of the first poem is the victim of madness because he breaks the regulative arrangements of marriage. By the same token, the first poem in *Maud* makes peace into disorganised war, and war into organised aggression or regulated madness. 'Is it peace or war? Civil war, as I think, and that of a kind/The viler, as underhand, not openly bearing the sword' (Part I, i, 27).

It is exactly such crossing-over of terms which makes the asylum, the place where the mad are cared for, a *home*. *Maud's* project is to negotiate contradictions of a structural kind which occur when madness and the norm merge into one another and become conflated. Questions of agency and choice become paramount as the madman becomes painfully responsible for the madness which is at the same time society's madness. If society is organised madness, how is power and legitimacy maintained and what confers right on legitimacy? The poem's answer is to explore the nature of the *will*. The will as the imposition of legal power controls inheritance, and the distribution of property. The will in the personal, ethical and psychological sense controls a biological inheritance, the blood and the nerves of the physical being with which the speaker is so obsessed. These two senses of the law of will emerge in the first poem. One is the law of inheritance which makes the 'old man' who 'Dropt off gorged from a scheme that left us flaccid and drained' now 'lord of the broad estate and the Hall' (Part I, i, 19–20). The second is the act of self-control: the speaker vows to 'hold by the law that I made, nevermore to brood/On a horror of shattered limbs and a wretched swindler's lie' (ll. 55–6). The freedom of individual self-mastery is set against the brute power which has manipulated the laws of property. The death of the father and economic loss are seen as impotence – 'flaccid and drained' – and castration. The 'shattered limbs' of the dead father figure a phallic loss. The 'dreadful hollow behind the little wood', with its 'red-ribbed ledges' becomes a destructive feminine symbol, the condition of being without. It is not surprising that violence is implicated in sexuality throughout the poem, for the erotic passion for Maud is one way of redeeming manhood, just as going to war is a form of self-mastery. They are both ways of reasserting the will. There is a supreme irony in the poem's title. The named, 'entitled' woman is spoken for by the unnamed, unentitled protagonist, who wants to come into identity and legitimate being through her. At the same time the feminine signifies a condition of lack.

By the end of the poem the text investigates what is involved in the freedom of the will against the necessity of what is willed in the inheritance determined by the law and by biology. The second poem of Part II, 'See what a tiny shell . . .', tries to bring the two into relation, and fails. The first part of the poem prepares for this moment by setting up a false dialectic between the will to privilege and power and the will to self-mastery. The more the speaker takes on the responsibility for rational control of melancholia to confront the powerful order of wealth and privilege represented by Maud and her brother, the more he identifies with them, reduplicating for himself the structures of family and ownership which exclude him. The attempt at self-mastery leads him further into irrational isolation, but at the same time his obsession with the life of the Hall has the effect of making that life itself manifestly irrational. Because it is reflected into a pathological world it cannot be seen in opposition to the speaker's violence but becomes a part of it. And the speaker in turn becomes an extension of that world. They become doubles of each other. Madness is not a contradiction of the life of the Hall but a confirmation of it. The Hall becomes the mirror-image of madness, not its rational opposite.

The topography of *Maud* strangely reproduces the spaces Allen advocated for the classification of the insane. Two establishments, sufficiently separated, but in the same grounds, were to house males and females and the proprietor was to reside in one of these. He was to inspire the inmates with a zeal for rational behaviour by admitting them to his company as a reward for self-discipline. The rational come to the 'front' of the house, the less rational remain behind and hidden.[41] In *Maud* the spaces that matter are those of the speaker's 'home' and the Hall. He retreats into one and longs for access to the other. Though the speaker is excluded like a stranger, viewing Maud's cold, clear-cut face in a passing carriage, seeing the flash of a bridle as she and her brother ride with the suitor, looking at Maud at church with hungry voyeurism, both home and Hall are isolated from the village community (it is simply the place where he can meet Maud accidentally, as it were, out of bounds), and from the *nouveau riche* towers of the suitor's abode. The excluded speaker is deeply complicit with the life of the Hall. He views the brother with dependent fascination, longing for fellowship: 'I longed so heartily then and there/To give him the grasp of fellowship' (Part I, xiii, 458–9). And though he is given the 'gorgonising stare' of the British upper classes, that stare is in alliance with his own 'heart of stone', just as Maud's 'null', stony face parallels his own 'set' 'flint'-like face (Part I, i, 31) and just as her blushes in I, viii and I, xvii reflect the feverish flush of blood in his own physical being.

The speaker is constantly situated at a boundary point in the Hall grounds, looking in from the outside, 'at the high Hall garden', outside the gate, outside the sleeping house, in the field below it.

Imagining that he is only noticed for the sake of his vote, uninvited to the great political dinner and dance, he marks the barriers and points of exclusion which possessions and property can establish. And yet the estrangement is for him simultaneously a participation in privilege. Ownership and power over the *ground* fascinate him. He is delighted that a stream crossing 'my ground' carries a rose in its current 'born at the Hall' (II, xxi) which he supposes to have been sent by Maud. In the triumphant lyric, 'I have led her *home*' (I, xviii), the certainty of feeling prevents the incipient questions from emerging: *whose* 'home', hers or his? The worst that can happen is that the 'solid ground' (I, xi) should give beneath one's feet and leave one *without* entitlement or security. His home, with its two servants, replicates the master–servant structure of the Hall. In the extraordinary deranged lyrics of Part II which mark the movement from morbidity to insanity the difference is one of degree rather than kind. The poems are obsessed with spaces. The market place, the 'squares and streets' (II, iv) are loathed spaces because they alienate him from the memory 'Of the old manorial hall' and its privileged enclosure. The living burial underground (II, v) simply reproduces the exclusion experienced earlier, but it too is an enclosure mimicking the confinement of both 'home' and 'hall'. The movement to open war in Part III simply extends these relationships to foreign ground. The passion for ownership is subsumed in national identity – 'I have felt with my native *land*' (III, vi, 58: emphasis mine).

A passionate concern with inheritance, genealogy and degeneration, which replicates the bourgeois family structure even when it proposes an alternative to it, is a parallel concern related to the consuming interest in ownership, land and the boundary which excludes. The speaker insists that he is cheated not only of a financial inheritance but of Maud herself, subject of a marriage contract (I, vii, xix). Maud is 'my bliss', 'my Maud', 'My bride to be . . . My own heart's heart, my ownest own' (Part I, xviii, 655, 656, 672–3), a possession by a parody of legal right as well as through the rights of love (Part I, xix, 722–6). In an inconsistent effort to evade the lineage of patriarchy, which actually confirms it by consolidating the idea of descent, he attempts a Schopenhauerian account of inheritance by proposing Maud's descent only through the mother's line, 'the sweeter blood by the other side' (Part I, xiii, 477). Such infantilised fascination with the mother, Maud's mother and his own, as the redeemer of patriarchy makes the speaker's passion regressive and strangely participates in the slide to a 'lower' form of life which he dreads. The 16-year-old Maud envisaged in her plain riding-habit or precociously seductive 'gipsy bonnet' (Part I, xx, 805) plays out contradictory roles of child, bride and mother, acting out the inconsistent needs of patriarchial ownership for both lover and brother. The gipsy bonnet, with its suggestion of degenerate ancestral blood, hints at one of the continual threats to the speaker, the recognition of degeneracy, inherited in his own mental and physical being, in Maud's family, in the working classes, in man as a whole. The speaker is constantly aware of his own hypersensitive nerves ('Prickle my skin and catch my breath' (Part I, xiv, 524)) and the blood which made his own father rage and rave. He attributes the degradation of deceit and 'inherited sin' to Maud's family (Part I, xiii, 484), theft and lies to the servants and 'Jack on his ale-house bench' (Part I, iv, 110) and baseness to man in general, 'Nature's crowning race' (Part I, iv, 134). In the first poem the poor have reverted to the condition of animals. Degeneracy is inherited by family and class, confirming a structure which is absolutely corrupt and absolutely fixed, yet somehow always in danger of becoming ever more degraded. War is a way of arresting this process, reaffirming the strength of Britain's ancient lineage – 'The glory of manhood stand on his ancient height' (Part III, vi, 21).

These dreads and fantasies of a universally-determined physical and moral degeneracy are accompanied by a phenomenon of behaviour which is equally hysterical and inconsistent – the assumption of absolute moral responsibility for the condition of madness. Madness is a disease of the will and the will can arrest the decay of biology. The need to be rational, to 'keep a temperate brain', to be 'passionless' (Part I, iv, 141, 151), to repress 'morbid hate and horror' (Part I, vi, 264), to control the 'splenetic', 'rancorous' 'war with myself' (Part I, x, 262–4), and, above all, the need for a new manhood, bespeaking both moral and sexual power and health to 'arise' in the self is paramount in the poem.

> And ah for a man to arise in me,
> That the man I am may cease to be!
> (Part I, x, 396–7)

Such a new man can arrest the dreaded slide to lower forms, the identification of the speaker with the swine-like classes, just as it can repress the outbreak of buried violence and anarchy which is a continual threat to political stability. In war we make good that power, Part III asserts, abandoning the 'old hysterical mock-disease' (III, vi, 33) of madness. By an ironic trick of syntax the imitation disease of madness gives way to the 'real' disease of war.

Yet a theory of reversible degeneracy and the belief in moral and rational responsibility for disease are incompatible. These are the contradictions of the false dialectic set up in the poem. Foucault sees the assumption of power as a pathological form of the 'apotheosis of the self', in the nineteenth-century, in which the imperative of rational responsibility for the self takes the form of paranoia.[42] The speaker's new man of power is the equivalent of the madman who becomes a 'lord of all things', a 'statesman', a powerful 'physician' (Part II, v, 270–4). Interestingly, the commonest instance of madness offered by Allen and Maudsley is this form of delusion. Allen describes a dissenting minister believing himself one of the elect, and a man who believed himself a genius – 'he was the greatest of men'. Maudsley remarks that the lunatic appeals to the evidence of his own consciousness for the truth of his hallucination or delusion. 'The only person who answers at all to the metaphysical definition of a self-determining will is the madman, since he exults in the most vivid consciousness of freedom and power.'[43] The apotheosis of subjectivity which calls for 'One still strong man in a blatant land . . . Aristocrat, democrat, autocrat – one/Who can rule and dare not lie' (Part I, x, 392–5), to match the speaker's new powerful self is an irrational cultural delusion. The strong man is the double of the wife-battering ruffian of the first poem. He is the product of an ideology which celebrates the individual will at the same time as it dreads the degeneracy which undermines the will.

The decision to be 'one with my kind' in the higher life of nation and war, to be 'noble still' and to find a name at last in the 'making of splendid names' (Part III, vi, 58, 55, 47) is a further manifestation of the apotheosis of subjectivity in delusion and not its transformation. A confirmation of this, if any is required, is the existence in Part III of the same compulsive linguistic patterns as those which occur earlier. The speaker discloses a libidinal fascination at the start of the poem with the mouth of the 'dreadful hollow' as erotic orifice reproducing *sound* which can be interpreted as he wills – 'And Echo there, *whatever is ask'd her*, answers "Death"' (Part I, i, 4: emphasis mine). The same oral and aural image returns in the figure of the 'dreadful-grinning mouths of the fortress' (Part III, vi, 52) at the end of the poem. To mix 'my breath/With a loyal people shouting a battle cry' (Part III, vi, 34–5) is to make the universe the servant of desire in language. Echo invariably answers 'Death' because she ventriloquises the speaker's obsessions, just as 'breath' rhymes with 'death' (l. 37) in the last poem. The unifying battle-cry is a linguistic figment appropriate to a consciousness which conceives all language and communication as pure *noise*, 'hubbub', 'chatter', 'babble', unless it will answer to his own moods. Maud, so much an extension of himself that he cannot remember what he has told her, is 'Not her, not her, but a *voice*' (Part I, v, 189), a voice like Echo's to 'answer' to needs, and perhaps a delusory voice: like the rose which can be read as the secret sign of a private assignation; like the voices of the non-human world where mice shriek (Part I, vi, 260) and the beach screams (Part I, iii, 98), where birds call 'Maud' (Part I, xii, 414), where passionate flowers speak (Part I, xxii, 912–15). The poem mobilises the pathos of the pathetic fallacy to explore the linguistic solipsism of madness, another manifestation of the will to power.

If the madman is replicating society's madness, the assent to war is a further assent to madness. War is the product of a deranged society. The last two parts of *Maud* are often thought to chart the speaker's collapse and reintegration in recovery, but if they are read like this, they become a successful attempt to conform to the war ethic.[44] On the contrary, they stand as an insane duplication of the incipient madness of Part I. Unlike *In Memoriam*, where a dialectical reading of collapse and recuperation is possible, *Maud* is not a dialectical poem. Its separate parts simply mirror each other. The question of the will becomes paramount for the last two parts of the poem. Is the assent to war a triumph of the self-determining will or is such an assumption of responsibility an illusion? The second poem of Part II, 'See what a lovely shell . . .', brings the exploration of will into explicit relation with the speaker's condition as the 'tiny cell' (l. 61) of the underwater mollusc, bearing an affinity with his underground state, becomes the object of contemplation. In its 'dim water-world' (l. 68) it is another of Lyell's subaqueous creatures without knowledge of the upper world, of the geological and biological processes to which it is subject, or even that it may be a 'miracle of design' (l. 56). It has an extraordinary resistance to shock and change despite its capacity to be 'crushed with a tap/Of my fingernail' (ll. 69–70). When it was not 'void' of the 'little living will' (l. 62), did volition enable it to have power over the environment, or was it always subject to external forces? Has the speaker, likewise, and we note the language of power, 'a spark of will/Not to be trampled out' (ll. 104–5)? Yet in a subsequent poem, 'Will', one of the most non-univocal words in Tennyson's vocabulary, is used in its opposite sense as that to which one is subject rather than volition. The vision of Maud is a 'blot upon the brain', an internal phantom or even a physiological mark objectified, which makes the self subservient to it – 'That *will* show itself without' (Part II, iv, 201).

The shell poem is taking part in a debate about the psychological, philosophical and cultural significance of the concept of 'will', which preoccupied both idealists and materialists in the latter part of the nineteenth century. Interestingly, both use the mollusc or crustacea as analogue of the will.

> On the lowest levels of animal life the motive is still closely related to stimulus: zoophytes and radiata in general, acephala among the molluscs, have only a feeble twilight of consciousness, just as much as is necessary to perceive their nourishment or prey and to snatch it when it offers itself . . . Who will dream of freedom here?[45]
>
> Arthur Schopenhauer, *Essay on the Freedom of the Will*, 1841

> Organised as we are we can no more know about it than an oyster in its narrow home and with its very limited sentiency can know of the events of the human world. . . .
>
> Henry Maudsley, *The Physical Basis of Will*, 1880[46]

In different ways both writers, the German idealist and the British empiricist, swing between the concept of will as necessity and will as choice. Rather than mediating between these notions, Tennyson's text uses both accounts of will to open up questions about the nature of madness and war in a deconstructive movement which makes the status of the speaker's commitment to war finally problematical.

For Schopenhauer, a war of antagonistic wills, a universe at war, is a biological necessity. Freedom is limited both by inheritance and the passions, insanity and mania being the most extreme. However, essence, not action, is the seat of the will. A man *is* what he does, but this can only be seen *a posteriori* and cannot involve intentional action. But it is precisely such *a posteriori* knowledge which liberates consciousness into an *idea* of the self. This can be turned against the determinations of the will. Freedom lies in reflexive contemplation rather than action.[47] There could be no freedom of action or choice in war, partly because transcendental contemplation constitutes freedom and partly because war is a condition of wills in conflict by necessity. To *decide* to fight would be a form of suicide.

With the same paradox that makes quietism the ultimate freedom of the will the latter part of the poem moves towards a gentler vision of Maud and her suffering. It accepts her as fate or necessity rather as Freud was to see the woman as law because she obeys the cycles of reproduction and death.[48] Maud's paleness and dumbness denote the absence which is death. Yet the way of transcendental quietism is to live with death, and ironically presages more violent derangement, as the last troubled poem of Part II suggests, 'Dead, long dead' (II, v). Nor does the Schopenhauerian solution produce an adequate account of war. For peace and war are alike the undifferentiated war of wills elided without distinction, the conflation seen as both cause and effect of madness in this text. If this *is* a Schopenhauerian poem, and there are certainly elements which suggest so, Tennyson has transposed the universal conflict of will, in which both peace and war are subsumed, into an ideological critique. We must differentiate between the hero's compliance in an account of universal war from the analysis of the text, which sees the madness of the 'civil' life of the Hall as an extension of and double of the hero's madness and not its opposite, and the madness of war as a double of both.

Does the poem, then, anticipate Maudsley's oyster as will, rather than Schopenhauer's mollusc? In many ways Maudsley adopts the impossible account of will which the text tries to negotiate, the threat of degeneracy coupled with the need for moral responsibility. In several works he argues emphatically against the freedom of the will and self-determining agency. Consciousness is not coextensive with mind. It responds to external stimuli but cannot know of 'preconscious' and 'unconscious' operations which are founded in physiological action 'which it receives unconsciously from other organs of the body'.[49] The influence of the sexual organs upon the mind is a prime example of such processes. Mind receives its life from the continuous cycles of repair and waste going on in the body. The most important part of our experience 'lies in the dark'.[50] Inheritance determines our nature, passed on from generation to generation. The 'anti-social conditions of one generation predetermine the social disintegration of following generations'.[51] Mania and monomaniac brooding are connected with the impairment of nerve centres whose 'solidarity' is undermined. Will is 'the character of every organ of the body'.[52] When physiological unity is damaged, the 'dissolution' of the 'conscious ego' follows. A 'double or divided personality', each speaking in a foreign language to the other, occurs when a morbid growth 'lives its own life apart' physiologically and mentally, often resolving into 'two different and hostile unities'.[53] The threat to unity and 'organisation' haunts his work. And yet he maintains that it is civilisation and the development of human culture in time which can prevent decadence and the dreaded disorganisation. The responsibility for coherence is displaced from the individual to human history, which might be capable of opposing the unbecoming of genetic weakness with the becoming of integration. The dark physiological writing of the body in *Maud* seems to be retrospectively theorised here.

Maudsley, however, writing a peculiarly Victorian version of civilisation and its discontents, does offer, perhaps unawares, a way of deconstructing his theory of unity. As well as describing the disorganisation which the culture struggles to repair, he does pay attention to the needs of those forces which lie 'in the dark'. The 'latent energies' of 'secret and silent courses, in infra-conscious depths' which lie beneath the surface of national consciousness, its traditions, opinions, institutions, open feelings and aims find expression in 'disorderly volcanic upheavals' unless they are recognised rather than repressed. The 'ignorant ruler' 'despises' them, but 'great pulses' and 'great sub-conscious social forces explode . . . if too much or too long repressed'.[54] This expressive politics has revolution in mind. In *Maud* the displacement of frustrated social energy into war is analogous to the 'volcanic upheavals' and their terrible catharsis predicted by Maudsley. The hero of *Maud*, experiencing the world from underground, yet living out the ideology of repression, colludes with the notion that war is the expression of national will and unity. Maudsley's writing allows that it can be the ultimate pathology of will in which war becomes a representation for deranged energy. On this reading *Maud* is closer to *Anti-Maud* than its 'hero' knows. The implicit debate on the will makes the confirmation of war deeply problematical.

It is tempting to feel that after *In Memoriam* and *Maud* Tennyson never achieved anything of quite the same concentration again. Certainly both are double poems of extraordinary complexity. Both drive towards the 'unity' and 'organisation' which Maudsley was to value so highly: *In Memoriam* by evolving through the vicissitudes of trust in love as 'creation's final law', *Maud* by the need to be 'one with my kind'. Both sanction conservative, not to say reactionary readings, and both investigate the contradictions on which these are founded. The need for continuity in *In Memoriam* and the need for violence in *Maud* are subjected to a rigorous analysis. Their way of combining expressive writing with critique is perhaps unparalleled in the nineteenth-century. Tennyson's capacity to be startling is evident in both, but the move from *In Memoriam* and the unseen workings beneath the earth's surface to the pathological geology of the self in *Maud* in which 'secret and silent courses' work darkly in the physiological cells and in the brain creates a Victorian writing of the body which is startling in the extreme. The throbbing pulses and coercive rhythms of *Maud* live in the writing of the next decades even when Tennyson was deemed old-fashioned and conventional. Published the year before Freud was born, *Maud*'s Victorian exploration of the unconscious is not to be identified with his, but it initiates the exploration of hysteria with which Freud's work began and brings this together with cultural critique and ideology in a way which he did not. Interestingly, *Maud* studies a hysterical man; Freud, more conventionally and in accord with nineteenth-century preconceptions, worked with hysterical women. As in the early poems, Tennyson's conservatism leads him towards radical questioning.

Notes

1. Charles Lyell, *The Principles of Geology, or, The Modern Changes of the Earth and its Inhabitants* (1830–33). All references to Lyell will be according to the 7th edition, London (1847). This, the first single-volume edition of *The Principles*, has been chosen on grounds of availability. Lyell revised his work, often substantially, with every edition, though his thesis remained the same. The Cambridge Apostles seem to have been well acquainted with his ideas at an early stage. My quotation from Lyell is intended to suggest Tennyson's grasp of his thesis rather than that *In Memoriam* is indebted to specific passages.
2. Arthur Hallam, 'On Some of the Characteristics of Modern Poetry', *Englishman's Magazine*, 1 (1831), pp. 616–28. In Isobel Armstrong (ed.), *Victorian Scrutinies: Reviews of Poetry 1830–1870* (London: Athlone Press, 1972), p. 90.
3. Ibid., p. 90.
4. Hallam developed his epistemology in his 'Essay on the Philosophical Writings of Cicero' and his views on the sexuality of God in 'Theodicaea Novissimo'. See T. H. Vail Motter (ed.) *The Writings of Arthur Hallam* (New York: Modern Language Association of America; London: Oxford University Press, 1943), pp. 142–81, 198–213, esp. 204–7.

5.   William Edmounstone Aytoun (*pseud.*, T. Percy Adams), *Firmilian; or, The Student of Badajoz: a Tragedy*, *Blackwood's Magazine*, 75 (1854), p. 550. For the psychological language of the Spasmodic controversy, see Isobel Armstrong, 'The Role and Treatment of Emotion in Victorian Criticism of Poetry', *Victorian Periodicals Newsletter*, 10 (March 1977), pp. 3–16. See also Mark A. Weinstein, *William Edmounstone Aytoun and the Spasmodic Controversy* (New Haven and London: Yale University Press, 1968).

6.   Henry Maudsley, *The Physiology and Pathology of the Mind* (London, 1867; 2nd edn. London, 1868), p. 257: 'there is, as it were, a loss of the power of self-control in the individual nerve-cell, an inability of calm self-contained activity, subordinate or co-ordinate, and its energy is dissipated in an explosive display, which, like the impulsive action of the passionate man, surely denotes an irritable weakness.'

7.   'Peace and War: A Dialogue', *Blackwood's Magazine*, 76 (1854), pp. 589–98. Author identified by the *Wellesley Index of Victorian Periodicals* as G. C. Swayne. This is a dialogue representing conservative and peace party (manufacturing and trade interests) views of the war. Here it is the peace party which is regarded as being feeble-minded. In *Maud* the movement to war is a movement to madness. R, ii, 520n refers to Valerie Pitt, *Tennyson Laureate* (London: Barrie & Rockliffe, 1962, p. 175) who discusses the relation between *Maud* and Carlyle's *Past and Present* (1843), where criminal poisoning in a sick society is described. Also relevant is Kingsley's *Alton Locke* (1850). See also James R. Bennett, 'The Historical Abuse of Literature: *Maud: A Monodrama* and the Crimean War', *English Studies*, 62 (1981), 34–45. I am grateful to Joseph Bristow for directing me to these discussions and for permission to read his unpublished article, 'Tennyson's *Maud* and War'.

8.   All references to Tennyson's poems will be according to Christopher Ricks, (ed.), *The Poems of Tennyson*, 3 vols (Harlow: Longman, 1987).

9.   Sigmund Freud, 'Mourning and Melancholia', in *The Standard Edition of the Complete Works of Sigmund Freud*, ed. James Strachey and Anna Freud (London: Hogarth Press, 1953–1966), Vol 14, p. 244. All references to Freud will be according to this edition.

10.   Lyell, p. 178.

11.   See A. C. Crowley, *The Politics of Discourse* (London: Macmillan, 1989), pp. 51–90, for an extended reading of Trench.

12.   R. C. Trench, *On the Study of Words* (London 1851), p. 5.

13.   Ibid., p. 23.

14.   Ibid., pp. 16–17.

15.   Robert Montgomery, *The Omnipresence of the Deity: A Poem* (1828). In this poem the believing mariner is saved from drowning for his equally believing loved one while the atheist dies. The verbal parallels are interesting: 'She blush'd an answer to his wooing tale': 'Clasp'd in his twining arms, her seaman now / Parts the sleek locks that nestle on her brow' (pt 2, p. 44).

16.   Tennyson, *The Letters of Alfred Lord Tennyson 1821–1850*, ed. Cecil Y. Long and Edgar F. Shannon Jr (Oxford: Clarendon Press, 1982), Vol. I, p. 337.

17. *Language as Living Form in Nineteenth-Century Poetry* (Brighton, Sussex: Harvester Press; New Jersey: Barnes and Noble 1982), pp. 187–90.
18. George Eliot translated Strauss' *Life of Jesus* in 1846, but the Apostles knew his work in the 1830s. Ludwig Feuerbach, in *The Essence of Christianity* (1841, translated by George Eliot in 1854), extended his account of Christian myth as the imaginative interpretation of a people by seeing myth as a construct made by the projection of desire on to its object.
19. Lyell, pp. 746–7.
20. Robert Chambers, *Vestiges of Creation* (1844). Published anonymously, this work argues for the origin of the species in evolutionary terms, but whereas Lyell's argument is about the retrospective construction of uniformitarian change from the ambiguous and discontinuous evidence of geological remains, Chambers is concerned with tracing progressive change from the beginning of creation onwards.
21. Lyell, pp. 170, 180, 186.
22. See, for instance, Lyell, pp. 172, 174, 182, 187–9.
23. Ibid., p. 70. Also: 'All geologists . . . must be conscious, therefore, that the inaccessibility of the regions in which these alterations are taking place, compels them to remain in ignorance of a great part of the working of existing causes . . .'. Ibid., p. 172.
24. Ibid., p. 70.
25. Ibid., p. 173.
26. Ibid., p. 186. Also: 'Organic remains . . . may abandon and revisit many spaces again and again . . .' (p. 187).
27. Ibid., p. 552.
28. Friedrich Nietzche, *Twilight of the Idols*, in *Twilight of the Idols and The Anti-Christ* (Harmondsworth: Penguin 1987), p. 38.
29. Lyell, p. 190.
30. John Keble, *Tract 89* (1841), in *Tracts for the Times* (London, 1833–41), Vol. 6, pp. 65–7, 144.
31. John Milton, *A Mask (Comus)*, 1. 476.
32. Rii, 413, xcv, 46.
33. Freud, *Civilisation and its Discontents*, Vol. 21, pp. 69–71.
34. Lyell: 'But if we may be allowed so far to indulge the imagination, as to suppose a being entirely confined to the nether world – some 'dusky melancholy sprite' like Umbriel, who could 'flit on sooty pinions to the central earth', but who was never permitted to 'sully the fair face of light', and emerge into the regions of water and of air; and if this being should busy himself in investigating the structure of the globe, he might frame theories the exact converse of those usually adopted by human philosophers' (p. 71).
35. *Anti-Maud* was written by W. C. Bennett.
36. See Brian Maidment, *The Poorhouse Fugitives: Self-taught poets and poetry in Victorian Britain* (Manchester: Carcanet Press, 1987), pp. 55–6, 312–14. A self-taught working man associated with the Christian Socialists, Massey was aware of European socialism and could write powerful lyrics on the redemption of the oppressed working classes, such as 'The Awakening of the People', reprinted by Maidment, who

sees Massey as a poet who gained a middle-class audience more easily than some working-class poets. It is interesting that Massey's poems on oppression and celebrations of the war were published virtually concurrently.

37. Michel Foucault, *Madness and Civilisation: A History of Insanity in the Age of Reason* (London: Tavistock Publications, 1987), pp. 241–78.

38. Matthew Allen, *Essay on the Classification of the Insane* (London, 1837), pp. 3–4.

39. Foucault, op. cit., p. 261: 'It was the man himself, not his projection in a delirium, who was now humiliated . . .'.

40. Allen, op. cit., pp. 20–1.

41. Ibid., p. 3. See also ibid., pp. 27–8 for a similar structure.

42. Foucault, op. cit., p. 264.

43. Allen, op. cit., p. 13; Henry Maudsley, *The Physical Basis of Will* (London, 1880), p. 11.

44. James Robert Mann, *Tennyson's 'Maud' Vindicated: An Explanatory Essay*, (London, 1856), p. 77. This work considers the poem as a case-study of the insane, demonstrating that 'acute eruptive disorder' is preferable to the 'chronic disease' of madness. Though Mann sees the response to the war as in some sense pathological, it produces a catharsis and thus constitutes a 'cure'.

45. Arthur Schopenhauer, *Essay on the Freedom of the Will* (New York: Liberal Arts Press, 1960), p. 40.

46. Maudsley, op. cit., p. 27.

47. All the movements of the will are the objects of self-consciousness, which can master actions retrospectively: 'He can *wish* two opposing actions, but *will* only one of them. Only the act reveals to his self-consciousness which of the two he wills' (op. cit., p. 117).

48. Freud, 'The Theme of the Three Caskets' (Vol. 12, p. 301).

49. Henry Maudsley, *On the method of the Study of Mind: An Introductory Chapter to a Physiology and Pathology of the Mind* (London, 1883), p. 18.

50. Maudsley, *The Physical Basis of Will*, op. cit., p. 16.

51. Maudsley, *Body and Will, being an Essay concerning Will in its metaphysical, physiological and pathological aspects* (London, 1883), p. 293.

52. Ibid., p. 302.

53. Ibid., p. 304.

54. Ibid., pp. 291–2.

6

Larger Hopes and the New Hedonism: Tennyson and FitzGerald

NORMAN PAGE

In defiance of both seniority and the alphabet, 'Tennyson and FitzGerald' is a formulation that shapes itself much more readily than 'FitzGerald and Tennyson'; and it is of course a very different kind of pairing from Pope and Swift, Wordsworth and Coleridge, Eliot and Pound. It is the disparities between Tennyson and his friend (and again one instinctively puts it that way round) that most quickly seize the mind: the whale and the minnow; the vastly prolific major poet dedicated to the bardic vocation, and the dilettante translator-cum-man-of-letters whose creative stream usually ran shallow and sometimes dried up altogether; the celebrity or national institution, cossetted by his family and besieged by admirers, and the lonely eccentric single gentleman living a life of obscurity and self-imposed monotony. Yet their lives touch at many points; and, unequal though their achievement is, if *In Memoriam* was the Victorian age's favourite poem, the *Rubáiyát of Omar Khayyám*, which appeared in the same decade, was surely a close runner-up. After glancing at the history and nature of the relationship between Tennyson and FitzGerald, and the surviving record on both sides, I would like to make some comparisons between these two poems, the most celebrated sets of quatrains of their period. And if I seem at times to dwell a little more on FitzGerald than on Tennyson, this will be because *In Memoriam* and its history have received the larger share of attention in the past and will probably be more familiar to readers.

First, then, let me recall the origins and progress of a friendship that, whatever else may be said of it, was one of the longest in the lives of the two men concerned. They were almost exactly the same age (within less than four months), – as Arthur Platt once said, everybody was born in 1809 – had a similar dark complexion, and were of about the same above-average height and build. They also share the same modern biographer, Robert Bernard Martin. Unsurprisingly, Martin's life of FitzGerald is much shorter than his earlier life of Tennyson, but there are one or two striking parallel passages. For example, of Tennyson's siblings:

> One of [his] brothers was totally insane most of his life, another suffered from some form of mental illness nearly as incapacitating, a third was an opium addict, a fourth was severely alcoholic, and of the rest of the large family each had at least one bad mental breakdown in a long life.[1]

While of FitzGerald's seven siblings, Martin writes:

> All his family were mad, FitzGerald used to enjoy saying, but at least he had the advantage of knowing that he was insane. The wryness of the statement nearly blinds us to its essential truth. All his brothers and sisters were, in one way or another, peculiar. Some of them suffered from periodic mental breakdowns, and one was so odd that he became the subject of a chapter in a book on English eccentrics.[2]

In rank and wealth the two families had little in common: the FitzGeralds had 'an enormous fortune', and Edward enjoyed a private income and, after the death of his mother, was a rich man.

What they did have in common, though, was Cambridge, where their periods of residence overlapped by more than two years. FitzGerald knew Tennyson only slightly at Trinity but was greatly impressed by him and later remembered him as 'a sort of Hyperion'. He also remembered his readings and recitations, and his account furnishes fascinating evidence of Tennyson's vocal and elocutionary powers and of his oddities of pronunciation. Later they met in London, and in 1835 were together for a memorable holiday in the Lake District; FitzGerald's comment on this time sets the tone for their later relationship for, while he believed his friend to be a great man, he was quite prepared to make fun of him – 'his little humours and grumpinesses were so droll that I was always laughing' (*Mem*, i, 152).

From 1837 they saw each other often in London, and there were boisterous bachelor dinners at The Cock near Temple Bar and at Bertolini's (which they nicknamed Dirtolini's) in Leicester Square.

FitzGerald brought out a vein of humour in Tennyson that was not always evident and that did not survive his youth undiminished. He recalls, for instance, his gifts as a mimic, 'tak[ing] off the voices and expressions of well-known public characters', and in particular one remarkable party-piece:

> He used also to do the sun coming out from a cloud, and retiring into one again, with a gradual opening and shutting of the eyes, and with a great fluffing up of his hair into full wig and elevation of cravat and collar; George IV, in as comical and wonderful a way (*Mem*, i, 184).

In their more serious moments, Fitz, as Tennyson called him, was a willingly captive audience for Tennyson's readings of his poems. In March 1841 Fitz saw him in London 'with a little bit of dirty pipe in his mouth; and a particularly dirty vellum book of MSS on the sofa'[3]. This was what Fitz elsewhere called the 'butcher's book', and it was Fitz who 'carried him off with violence' to the publisher Moxon to arrange for publication of what became the 1842 volumes. His faith in his friend's poetic powers must have been gratifying and may have been crucial: Alfred, he declared, 'will publish such a volume as has not been published since the time of Keats; and which once published, will never be suffered to die'. This, at least, is the version loyally given in Sir Charles Tennyson's biography of his grand-father;[4] actually FitzGerald seems to have prefaced his tribute with the phrase 'with all his faults' (*Letters of EF*, i, 315) – and the point is worth making, since his admiration, though genuine, was not un-critical.

In the mid-forties Tennyson's poor health and his indulgence in tobacco and port caused concern to his friend. Already, though, they were drifting apart: FitzGerald was making new friends, and the epoch of the closest intimacy was over. After Tennyson's marriage they saw very little of each other: apart from one visit to Farringford in 1854 Fitz seems to have consistently declined invitations. He was clearly not keen on being just a member of a house-party; he was slightly jealous of Tennyson's other friends and impatient with his admirers; and he did not much care for Mrs Tennyson. What he longed for was a return to what he rather poignantly called the 'ante-laureate days' (*Mem*, i, 184), and in doing so he was of course not only yearning for a revival of their vanished intimacy but hankering after a return of his own vanished youth.

The relationship that I have so far, and so baldly, summarised can also be traced through the letters that passed, or failed to pass, between the two of them over a period of nearly fifty years. As one would expect, there are some evident gaps in the surviving record; but enough is available to tell its own story and convey its own suggestive implications. Of FitzGerald's letters to Tennyson, a total of 50 survive, of which all but one were written after Alfred's marriage. The solitary exception is a letter of 1835 in which, with exquisite tact, he offers to lend money to his friend; the offer seems to have been taken up, and the letter may have been carefully preserved for this reason. There were certainly others, but Tennyson presumably saw no reason to retain them. To the 49 letters from the period after 1850, and covering the last 33 years of FitzGerald's life, must be added a further 31 written to Emily and usually intended also for Alfred's eyes or ears. With Tennyson the tally is much smaller and the balance the other way round, since 11 letters survive (some mere notes, and not all of them complete) from his bachelor years but only two from the years after 1850. There may have been others but they can hardly have been numerous, for in 1869 we find Fitz remarking that he has just received the first letter from Alfred for fifteen or twenty years. We know that Fitz told Thackeray in 1852 that he had just burned most of *his* letters, partly to avoid the risk of eventual publication 'according to the vile fashion of the day' (*Letters of EF*, ii, 51); and some of Tennyson's may have received similar treatment; but there are few references to letters that have failed to survive and many allusions, teasing or mildly reproachful, to Tennyson's lack of eagerness as a correspondent. 'Do let me have a line from one of you one day,' he writes in 1854; 'at least let me have a line to tell about yourselves' in 1856; 'Write as little as you please, only write' in 1867; and, forgivingly, in 1872, 'I think you would generally give £100 sooner than write a Letter' (*Letters of EF*, ii, 135, 211; iii, 57, 346).

Remembering that Tennyson's pen was far from idle in other respects, we may be inclined to forgive his shortcomings as a correspondent; and Fitz would have known that they were nothing new, for as early as 1842 Tennyson had asked pardon for his 'ungracious silence in return for so many kind letters', pleading 'I know you like writing which I hate mortally', and in 1847 he had declared 'Aint I a beast for not answering you before?' (*Letters*, i, 204, 281). What must have been harder to stomach was the way in which Emily Tennyson interposed herself between her husband and his old friend: it was she who answered Fitz's letters, and she to whom, as we have seen, many of his were addressed. His situation resembled that of one who, hoping to have a word with the great man, has to make do with his polite but firm secretary; and although Fitz is invariably courteous and good-humoured in writing to Emily (though not always in what he said about her to others), he may well have felt sadness and even humiliation at his treatment. Even Tennyson's enthusiasm for the *Rubáiyát* must have lost some of its power to delight by being communicated through Emily. (It is pleasant to know that in about 1860 Tennyson was not only praising Fitz's Cambridge idyll in prose, *Euphranor*, to F. T. Palgrave but also 'commended to me warmly FitzGerald's famous *Omar* paraphrase' (*Mem*, ii, 505) – but the private praise did not of course appear in print until after Fitz's death.) Tennyson's earliest surviving letter to him, dating from 1835, is a touching tribute to their friendship at that period, though characteristically occasioned by Fitz's reproach that an earlier letter has gone unanswered. Relaxed, affectionate and humorous, it implies a rewarding relationship and, perhaps giving away more than was intended, casts Fitz in the role of Horatio to Tennyson's Hamlet by applying to him the lines 'as just a man/As e'er my conversation coped withal' (*Letters*, i, 132). But while Tennyson, married and famous, continued to play Hamlet, Fitz had been demoted to an attendant lord; if he ever re-read the letter he might have murmured 'Oh Alfred, what a falling off was there!'

FitzGerald's later letters resort to some odd contortions in response to the curious epistolary situation wherein his letters addressed to his friend would normally be opened and answered by another. A letter of 1881 begins touchingly, 'My dear old Alfred, I suppose that scarce a day passes without my thinking of you', but then perforce continues, 'I have told you why I do not write to you; because of Mrs Tennyson's having to reply, which I do not like troubling her to do' (*Letters of EF*, iv, 455–6). If Emily or Alfred had cared to read between the lines they would have found plenty of food for thought; and such moments are numerous – in 1870, for instance, a letter ends, 'Do not trouble the Mistress to write in reply' (ibid., iii, 220).

Tennyson's lament for 'the days that are no more' would have found a ready echo in Fitz's bosom, and indeed he quotes the line in a letter written (not to Tennyson) at one of the few emotional crises of his life. One result of his feeling that the best days of their friendship were over was an impatience with Tennyson's later poetry – with nearly everything, in fact, later than the 1842 volumes in the birth of which he had had a hand, though he made a partial exception in the case of *Maud*. As early as 1851 he avows a fondness for 'Tennyson's *old* poems' (ibid., ii, 28), pointedly underlining the adjective and implicitly showing scant respect for Tennyson's new poem, *In Memoriam*. When *Maud* appears he admits to liking its '*Drama*' but draws the line at what he calls 'the Lyrical Execution' – though even that, he quickly adds, is better than 'Princess and Memoriam' (ibid., ii, 234). With a consistency that must have been less than gratifying to Tennyson, he praises what he calls 'the old 1842 Volumes'; and a phrase in another letter brings his barely hidden motives right to the surface: 'Oh the dear old 1842 Days and Editions!' (ibid., iii, 59, 106). Elsewhere he recalls 'having heard nearly all I care for . . . from your own Lips' (ibid., ii, 413). In 1876 he tells Hallam that he 'gave up all hopes of [Tennyson] after "The Princess"' – and again we may note that this uncompromisingly dismisses *In Memoriam* – adding that 'none of the songs had "the old champagne flavour"' (*Mem*, i, 253). On the same page of the *Memoir* Hallam Tennyson records that the only song in *The Princess* for which FitzGerald had a good word to say 'was "Blow, Bugle, Blow," commemorating the echoes at Killarney', and he claims plausibly that 'Nothing either by Thackeray or by my father met FitzGerald's approbation unless he had first seen it in manuscript'.

Tennyson went on sending him his new volumes as they appeared, and they were politely acknowledged but received without enthusiasm. To Frederick Tennyson he wrote at the beginning of 1881:

> Alfred sent me his last Volume [*Ballads and Other Poems*], which to say the most of it, did not in my opinion add anything to what he had done before, and so (as I think) might as well have remained unpublished. (*Letters of EF*, iv, 388).

It was understandable that FitzGerald should think poorly of poems that came to him in the cold formality of print compared with those he had seen in manuscript and heard from the poet's lips – and which moreover were inseparably associated with the days of their youth and their closest friendship. Tennyson's marriage, the laureateship, his growing fame and his grander lifestyle must have produced in his friend a sad and painful sense of being left behind, stranded on the margin when he had once been close to the centre. He made no secret of his dislike of those he called Tennyson's 'aesthetic Worshippers'; and the same disapproving epithet was applied to Emily: telling his friend Pollock in 1864, with an unusual touch of sharpness, that he had received 'a kind letter from Mrs AT – who answers my yearly letter to her husband', he permits himself to add:

> She is a graceful lady, but I think that she and other aesthetic and hysterical Ladies have hurt AT, who, *quoad* Artist, would have done better to remain single in Lincolnshire, or married a jolly Woman who would have laughed and cried without any reason why. (Ibid., ii, 538)

A letter of 1874 to Richard Monckton Milnes sums up his grievances:

> I used to tell Tennyson thirty years ago that he should be a Dragoon, or in some active Employment that would keep his Soul stirring, instead of revolving in itself in idleness and Tobacco smoke. And now he has sunk into Coterie-worship, and (I tremble to say it) in the sympathy of his most Ladylike, gentle, Wife. An old Housekeeper like Molière's would have been far better for him, *I* think. (Ibid., iii, 487)

In the light of what has been said, it is difficult to endorse Sir Charles Tennyson's claim that 'the two friends had never known any weakening of the bond between them'.[5] As we shall see later, their friendship was to have an unpredictable and touching epilogue; but for the last two-thirds of the half-century they knew each other it is hard not to believe that the 'bond' meant much more to FitzGerald than to Tennyson. It is his life of FitzGerald, not his life of Tennyson, for which Martin uses as a title the Shakespearian phrase 'with friends possessed', but FitzGerald's kind of possessing was an anxious, emotional preoccupation or possessiveness rather than a tranquil and secure enjoyment; and one wonders whether Tennyson's perhaps slightly conscience-stricken remark on hearing of Fitz's death – 'I had no truer friend' (*Letters of EF*, iv, 598) – could have been used by Fitz if *he* had been the survivor.

All of this might lead one to suggest that it ought to have been FitzGerald rather than Tennyson who produced an *In Memoriam*, a painfully wrought monument to a friendship, though of course Tennyson's poem, like 'Lycidas', is a good deal more than a lament for or a tribute to an individual. What I want to suggest now is that

FitzGerald's own masterpiece is, less overtly, itself a commemoration of an intense friendship and the expression of a sense of loss, and that in some respects its origins curiously resemble the more familiar ones of Tennyson's poem. The genesis and the 17-year gestation of the latter need not be rehearsed; but the birth of the *Rubáiyát* is a less familiar story, and, though Martin's recent biography reports the relevant facts, he does not, it seems to me, fully bring out the underlying pattern or draw attention to the significant conclusions.

'FitzGerald's translation of Omar Khayyám': the idea is such a tritely familiar one to us that it is easy to forget its inherent strangeness – the phenomenon of such a man producing such a work needs to be accounted for. There is nothing in FitzGerald's literary track-record before or after to encourage the supposition that he might be capable of producing one of the most widely admired, most oft-quoted and most frequently reprinted poems of the Victorian age. Most of his undertakings were little more than the recreations of a bookish gentleman with too much time on his hands: a glossary of nautical expressions, a calendar of Charles Lamb's life, a dictionary of the characters referred to by Madame de Sévigné, a children's version of the story of Little Nell, translations from Greek and Spanish. There is not a shred of evidence of that 'incessant activity of mind' that V. S. Pritchett has identified as the hallmark of genius; and FitzGerald, who was wont to refer to himself as 'poking out' or 'puddling away at' or 'trifling with' his literary and philological enterprises, seems to have accepted at an early stage that his talents were of a minor order. As he told Frederick Tennyson in 1850, 'I pretend to no Genius, but to Taste: which, according to my aphorism, is the feminine of Genius' (ibid., i, 664). And yet, against all probability, this rather lethargic man tackled the daunting task of learning Persian; translated a medieval Persian poet into verse that became so widely known that it fills three columns in the *Oxford Dictionary of Quotations* (nearly as much as *In Memoriam*); and went on revising his poem over a period of twenty years. What can it have been that uniquely jolted FitzGerald out of his indolence and dilettantism?

The answer lies in his personal life; for the most emotionally turbulent period of an existence otherwise placid to the point of tedium was the years from 1852 to 1857, and especially 1856–71, and this precisely corresponds to his study of Persian and his translation of Omar Khayyám. The story of these years is one of deep attachment followed by loss and deprivation; but to understand it we need to go back nearly a decade to 1844, when FitzGerald made the acquaintance of a brilliant 18-year-old called Edward Cowell.

Cowell was to become a Cambridge professor and one of the founding members of the British Academy, but his origins were humble, and his early career testifies both to the effectiveness of self-help and to the vitality of provincial culture in the early Victorian period. The son of an Ipswich maltster, he left the local grammar school at 16 on the death of his father and entered the family business; but, well before this time, he had discovered in a local library the work of the eighteenth-century orientalist Sir William Jones and, at the tender age of 14, had become fired with an enthusiasm for Persian and Sanskrit. He taught himself Persian – as he casually observed nearly sixty years later, 'I soon learned the character'[6] – and at sixteen was already contributing verse translations to the *Asiatic Journal* and elsewhere. By a stroke of good fortune, orientalists and linguists were surprisingly thick on the ground in East Anglia in the 1840s, and Cowell took lessons from Major Thomas Hockley, who had retired to Ipswich after service in India. Another scholarly Anglo–Indian, Edward Moor, author of the popular *Hindu Pantheon*, was not far away, and George Borrow after his wanderings had married and settled at Oulton Broad.

FitzGerald met Cowell through a local clergyman; a close friendship based on a common enthusiasm for languages and literature developed between them; and FitzGerald, always ready to idealise someone who possessed the intellectual powers or the physical prowess that he felt himself to lack, looked up to the boy who was half his age as his natural superior. The friendship survived Cowell's early marriage, and did not flag when, at the age of 24, he went to Oxford as a specimen of a rather rare Victorian species, the married undergraduate. It was Cowell who in 1852 suggested to FitzGerald that he should take up the study of Persian. FitzGerald's father had died earlier in the year, and perhaps his friend sensed that he needed a new interest in life to cheer him up. FitzGerald's initial enthusiasm was not great, but he persisted in what amounted to a correspondence course conducted from Oxford. By the end of 1853 he was doing 'a little every day' (ibid., ii, 116) and sending his translations for correction.

After graduating, Cowell remained at Oxford as a part-time employee in the Bodleian, and there in 1856 he came across an uncatalogued manuscript of some quatrains by a poet named Omar

Khayyám who had received very little attention from scholars and to most educated men at that date was not even a name. These he promptly transcribed and sent to FitzGerald. The timing of events at this turning-point of FitzGerald's quiet life is significant. In January of 1856 he had learned to his dismay that his energetic and ambitious young friend was applying for a post in India; he had written to him on the 12th of that month that 'Your talk of going to India makes my Heart hang really heavy at my side' (ibid., ii, 194) and had tried – in vain, and not altogether disinterestedly – to persuade him to change his mind. In February Cowell accepted the appointment to Calcutta. Meanwhile, he was continuing to provide long-distance supervision of FitzGerald's Persian studies, and letters were passing frequently between Suffolk and Oxford: of FitzGerald's to the Cowells nearly thirty survive from the first four months of the year. Early in April, Cowell told his friend about his transcription of the Omar manuscript. At the end of June, FitzGerald went to spend a fortnight with the Cowells: a farewell visit, for they sailed for India on 1 August; and it was during this visit that Cowell gave FitzGerald a complete transcript of the manuscript of the *Rubáiyát*. It was in fact, and poignantly, a parting gift; for though pressed to go to see them off, FitzGerald declined, feeling that it would be unbearably painful (as he told Cowell at the end of July) 'to say a Good-Bye that costs me so much' (ibid., ii, 236).

But the most revealing document from this period is a letter that FitzGerald wrote to Tennyson on the day after leaving the Cowells at the end of his farewell visit. FitzGerald's friendships were passions – and tragic passions, since even their sunniest moments were haunted by the thought of the inevitability of separation. At what must have seemed like the desolating termination of an intense friendship (for he was not to know that the Cowells would survive the hazards of life in Calcutta and eventually return), it was natural that he should have turned for consolation to one of his oldest friends. In that letter he tells Tennyson that while staying with the Cowells they read together 'some curious Infidel and Epicurean Tetrastichs by a Persian of the 11th Century – as savage against Destiny, etc., as Manfred – but mostly of Epicurean Pathos . . .'. (It is, incidentally, in this same letter that he confesses his lack of enthusiasm for 'Princess and Memoriam' (ibid., ii, 233–4).)

Three months after the Cowells sailed, FitzGerald married Lucy Barton, daughter of the deceased Quaker poet and friend of FitzGerald, Bernard Barton. This disastrous and short-lived venture can perhaps be partly explained by his state of emotional confusion after their departure. What he did cleave to was Omar: his first letter to Cowell in India refers to his Persian studies, and his second and third discuss his reading of Omar in detail. 'It is very pleasant to think,' he writes early in 1857, 'that we can go on exchanging our notes – in which you will still be Teacher – almost as easily as if we were only London and Oxford apart' (ibid., ii, 252). By a stroke of luck Cowell discovered in a Calcutta library another manuscript of the *Rubáiyát*, and sent a transcription of it to England, enabling FitzGerald to commemorate the anniversary of his farewell to Cowell by completing his first perusal of this new source. At about the same time we find the first references to his attempts at translation.

To FitzGerald, it seems clear, Omar Khayyám provided a lifeline to keep afloat a friendship that might otherwise have sunk without trace. To Cowell he confessed that he was 'still harping on our old Studies' and that 'Omar breathes a sort of Consolation to me!', while to Tennyson he was more explicitly self-aware: 'I keep on reading foolish Persian . . . chiefly because of its connecting me with the Cowells' (ibid., ii, 273, 291). Before the end of the year he is thinking of sending to *Fraser's Magazine* 'a few Quatrains in English Verse' (ibid., ii, 305), the first fruits of a highly uncharacteristic burst of creative energy. In the context of what Carlyle once called FitzGerald's 'innocent *far niente* life' it is truly startling to find him telling Cowell, once the version of the *Rubáiyát* is completed, 'I supposed very few People have ever taken such Pains in Translation as I have . . .' (ibid., ii, 335).

This bare summary perhaps makes the essential points sufficiently clear. For FitzGerald the study of Persian in general and of Omar Khayyám in particular were closely woven into the texture of his friendship with Cowell: his *Rubáiyát* might later be taken as an expression of the *Zeitgeist*, but its origins were intimately personal. FitzGerald's friend had not died of a stroke in Vienna, but his departure must have seemed almost as final ('Shall we ever meet again? I think not . . .', he writes gloomily in one letter (ibid., ii, 260)); and, though less shocking, it was more painfully prolonged. Nor is it absurd to compare Tennyson's attitude towards the brilliance and promise of Hallam with FitzGerald's hero-worship of one whom an obituarist was much later to describe as 'not only the greatest Oriental scholar that England has produced, but probably also the most widely learned man of our time' (*Athenaeum*, 14 February 1903, p. 209). It also seems undeniable that, just as the excessively long-drawn-out labours on *In Memoriam* were a means of sustaining a kind of relationship with a dead man, FitzGerald turned to Omar – given to him by Cowell, read together at their last meeting, and a continuing justification for frequent letter-writing – as a link with the friend from whom he was separated not indeed by the grave but by what Matthew Arnold had a few years earlier called the 'estranging sea'.

But the two poems have more in common than a shared impulse to commemorate an intimacy terminated in its prime. Both were published anonymously (though Tennyson's authorship was common knowledge); both continued to grow after the original publication (though FitzGerald's expanded more dramatically, from 75 to 110 quatrains in the second edition); both were found to provide consolation (though, as we shall see, not for the same readers). The *Rubáiyát* is ostensibly a translation but takes such liberties with both the structure and the details of the original as to entitle us to regard it as substantially an original work. *In Memoriam*, it is true, is more obviously autobiographical; but as Susan Shatto and Marion Shaw have recently shown, Tennyson's successive revisions tended to make it appear less personal.

When all is said and done, however, the differences (which sometimes amount to antitheses) are more important than the resemblances. Tennyson, after all, was famous (as I have pointed out elsewhere, the epithet 'Tennysonian' was current at least as early as the mid-forties), while FitzGerald was unknown and seems not to have been named as the author of his poem until nearly 16 years after its original appearance. *In Memoriam* was an instant success, but the *Rubáiyát* had a long wait for recognition. That delay was surely not just the result of FitzGerald's obscurity and disinclination for self-advertisement: his poem had to create the taste by which it could be enjoyed, or at the very least had to bide its time until there occurred a change in the intellectual and spiritual weather favourable to its flourishing. With remarkable appropriateness, Tennyson's poem appeared in the first year of the new decade and 11 months before the opening of the Great Exhibition; FitzGerald's appeared in the last year of the decade, the year of *On the Origin of Species*. Even as he confronts the threats to faith posed by the new science, Tennyson is conservative and reassuring with the strength of his convictions; the *Rubáiyát*, a *fin-de-siècle* poem born before its time, is uncompromisingly unorthodox and challenging with the power of its scepticism.

The steady increase in FitzGerald's popularity during the remaining decades of the century was partly at Tennyson's expense. 'Every-

body admires Tennyson now,' Walter Bagehot had declared in the
year in which the *Rubáiyát* appeared; but John Jump has pointed out
that criticisms of Tennyson became common, especially among the
younger generation of readers, from about 1860.[7] A writer in the
North British Review in 1864 drew attention to Tennyson's 'empire
over some, and the indifference to his poetry of other by no means
less able judges';[8] and things went far enough for Gerard Manley
Hopkins, writing in 1879, to express his grief 'to hear [Tennyson]
depreciated, as of late years has often been done'. Grieved or not,
Hopkins had not a few reservations of his own: while (with ecu-
menical generosity) he thought *In Memoriam* 'a divine poem', he
suggested that the *Idylls* should be called *Charades from the Middle
Ages* and dismissed *Maud, The Princess* and other poems as 'an un-
gentlemanly row'. Ten years earlier, Alfred Austin claimed that
Tennyson's 'fame has steadily increased precisely as his genuine
poetical power has steadily waned', and (unconsciously echoing
FitzGerald) suggested that 1842 represented the climax of his real
achievement. Soon afterwards Swinburne – a notable early admirer
of the *Rubáiyát* – attacked the ethical pretensions of the *Idylls of the
King*.[9]

These were, of course, precisely the years that saw the rise in
popularity of FitzGerald's poem. Charles Eliot Norton contributed a
long essay to the *North American Review* in 1869 in which, reviewing
the second edition, he declared that 'The prevailing traits of Omar
Khayyám are so coincident with certain characteristics of the spiritual temper of our own generation'[10] – a point that was to recur
frequently in subsequent criticism, and a clue to the growing popularity of the poem as the end of the century hove in sight. In the next
decade a contributor to *Fraser's Magazine* (identified as Jessie E.
Cadell) observed somewhat disapprovingly: 'That we have heard a
good deal of late about Omar Khayyám is not due, we fear, to any
increase in the number of Persian scholars, but to the fact that the
existing translation harmonizes with a special phase of modern
thought'.[11] On a less magisterial level, copies of the *Rubáiyát* became
familiar items in the middle-brow cultural scene. Writing after the
turn of the century, FitzGerald's great-niece testified to the popularity of the poem in her own generation:

Quotations from Omar are in the mouth of every cultured 'miss'
in real life and in fiction. Half-crown and penny magazines alike
drag in his name. No novelist of pretension is happy unless one
chapter boasts a quotation as headline or some heroine goes

through the psychological moment of her existence with the *Rubáiyát* at hand on her dressing-table to point out to her the nothingness of all things. In every conceivable binding and at all variety of price it lies on bookshop counters and railway stalls.[12]

One more recent commentator speaks of 'the extraordinary rage [in the 1890s] for FitzGerald's *Omar*'; another refers to the widespread use of Omar Khayyám's name for cigarettes, cigars, pipes, tobacco, wines, soaps, pens, and dozens of other commercial items, both in England and in America'.[13] One offshoot of the Omar cult was the foundation in 1892 of the Omar Khayyám Club, the list of whose members included some of the best-known authors and critics of the day, among them Hardy, Gissing, Newbolt, Conan Doyle, Gosse, Lang and Clodd. Hardy's autobiography records that he attended a meeting in 1895 in the company of Meredith and made his first public speech (and one of the very few he ever delivered) on that occasion; later he visited FitzGerald's grave; and it was a favourite stanza from the *Rubáiyát* that he asked his wife to read to him on his deathbed.[14]

So that when Hardy, in his first great novel of the nineties, speaks of Angel Clare as one who 'persistently elevated Hellenic Paganism at the expense of Christianity' (*Tess of the d'Urbervilles*, ch. 49), we may well be justified in enlarging 'Hellenic' to embrace Omar's Persia as well as in seeing this as a declaration of personal faith on the part of the author. During his last minutes of consciousness, Hardy seems to have felt no craving to hear a stanza from *In Memoriam*, and there is a sense in which he and his contemporaries had to choose between FitzGerald and Tennyson as they had to choose between Disraeli and Gladstone or between Huxley and Wilberforce, since the two poets could be seen as standing for contrasting responses to the anxieties of the age. Whatever it may be for us, for Tennyson's contemporaries, as Humphry House has pointed out, *In Memoriam* was primarily 'a great poem of spiritual and emotional victory.'[15] Victoria herself had found 'comfort' in the poem after Albert's death; and A. C. Bradley was to imagine 'readers who never cared for a poem before' turning to it at a time of grief and murmuring '"This . . . is what I dumbly feel"'. But as the century wore on, an increasing number found their instinctive convictions expressed – strikingly, memorably, and eminently quotably – in the pagan *Rubáiyát* rather than in Tennyson's Christian poem. Leslie Stephen and Charles Eliot Norton, who both lost their wives in the seventies, opted for FitzGerald to provide solace; and Stephen's *An Agnostic's Apology*, published in the year after his wife's death, seems not only to reflect his bereavement but to echo the pessimism of Omar as transmitted by FitzGerald:

> There is a deep sadness in the world. Turn and twist the thought as you may, there is no escape. Optimism would be soothing if it were possible; in fact, it is impossible, and therefore a constant mockery.[16]

A revealing case-study of changing taste is furnished by Meredith, whose early enthusiasm for Tennyson evaporated far enough for him to declare at the end of the sixties that Tennyson was 'twenty years behind his time' and to speak of his latest work as 'lines like yards of linen – drapery for the delight of ladies who would be in the fashion'. Earlier in the decade he had been one of the first to respond enthusiastically to the *Rubáiyát*: as he recalled in a letter written only a few weeks before his death, the unknown poem had been brought to his attention in 1862 by Swinburne:

> It happened that he [Swinburne] was expected one day [14 June 1862] on a visit to me, and he being rather late I went along the road to meet him. At last he appeared waving the white sheet of what seemed to be a pamphlet. He greeted me with a triumphant shout of a stanza new to my ears. This was FitzGerald's *Omar Khayyám*, and we lay on a heathery knoll beside my cottage reading a stanza alternately, indifferent to the dinner-bell, until a prolonged summons reminded us of appetite. After the meal we took to the paper-covered treasure again. Suddenly Swinburne ran upstairs, and I had my anticipations. He returned with feather-pen, blue folio-sheet, and a dwarf bottle of red ink. In an hour he had finished thirteen stanzas of his 'Laus Veneris', and rarely can one poet have paid so high a compliment to another as FitzGerald received.[17]

Both Meredith and Swinburne, we may reflect, belonged to a younger generation than Tennyson, and Swinburne was barely in his teens when *In Memoriam* appeared. For them, and for many others of their generation, Tennyson's reassuring surveyor's report that in spite of surface-cracks the edifice of faith was structurally sound must have seemed to belong, like the traditionalism of the laureateship and the optimism of the Great Exhibition, among the outmoded notions of their elders, while the pessimism and hedonism of the *Rubáiyát* were much more in tune with their own worldview. It was in fact in the mid-fifties, between the appearances of the two poems I have been discussing, that the words 'hedonism' and 'hedonist' seem to have entered the language: the *OED* records their first use in 1856, the year in which FitzGerald encountered Omar.

But 'the new hedonism', as Grant Allen called it in an essay contributed to the *Fortnightly Review* in 1894, came into its own in the eighties and nineties. Writing in the same journal in 1889, Edmund Gosse was able to look back on the causes for the *Rubáiyát's* rise to fame:

> Whether it accurately represents or not the sentiments of a Persian astronomer of the eleventh century is a question which fades into insignificance beside the fact that it stimulated and delighted a generation of young readers, to whom it appealed in the same manner, and along parallel lines with, the poetry of Morris, Swinburne, and the Rossettis. . . . The same reassertion of the sensuous elements of literature, the same obedience to the call for a richer music and a more exotic and impassioned aspect of manners, the same determination to face the melancholy problems of life and find a solace for them in art. . . .[18]

Gosse's unintentionally ironic claim is that FitzGerald, the most reactionary of men, had written a modern poem without knowing it and had anticipated the aestheticism that he never lived to see but would certainly have taken a dim view of.

In the closing decades of the century, then, FitzGerald's stock was steadily rising, and for a generation or two his poem must have been a serious contender for the title of the most popular longer poem in English, with perhaps only Gray's *Elegy* (of which FitzGerald was a passionate admirer) and Housman's *A Shropshire Lad* (not very dissimilar to the *Rubáiyát* in its broad appeal) as non-Tennysonian rivals. (Housman, incidentally, who must have found FitzGerald deeply congenial, once observed of *In Memoriam* that its argument could be summed up as 'things must come right in the end, because it would be so very unpleasant if they did not'.) 'All the English are crazy for Omar' says an Arab character in Muriel Spark's *The Mandelbaum Gate*, and although the claim hardly holds good in a novel set in 1961, it faithfully echoes the reality of an earlier age.

Modern criticism and scholarship has, of course, reversed the process I have been describing: it is Tennyson, not FitzGerald, who is the hero of theses and conferences – and not unreasonably so, since beside the massiveness of his achievement even the *Rubáiyát* seems puny and anorexic. FitzGerald remains a one-poem man; the *Rubáiyát* in its final version is less than half the length of *Enoch Arden*; and the story of its birth is largely contained in less than three years of FitzGerald's long life, between that painful and creatively fertile visit to the Cowells in the summer of 1856 and the publication of the first edition. Still, he may be more of a presence in the twentieth-century than has sometimes been supposed: it has been suggested, for example, that T. S. Eliot not only unblushingly plagiarises A. C. Benson's biography of FitzGerald in the opening lines of 'Gerontion' but is 'greatly influenced' by FitzGerald's letters through-out his early poetry.[19] And it is worth remembering that Tennyson himself commemorates their long friendship in what has sometimes been regarded (in my view rightly) as one of his finest shorter poems. 'Ally has been finishing one of his old world poems begun about the Ulysses period and discarded', wrote Emily Tennyson to Edward Lear in 1883.[20] The 'old world poem' was 'Tiresias', and Tennyson may have been partly prompted by the reflection that exactly half a century had passed since he had begun it. In these circumstances it was natural to think of dedicating the finished poem to the surviving friend closely associated with that period of his life, 1883 being also the fiftieth anniversary of their meeting. The dedicatory poem 'To E. FitzGerald' commemorates both their long friendship and their last meeting seven years earlier. That FitzGerald, who by an uncanny coincidence died a few days after the poem was written, never read it was perhaps on the whole a good thing, since (as Christopher Ricks has pointed out) his oldest friend, born in the same year as himself, had contrived to get his age wrong. But this final piece of thoughtlessness, so characteristic of Tennyson's side of the relationship, hardly mars a magnificent memorial that has some-thing of the quality of an act of atonement.

Charting the currents of nineteenth-century belief and feeling, David Daiches has drawn attention to the changes that took place from the 'moral dandyism' of Byron's 'pre-evangelical sensibility' to the 'activist stoicism' of Henley and Housman: by the end of the century, he argues, it was no longer possible 'for a sceptic such as Housman to use his scepticism as a passport to hedonism'.[21] FitzGerald, born in the year in which *Childe Harold* was begun, seems

closer to Byron than to Henley or Housman in temperament as well
as background – which perhaps makes it all the more paradoxical
that his greatest popularity should have been in the *fin-de-siècle*
years. In the last third of the century the *Rubáiyát* advertises the
hedonistic alternative; but FitzGerald's own distaste for the Laureate's unrelenting seriousness was articulated long before his own
poem was even begun – to be precise, on the last day of the
Tennysonian *annus mirabilis* of 1850, in a letter to Frederick Tennyson
– and since the passage also conveys in a few lines the essence of
their relationship it will serve as a fitting conclusion to these com-
parative observations:

> But you know Alfred himself never writes, nor indeed cares a
> halfpenny about one, though he is very well satisfied to see one
> when one falls in his way. You will think I have a spite against
> him for some neglect, when I say this, and say besides that I
> cannot care for his In Memoriam. Not so, if I know myself: I
> always thought the same of him, and was just as well satisfied
> with it as now. His poem I never did greatly affect: nor can I learn
> to do so: it is full of finest things, but it is monotonous, and has
> that air of being evolved by a Poetical Machine of the highest
> order. (*Letters of EF*, i, 696)

Notes

1. Robert Bernard Martin, *Tennyson: the Unquiet Heart* (Oxford and London: Clarendon Press and Faber & Faber, 1980), p. 10.
2. Robert Bernard Martin, *With Friends Possessed: A Life of Edward FitzGerald*
   (London: Faber & Faber, 1985), p. 22.
3. *The Letters of Edward FitzGerald*, ed. A. M. and A. B. Terhune (Princeton,
   NJ: Princeton University Press, 1980), 1. 272; hereafter cited as *Letters of
   EF*.
4. Charles Tennyson, *Alfred Tennyson* (London: Macmillan, 1949), p. 191.
5. Ibid., pp. 467–8.
6. Quoted in Cowell's obituary (*Athenaeum*, 14 February 1903, p. 209)
   from 'a memorable address given to the Royal Asiatic Society in 1898'.
7. *Tennyson: the Critical Heritage*, ed. J. D. Jump (London: Routledge &
   Kegan Paul, 1967), pp. 12–13, 216.
8. Quoted by Humphry House in 'Tennyson and the Spirit of the Age',
   All in Due Time (London: Rupert Hart-Davis, 1955), p. 123.
9. *Tennyson: the Critical Heritage*, pp. 295, 319, 334–5.
10. *North American Review*, cix (October 1869), p. 565. Norton's review,
    published anonymously, is, according to A. M. Terhune (*The Life of*

Edward FitzGerald [New Haven Conn.: Yale University Press, 1947], p. 209), the first review of FitzGerald's poem to appear. It was prompted by the second edition of the *Rubáiyát* (1868), which is discussed in tandem with J. B. Nicolas's *Les Quatrains de Khàyam, traduits du Persan* (Paris, 1867). The first review to appear in England seems to be that in *Fraser's Magazine*, n. s. i (June 1870); the anonymous reviewer was Thomas W. Hinchliff, who draws a comparison between some of FitzGerald's stanzas and the 'infant crying in the night' stanza of *In Memoriam*.

11. J. E. C[adell], 'The True Omar Khayam', *Fraser's Magazine*, n. s., xix (May 1879), p. 650. The reviewer notes of the translation that 'its inexactness has allowed for the infusion of a modern element'. FitzGerald himself describes the review as 'a temperate and just Article' (to E. B. Cowell, June 1879: *Letters of EF*, iv, 225). It is perhaps not unfair to mention that Mrs Cadell was herself at work on a text and translation of Omar that remained unfinished at her death in 1884.

12. Mary Eleanor FitzGerald-Kerrich, 'Edward FitzGerald: a Personal Reminiscence by his Great-Niece', *Nineteenth Century*, lxv (1909), p. 468.

13. John A. Lester, Jr, *Journey through Despair 1880–1914: Transformations in British Literary Culture* (Princeton, NJ: Princeton University Press, 1968), p. 8; Sol Gittleman, 'John Hay as a Critic of the Rubáiyát', *Victorian Newsletter*, xxiv (1963), p. 26.

14. F. E. Hardy, *The Life of Thomas Hardy* (London: Macmillan, 1962), pp. 268, 446.

15. *All in Due Time*, p. 135.

16. *Fortnightly Review*, n. s., xix, 1 June 1876, p. 857.

17. *The Letters of George Meredith*, ed. C. L. Cline (Oxford: The Clarendon Press, 1970), i. 407, ii. 1692.

18. 'Edward FitzGerald', *Fortnightly Review*, xlvi (July 1889), pp. 65–6.

19. J. A. Clark, 'On First Looking into Benson's FitzGerald', in *Fifty Years of the South Atlantic Quarterly*, ed. W. B. Hamilton (North Carolina: Duke University Press, 1952). The facetious tone of this essay makes it difficult to know how seriously Clark means to be taken: some of the alleged echoes are unconvincing, but others are undeniably startling.

20. *The Letters of Emily Lady Tennyson*, ed. James O. Hoge (Pennsylvania State University Press, 1974), p. 327.

21. David Daiches, *Some Late Victorian Attitudes* (London: André Deutsch, 1969), pp. 15–16.

7

Tennyson and Victorian Balladry

W. W. ROBSON

I

Could Tennyson write good ballads? To answer this question we must first decide what is meant by 'ballad'. The word has been applied to various kinds of verse, but they all have a family resemblance. For English-speaking readers the Border Ballads represent the prototype. In this kind of poetry the intention is to tell a story, and at the same time to arouse the emotions appropriate to it. Poetic 'beauties' are sometimes present but always seem incidental, even unintentional: the attention of the reader or hearer is directed to the story and the characters. The verse-form is short rhymed stanzas. The metre is simple and does not call attention to itself, though repetitions and refrains may create an effect of incantation. There are no complications of rhythm, corresponding to subtleties of feeling, that cannot be taken in at the first hearing. Some ballad verse is old and it can be regarded as a primitive form, but it has not been superseded: the ballad has persisted, it has developed in its own way, it has its own history. T. S. Eliot, however, thought that it is difficult to write in the conditions of present-day society, pointing out that the greatest of modern balladists, Rudyard Kipling, had an advantage over more recent poets of this kind because he still had the living music-hall behind him.[1]

There is still no agreement among scholars about the origin of ballads. But about one of their qualities there is no dispute. They are impersonal. It is not merely that the poets' names are unknown: the absence of the poet is, so to speak, a requirement of the form. If 'poem', as it surely does, implies 'poet' (*das Volk dichtet* cannot be literally true) a ballad must have had an author. But, as G. L. Kittredge said, it has the effect of appearing to tell itself, without the instrumentality of a conscious speaker.[2] 'The style is the man' does not

160

apply here. The teller of the tale has no role in it. Unlike other songs, it does not purport to give utterance to the feelings of the speaker. The first person does not occur, except in the speeches of the characters. The narrator offers no comments or reflections, does not analyse the characters psychologically. Nor does he take sides for or against any of them. He merely tells what happened, and what people said. The dialogue is confined to its simplest and most inevitable elements. The story exists for its own sake.

This kind of popular poetry, impersonal and enigmatic, has often appealed to sophisticated poets, but, as Albert B. Friedmann shows in *The Ballad Revival* (1961), they have found it tricky to handle. Friedmann's last chapter is, significantly, entitled 'The Difficulties of Imitation.'[3] It tells the story of the ballad revival, starting from Percy's *Reliques of Ancient English Poetry* (1765), and it makes clear the uneasiness of many poets with the ballad and the problem that both the early and the late Romantics and the Pre-Raphaelites encountered when they tried to assimilate it into their personal styles. Sir Walter Scott, the great collector of ballads, noted that a good many readers did not find them attractive in their original form. Sometimes they were so crude and harsh as to be repellent. His own solution was to cross them with romance. Scott is often credited with initiating this confluence. But he had been anticipated by Percy. Some of the best-known and most influential ballads in Percy's collection, like 'The Hermit of Warkworth', were largely fabricated by him. W. J. Mickle's ballads, with their Spenserian locutions and archaic spellings, have a similar manufactured quality. So do the romance-ballads fathered by Thomas Chatterton on 'Rowley', though the completeness of Chatterton's delusion gives a charm to the pseudo-antique style which is merely tiresome in Mickle.

And so it came about that two of the traditions of medieval storytelling were given a new life by the Romantic movement. 'The penetration of the ballad by romance' is an appropriate formula for the wave of nineteenth-century poetry launched by Scott's *Lay of the Last Minstrel* (1805) and other poems by him and by other poets – Coleridge, Southey, Wordsworth, Keats. These poets do not always mingle the two traditions. Southey was well-versed in chivalry and studied the metrical romances, but he did not draw on this knowledge when he was writing his ballads. Wordsworth explicitly renounces romance at the beginning of *Peter Bell* (written 1798), though it is still plausible to argue, as Hugh Sykes Davies did, that Wordsworth is a greater master of the eerie and strange than Coleridge or

Keats or Shelley. In other poems he shows a continued liking for romance. His 'Song at the Feast at Brougham Castle' is, stylistically, a curious mixture. The minstrel, expressing warlike emotions, speaks in Scott's manner, in the short rhymed couplets of a romance, but Clifford's response is made in long meditative lines and sounds a more characteristically Wordsworthian note of thoughtfulness and limpid gravity:

> The silence that is in the starry sky,
> The sleep that is among the lonely hills.

The romances are not an important source for Coleridge in his 'Ancient Mariner'. His most famous romance-ballad is 'Christabel' (1797), influenced by Percy's 'Sir Cauline'. But 'Christabel' is much more romance than ballad. If literary historians still call it a ballad, this is perhaps on account of its sensationalism about snakes, which links it with 'Gothic' ballads, or because of its metre, which derives from Coleridge's study of the irregularities of the older ballad verse. A poem of this period that exhibits a more balanced blend of romance and ballad is Keats's 'La Belle Dame sans Merci' (1819). Keats loved the old ballads for their dramatic effect and air of mystery. In this respect his poem is a distillation of the ballad spirit. It is written in a modified form of the ballad stanza, opens abruptly as they do, with the ballad formality of the query:

> O what can ail thee, knight-at-arms . . .?

and uses dialogue as the means of revelation. But unlike the ballads, 'La Belle Dame sans Merci' is not a tale of action. It is more like an allegorical episode in a romance. As Albert Friedmann says, the lady is more like Spenser's Phaedria or Duessa than like the Queen of Elfland. The effect of the poem is the evocation of a state of strange indefinable anguish. The situation, unlike those in the ballads, remains unresolved. The poem is like the ballads in being concentrated and elliptical, but the setting, weird and desolate, and the languid, dream-like atmosphere, are properties of a suggestive, subjective kind of poetry, not of old balladry.

So many poems were written in this tradition – for example, by Tennyson, Gabriel and Christina Rossetti, Swinburne, Morris, and

Yeats – that it looks like the main line in Victorian balladry. So atmospheric, so centred on mood rather than action are some of Tennyson's poems in this manner that Eliot in 1932 said that Tennyson could not tell a story. Whether this is true of the whole of Tennyson's balladry is a question I shall return to. Certainly the story is only hinted at in 'Mariana' and 'Oriana', for example, and it is hardly the main interest in 'The Lady of Shalott'. But there is some Victorian balladry which, though suffused with romantic colouring, manages to tell a story.

An example is the once very well-known poem of Jean Ingelow, first published in 1863, 'The High Tide on the Coast of Lincolnshire, 1571'. Born at Boston, Lincolnshire, Jean Ingelow (1820–97) belonged to Tennyson's native region and had some personal acquaintance with him (he expressed mild approval of some of her poetry, while deploring 'cockneyisms' in her rhymes). The 'High Tide' is a 'period' narrative, with suggestions of Elizabethan spelling and diction, but it is not primarily a pastiche but obviously a nineteenth-century poem, with Scott and the Romantics and the Pre-Raphaelites behind it. (Jean Ingelow in her time was a more popular practitioner of Pre-Raphaelite poetry than Christina Rossetti, as Christina ruefully noted.) The poem opens with the promise of a gripping narrative:

> The old mayor climb'd the belfry tower,
>   The ringers ran by two, by three;
> 'Pull, as ye never pull'd before;
>   Good ringers, pull your best,' quoth he.
> 'Play uppe, play uppe, O Boston bells;
> Ply all your charges, all your swells,
>   Play uppe 'The Brides of Enderby'.

I used to wonder just how the farmers, as they struck out with stout breast-strokes, were helped by being informed that there was a flood: perhaps it was some sort of early warning system. Anyway that brisk start is in the ballad manner. But the 'High Tide' makes no attempt at a 'Border' starkness of style. There is an emotionally involved narrator, the heroine's mother-in-law, and the tone of the poem soon becomes elegiac and pathetic: the refrain, the calling of the cows by 'my son's wife Elizabeth' has the effect of a lament. The power of the poem comes from the evocation of the flood:

> For lo! along the river's bed
> A mighty eygre reared his crest.
> And uppe the Lindis raging sped.
> It swept with thunderous noises loud;
> Shaped like a curling snow-white cloud,
> Or like a demon in a shroud.
> . . . .
> So farre, so fast the eygre drave,
>   The heart had hardly time to beat,
> Before a shallow seething wave
>   Sobbed in the grasses at oure feet:
> The feet had hardly time to flee
> Before it brake against the knee,
> And all the world was in the sea.

'Sobbed' is a well-chosen and thrilling word here, but a traditional ballad would have been more literal. The details are rendered from within the subjective experience of the human-beings concerned: again, not in the manner of the old ballads.

Victorian debate about modernising the ballads was sharpened by Swinburne's review of Rossetti's first volume of original poetry.[4] Swinburne laid down the requirements for sound balladry. The form demands from a poet, he says, 'narrative power, lyrical, and dramatic', and all three at once. It must condense the loose fluency of romantic tale-telling into tight and intense brevity. It must give 'as in summary' the result and the essence of events and emotions, without the exhibition of their gradual changes and growth which 'a romance of the older or the newer type' must lay open to us in order. 'There must be no pause in a ballad', no excess, no 'waste of a word or a minute in the course of its rapid and fiery motion.' Swinburne thought Rossetti had reproduced these qualities of the old ballads. Andrew Lang disagreed. He was probably right. But he may have been unfair to Rossetti. Faithful imitation of the old ballads was not Rossetti's purpose, which he disclosed when he described his very remarkable narrative poem 'Stratton Water' as 'a modern antique'. A 'modern' element is present in all his balladry, revealing itself in a sophisticated psychological interest, and a romantic antiquarianism, which are both alien to the ballad spirit. He was an excellent story-teller in 'The King's Tragedy' and 'The Bride's Prelude', but they are purely romances.

How far Swinburne's own specialist connoisseuring of the ballads influenced his own poetry is not an easy question to answer. It

seems, at any rate, to be agreed that he did not do his best work in
the poems of his that can strictly be described as ballads. I have come
across no ballad by Swinburne that can compare with the tense
grimness and mounting horror of Kipling's ballad 'Heriot's Ford',
the one that ends with the line

'You've finished with the flesh, my Lord.'

Gerard Manley Hopkins achieves an urgent and stark horror in his
unfinished poem 'Margaret Clitheroe', but it is not in the ballad
manner. His ballad 'The Queen's Crowning' has a mainly decorative
effect: Rossetti could have written it.

More real affinity with the Border Ballads is to be found in some
of William Morris's poems, such as 'The Haystack in the Floods', or
'Sir Peter Harpsdon's End'. Morris's medievalism belongs to a different ethos from that of 'La Belle Dame sans Merci' or 'The Lady of
Shalott'. Interested as he is in the picturesque details of medieval life,
he uses them, not as Rossetti does for romantic antiquarianism, but
to convince modern readers of the human realities (often very harsh
ones) of medieval life. His stories themselves may belong to romance, but the hard-bitten style in which he tells them surely owes
much to the Border Ballads.

But Morris is also the poet of 'The Nymph's Song to Hylas' and
'The Blue Closet', preoccupied, as Eliot said, with the creation of a
dream world. He is also part of the tradition of Victorian balladry we
have been considering, the line that runs from Coleridge and Keats
through Tennyson to the Pre-Raphaelites and Yeats: introverted
poetry, foregrounding the individual poet's reactions to what he
describes or evokes. It is time to look now at a more outward-
looking, publicly-orientated kind of nineteenth-century balladry,
playing for a communal rather than an individual response, and
more concerned with external action, events that are exciting in
themselves, than with the poet's moods or reveries.

II

Of this realm Walter Scott was for long the king. Then Byron's verse
romances stole the affections of the reading public, and Scott turned
to prose fiction. The supremacy in narrative verse passed eventually
to Thomas Babington Macaulay (1800–59), with his *Lays of Ancient
Rome* (1842). Macaulay was influenced by Scott. His praise of Scott in

his early essay on 'History' is a salute to Scott's power in the imaginative recreation of the past. In his youthful poem 'The Battle of Bosworth Field' he plunges into Scott's own domain, the world of chivalry. But though the great Whig owed much to the great Tory he was more at home in a different country of the mind: Ancient Rome as he imagined it. And this suggests another influence. In his preface to the *Lays*, while acknowledging his debt 'to our own old ballads', and his larger debt to Scott, 'the great restorer of our ballad poetry', Macaulay adds: 'To the *Iliad* still greater obligations are due.' We touch here on the fringe of an extensive subtext of Victorian poetry, the struggle for the mantle of Homer. It was widely believed that the *Iliad* and the *Odyssey* were based on primitive lays, and probably Macaulay was offering, in a modern English version, a suggestion of what they might have been like. The *Lays of Ancient Rome* were very popular. Published in 1842, the year of Tennyson's *Poems* and Browning's *Dramatic Lyrics*, they outstripped all competitors and had reached the 100 000 mark by 1875. Why was this? Many other collections of historical ballads were published in those days. The explanation perhaps is that Macaulay's imagination was not so much historical as contemporary. The world he wrote about was an immediate reality to him, and he brought to it the zeal of a political partisan. 'Horatius' and 'Lake Regillus' are about the struggle of liberated peoples to prevent the reimposition of alien rule.

> 'Hear, Senators and people
>   Of the good town of Rome,
> The Thirty Cities charge you
>   To bring the Tarquins home:
> And if ye still be stubborn
>   To work the Tarquins wrong,
> The Thirty Cities warn you,
>   Look that your walls be strong.'
>   ('The Battle of the Lake Regillus')

Kingsley Amis included 'Horatius' entire in his *Faber Popular Reciter*. He aptly suggests the quality of this splendid poem when he notes that its Rome has the appeal of a golden-age England (though there are English ideas in the ranks of Tuscany also). Yet, he adds, 'there is something unreal, something almost ritualized about ['Horatius'], not vulgar or sentimental as these words are normally applied, something not of pretence but of let's-pretend. The brave

days of old belong to a time when all the world was young.'[5] This is
well said. But Macaulay's partisan fervour is at least as prominent as
his nostalgia. In the preface to 'Virginia' he extends his partisanship
into the class war. He points out that the heroic warriors of the two
preceding Lays were all members of the dominant order. 'A poet
singing their praises, whatever his own political opinions might be,
would naturally abstain from insulting the class to which they belonged, and from reflecting on the system which had placed such
men at the head of the legions of the Commonwealth.' 'Virginia' is to
be seen as one of a group of compositions that attacked the privileged families by relating the bitter contest between the great houses
and the commonalty, 'whose position bore some resemblance to that
of the Irish Catholics during the interval between the year 1792 and
the year 1829'. The villain, Appius Claudius, represents unbridled
government authority:

He stalked along the Forum like King Tarquin in his pride . . .
For never was there Claudius yet but wished the Commons ill.

The plebeians dared not oppose his seizure of the lovely Virginia:

For then there was no Tribune to speak the word of might,
Which makes the rich man tremble, and guards the poor man's
    right . . .
But all the city, in great fear, obeyed the wicked Ten.

  Macaulay's exclusive concentration on the political issue means
the extinction of Virginia as a character. As a youthful reader of the
poem I used to wonder whether the fate Appius Claudius had in
store for her really was worse than death, and even so, whether she
might not have been allowed to find out for herself. Virginius was
one of the stern Roman fathers I had already learned to dislike in
Corneille. Virginia is not allowed to say or do anything in the poem,
and to the attempt of Appius' henchmen to seize her betrothed
Icilius responds not with swift and terrible anger but with a long
revolutionary speech about freedom. This has been thought an artis-
tic mistake, yet in a sense it is the point of the poem: the child
Virginia has no significance except as a symbolic focus for the patri-
cian/plebeian opposition. The subtlety of historical perspective of
which a Lay of Ancient Rome is capable is illustrated here. The
implicit author, i.e. Macaulay himself, is using the *persona* of a propa-

gandist of Catholic Emancipation in the 1820s looking back at an Ancient Roman narrator who is himself looking back, from a fiercely anti-Claudian point of view, at a legendary past.

The other Victorian master of this kind of poetry was William Edmundstoune Aytoun (1813–65), with his *Lays of the Scottish Cavaliers* (1849). Mark Weinstein in *W. E. Aytoun and the Spasmodic Controversy* (1968), to which I am much indebted, calls it a Victorian bestseller. In 15 years there were 15 British editions, and 32 editions in 32 years. Blackwood & Sons sold over 60 000 copies in the Victorian period alone; including foreign editions, the final total approached 100 000. The greatest vogue of these *Lays* was in Scotland, where selections from them were included in students' reading books. Aytoun's model was Scott. Scott had changed the nature of the old ballad, lengthened it to a Lay, removed its 'coarseness', and glamourised the life and manners of olden times. He had innumerable imitators, but none so successful in his own day as Aytoun. Aytoun also owed much to Macaulay, and his *Lays* can be seen as a Tory answer to Macaulay's. He was fixated on the Stuarts: six of the eight Lays deal with the fortunes of that family. Obviously this put him in opposition to Macaulay's reading of British history. But the situation is complicated by the fact that Macaulay himself had some sympathy – imaginatively if not politically – with the defeated side; especially when they were brave and loyal Englishmen, as in 'A Jacobite's Epitaph'. This motif, marginal in Macaulay, is central in Aytoun. He had a personal devotion to the defeated royal house. His use of the ballad form is centred on the Scottish cavalier, seen as a romantic figure, always in defeat, killed, like James IV, Montrose, Dundee, or the Old Scottish Cavalier, bereaved, like the Widow of Glencoe, or in exile, like Charles Edward and Dundee's Scottish regiment. Aytoun's emphasis on defeat may explain why his ballads so often end on a religious note, invoking the peace and calm of Heaven. This is as alien to the ballad tradition, which is this-worldly, as it is to Macaulay's *Lays*. Aytoun is like Macaulay, and unlike the old ballads, in making the narrator often an active participant. And, like Macaulay, he is a partisan. The soldier who narrates Dundee's conduct and death in 'The Burial March of Dundee' makes the greatness of Claverhouse more real to us by relaying it through his account of its effect on him.

As a champion of the ballad Aytoun, from his professorial chair in Edinburgh, was engaging both in academic power-politics and in current literary controversy. The contradictory tendencies of the

Romantic Movement were thrown into relief by the ballad revival. Both in theory and practice Aytoun stood for action in poetry and the expression of strong simple passions; for the Scott tradition, as against Wordsworthian introspection. In opposition to the Wordsworth who favoured meditation, sentiment, and a concern with modern subjects, he extolled Homer and Greek tragedy and the ballads, because of what he thought their universal appeal. This makes his critical position look like that of Matthew Arnold, in the Preface to his *Poems* (1853), in which Arnold deprecated modern introversion and called for a return to the objectivity of the old masters. But Arnold thought poorly of the traditional ballad. In his lectures on translating Homer (1861, 1862) he discouraged the use of the ballad style for that purpose, making game of the *Homeric Ballads* of Maginn (which were to have a successor in our own time in Robert Graves's translation of the *Iliad*). He spoke of Macaulay's *Lays* as 'pinchbeck', and he said of these lines in 'Horatius':

> Then out spake brave Horatius,
>   The Captain of the gate:
> 'To every man upon this earth
>   Death cometh soon or late.'

that they were 'hard to read without a cry of pain'. In contrast, in his lectures of 1853, Aytoun drew a distinction between the 'minstrel', whose poetry is read aloud to a group, and the 'poet', whose works are perused by the individual in solitude. Aytoun ranks the minstrel above the poet, because of his more general appeal.

In doing so he was taking sides in a dispute which has flared up from time to time down to the present day: the opposition, sometimes bitter, on the part of readers and critics, to the trend of withdrawal in poetry, the abandonment of that 'common world' which Wordsworth, whatever his own subjectivism, had called 'the place where in the end/We find our happiness, or not at all!' Aytoun exalted the ballad in his lectures in England and Scotland. He may have formed the taste of a generation of students; or perhaps he was merely responding to it. In reviews and articles on contemporary poetry in the *North British Review* he constantly returned to the topic of balladry. Aytoun in Edinburgh had the practical advantage over Arnold in Oxford of knowing whom he was addressing (i.e. undergraduates studying English and Scottish Literature). Arnold, twice Professor of Poetry at Oxford, had no such definable audience: the

Chair of Poetry had no connection with any distinct 'English' course. He himself was the first Professor of Poetry to lecture in English (rather than Latin), and most of his examples were drawn from outside the English tradition. In later years, when the possibility of establishing a School of English at Oxford was mooted, Arnold refused to support it, on the ground that it would endanger the supremacy of Classics. It is ironical that Aytoun is now almost forgotten, while Arnold is revered as a pioneer of Eng. Lit. But in his day the conflict between Aytoun's supporters and the Arnoldians gave an edge to the growing debate about 'English', and it can be seen now and then to impinge on the concerns of Tennyson.

Aytoun's sympathies with the common world and the common reader brought him into the great Victorian flowering of parody and burlesque. With Theodore Martin he published *A Book of Ballads* (1845) under the pseudonym 'Bon Gaultier', parodying various poets and styles of the time. They were very popular, and both Saintsbury and Mark Weinstein, a modern authority on Aytoun, speak highly of them, but they have not outlasted the century: their targets have dated, and their humour, while agreeable enough, is at the same time too gentle and too broad for our tastes. In view of Aytoun's ballad sympathies it is noteworthy that the old ballads are parodied in 'The Queen in France' (Queen Victoria had recently visited France). Tennyson provides one of the targets, with the exaggerated sensibility of 'The May Queen'. The parody ends: 'Draw me a pot of beer, mother, and mother, draw it mild.' The young man of 'Locksley Hall' is also parodied, and it may be noted that he is an anticipation of the (unnamed) hero of *Maud* (1855), round whom the 'Spasmodic' controversy was to simmer. Aytoun owes his own niche in literary history to his satire on the Spasmodics in *Firmilian*: its imaginary author, T. Percy Jones, is clearly a literary descendant of Bon Gaultier.

III

I now leave the literary and academic cross-currents round Tennysonian balladry for the poems themselves. The tradition of languid *Angst* associates several of his ballads with 'La Belle Dame sans Merci'. Deserted lovers, hopeless passion, beautifully described settings, and self-absorbed sad music, are pervasive in 'Mariana', 'The Lady of Shalott' and 'Oriana'. The first two of these are agreed to be among Tennyson's best poems in this kind. The mood is skilfully conveyed by the refrains, linking 'aweary' and 'dreary' in 'Mariana', while in 'The Lady of Shalott', written in the tail-rhyme of the romances, the tags in each stanza alternately join together and separate Camelot and Shalott, the poles on which the poem turns. It would be an exaggeration to say that folk ballads never use atmospheric effects, but they are never the main point, as they are here. The action consists of little more than vague gestures, indicative of inner suffering. The description of battle in 'Oriana' is not there for its own sake but as a pretext for grief. The interest centres on the teller, not the tale. The poem suffers from Tennyson's characteristic fault of overdoing it. 'Oriana' is metrically coarser than the other two. If Robert Graves has destroyed this poem by his suggestion that we should substitute 'Bottom upwards' for 'Oriana' every time the refrain occurs,[6] Tennyson had invited vandalism by making the speaker repeat it so often. 'St Agnes Eve' has an austere simplicity of diction which is like the ballads, and there is some vigour in the writing ('He lifts me to the golden doors', etc. [R i, 606, l. 25]). But it is too introspective, too lacking in narrative, to be really like a ballad. In most poems it was romance that suited Tennyson better, with his slow movement, his involved sentences, his habit of pausing to paint verbal pictures. His liking for the old metrical romances is especially clear in the Arthurian poems he wrote in preparation for the *Idylls of the King*. 'Sir Galahad' begins like a ballad but soon settles down to a more sedate pace as the hero's bravado is subdued to his sense of religious dedication. In 'Morte d'Arthur' the poet looks beyond Romance to Epic, but his doubts are unconcealed in the prefatory poem:

> Why take the style of those heroic times?
> For nature brings not back the Mastodon,
> Nor we those times; and why should any man
> Remodel models?
>   ('The Epic' [1842], R ii, 2, ll. 35–8)

In 'Morte d'Arthur' the epic style is muffled by decoration: jewellery, white samite, sumptuous materials. Malory has prevailed over Homer. It looks as if Tennyson's doubts about the possibility of epic extended to the ballad, for the poems of his that come nearest to that model lack conviction. 'Lady Clare', with its anti-snobbery overtone, comes nearer to a middle-class homily like 'Lady Clara Vere de Vere' than to the high tragedy and the elemental simplicities of the old ballads.

'The Sisters' repays special attention. It has never been regarded as one of Tennyson's best poems: it is mostly ignored by critics, or disparaged in passing. Yet it is not easy to say just why.

> We were two daughters of one race.
> She was the fairest in the face:
> > The wind is blowing in turret and tree.
> They were together, and she fell;
> Therefore revenge became me well.
> > O the Earl was fair to see!
>
> She died: she went to burning flame:
> She mixed her ancient blood with shame.
> > The wind is howling in turret and tree.
> Whole weeks and months, and early and late,
> To win his love I lay in wait:
> > O the Earl was fair to see!
>
> I made a feast; I bade him come;
> I won his love, I brought him home.
> > The wind is roaring in turret and tree.
> And after supper, on a bed,
> Upon my lap he laid his head:
> > O the Earl was fair to see!
>
> I kiss'd his eyelids into rest:
> His ruddy cheek upon my breast.
> > The wind is raging in turret and tree.
> I hated him with the hate of hell,
> But I loved his beauty passing well.
> > O the Earl was fair to see!
>
> I rose up in the silent night:
> I made my dagger sharp and bright.
> > The wind is raving in turret and tree.
> As half-asleep his breath he drew,
> Three times I stabbed him through and through.
> > O the Earl was fair to see!

> I curled and combed his comely head,
> He looked so grand when he was dead.
>   The wind is blowing in turret and tree.
> I wrapt his body in the sheet,
> And laid him at his mother's feet.
>   O the Earl was fair to see!

(R i, 434–5)

Tennyson adopts here the laconic manner of the old ballads. The use of the two refrains which bind the poem together is ingenious. The second refrain, identical throughout, keeps the beauty of the Earl before us right to the end, when he has been killed and become an erotic–aesthetic object to his murderess. The first refrain cleverly dramatises the emotional curve of the action through the changes in the verb used to describe the wind: 'blowing', 'howling', 'roaring' 'raging', 'raving' – the climax – and then back to 'blowing' again, when the story is over. This is the kind of stylistic effect not found in the old ballads, but that is not a sufficient reason for condemning it. 'The Sisters' could still have been an effective poem. But the judgement of readers and critics, if we may infer it from their collective silence, is that it is not. Perhaps this is because the story is gruesome and sensational: it is a 'Gothic ballad'. But these were written competently by Victorian poets: Rossetti and Morris succeeded with similar stories. They may not greatly appeal to twentieth-century readers, but they do not seem silly, as Tennyson does here. The only explanation I can suggest is that the terse manner has misfired.

> They were together, and she fell.

'So what?' is the natural reaction. How much better the line sounds when Eliot adapts it for the demure gaiety of 'Burbank with a Baedeker: Bleistein with a Cigar':

> Burbank crossed a little bridge
> Descending at a small hotel;
> Princess Volupine arrived,
> They were together, and he fell.

The telegraphic manner makes for comedy, whereas in 'The Sisters' we feel that the poet has not given himself enough time to create a thrilling atmosphere.

It is time now to look at Tennyson's performance in a different kind of Victorian balladry, the popular or demotic. The decline of poetry as a public art has long been lamented by people who care about such things. America's first-ever Poet Laureate, Robert Penn Warren, was quoted in 1986 as regretting that schools today provide no general education in poetry, and students are not exposed to it.[7] Whether as a cause or effect of this situation, or both, many modern poets seem to ignore the origins of poetry in song, riddle and proverb, and to discard its ancient devices of rhyme, metre and cadence. There has been a constant emphasis on the world of private experience, on the isolated 'image', and a manifest diminution of emotional and intellectual force and of substance, in the work of poets. They reject general truths and common experience in favour of a purely personal reality. Old-fashioned talk of 'pleasing the ear' and 'stirring the blood' is scorned. The appeal to ancient communal or 'stock' responses, physical, emotional or social, is rejected as vulgarity. The result has been that poetry is not read or taken account of by the generality of human beings. It plays no part in their lives. The chasm between the artist and the public continues to widen. Evidence seems continually to mount against the truth of Vico's saying, made current by Croce, that poetry is 'the primary activity of the human mind'. Yet some of us go on feeling that this is not just the sort of thing that is said on suitable public occasions, with no expectation that anyone will take it seriously, but that in some mysterious way it is *true*. And while that feeling persists there may be still hope for poetry.

Its future turns on the survival of what Kingsley Amis calls 'reciter' verse and I have referred to as balladry. George Orwell made current the description of this kind of verse as 'good bad poems'. This expression is obviously unsatisfactory, but it seems to have stuck. It refers to poems which the current critical orthodoxy disapproves of, or professes not to take seriously, yet shrinks from calling bad (it is indeed hard to see in what possible sense Byron's 'So we'll go no more a-roving', or Belloc's 'Ha'nacker Mill', could be judged bad). Orwell called a good bad poem 'a graceful monument to the obvious. It records, in memorable form, . . . some emotion which nearly every normal human being can share'.[8] It is a kind of rhyming proverb, founded on values which are straightforward and unchallenged. Leslie Fiedler, speaking of the old anthology favourites of American poetry, calls them the Lovely Commonplaces. Kingsley Amis thinks that in Britain this whole genre disappeared during the 1930s. The great themes of popular verse had been the nation and the Church. Today these, together with such minor themes as the desire for a simple rustic existence, have disappeared. To see why this is so we need only refer to the title of one of Philip Larkin's poems, 'MCMXIV': the year when the Great War broke out. 'Never such innocence again.' Yet it would be wrong to suppose that since the 1930s there have been no poets who could have written good balladry. Auden wrote 'Victor'; Empson (so often abstruse and eso- teric) wrote his 'Chinese Ballad'; Graves wrote 'The General Elliott'; Betjeman wrote 'The Arrest of Oscar Wilde at the Cadogan Hotel'. But all these have a jocular or ironic or oblique quality alien to the good bad poem. As for serious or tragic balladry, it seems to have vanished altogether.

In the nineteenth century it was abundant. Wordsworth, Coleridge, Scott, Mrs Hemans, Campbell, Southey, Longfellow, Whittier, Kingsley, and others, all wrote that kind of poetry, and some of their pieces survive in anthologies and in ordinary speech. But a question- mark hangs over the name of Tennyson. Some of his good bad poems are remembered, but not with affection. They are disliked, or ridiculed. Nor do they have a McGonagall sort of reputation. As we should expect from Tennyson, they are very competent technically. If they are bad, it is not because they fail to be good, but because they do successfully something that critics do not like.

To many of Tennyson's admirers they are merely an embarrass- ment. And as no one today thinks they are his best poems it might be asked why they should be discussed at all. I do not dispute that parts of *In Memoriam*, and some of the personal lyrics, represent Tennyson's poetry at its supreme height. But there are many areas of his work that need reappraisal. There has been a great increase in literary scholarship devoted to Tennyson, and much new information has come out about him, but there is no influential modern critique. I have the impression that Harold Nicolson's study of 1923 is still a potent influence. In some ways this is not a bad thing. Nicolson's book is enjoyable and elegantly written. Like his master, Lytton Strachey in *Queen Victoria* (1921), Nicolson may have begun with the intention of debunking, but then came to feel both affection and respect for his subject. I finished the book with the conviction (clearly shared by the biographer) that in spite of all Tennyson's pettinesses and pettishness and absurdities he was a great man. But much has changed in English literature since 1923, and the image of Tennyson needs adjustment. To explore the Collected Works is to be immersed in Victoriana, some morbid, some mawkish, some quaint, some positively bizarre, some endearing. And now and then there is the

poetry that speaks to us directly, requiring no extenuation. I suggest
that some poems in the extroverted part of Tennyson's work need to
be looked at again, without either the preconceptions of Tennyson's
own time, or of the 1920s and 'Modernism'. Nicolson himself, while
deprecating the 'Laureate' work (the 'Farringford period') had already praised some of the demotic poems. This is the poetry I will
now look into.

   Among the various kinds of popular poetry Tennyson wrote I
will refer to three: the homiletic; the celebratory; and the dramatic
monologues of common life. The homilies include some poems which
dramatise the hostility between the bourgeois and the aristocrat,
always from an anti-aristocratic point of view. This links them with
Maud. One of them is 'Lady Clara Vere de Vere'. The speaker, a
'yeoman', exhorts the tease Lady Clara to remember that

> Kind hearts are more than coronets,
> And simple faith than Norman blood.
>   (R ii, 64, ll. 55–6)

'School-miss Alfred' is not far enough away here. Good advice has
a harder thrust in Tennyson when it is shrewdly prudential and
delivered in a regional accent:

An' thou'll be his Curate here, but, if iver tha means to git 'igher,
Tha mun tackle the sins o' the wo'ld, and not the faults of the Squire.
         ('The Church-warden and the Curate', R iii, 229, ll. 45–6)

The celebratory poems are more problematic today.

> A voice by the cedar tree
> In the meadow under the Hall!
> She is singing an air that is known to me,
> A passionate ballad gallant and gay,
> A martial song like a trumpet's call!
> Singing alone in the morning of life,
> In the happy morning of life and of May,
> Singing of men that in battle array,
> Ready in heart and ready in hand,
> March with banner and bugle and fife
> To the death, for their native land.
>   (*Maud*, I, v, 162–72, R ii, 532–3)

This beautiful description of Maud singing arouses mixed feelings. We are exhilarated by the springiness of the versification, but we fear that the song itself would have been Tennyson at his worst. He could be bellicose, even bloodthirsty, and he certainly did what he could to get us into war with Napoleon III. But he also wrote 'The Voyage of Maeldune', years later, expressing the futility of hatred and the value of forgiveness.

Tennyson's most famous military poem was topical, 'The Charge of the Light Brigade'. Technically it is superb. The ominous opening ('Half a league, half a league') puts us at once in the midst of things. Jerome McCann has analysed the use in the poem of battle-stereotypes like the paintings of Meissonier. But, though distributed on broadsheets to the troops in the Crimea, the 'Charge' remains a Home Front poem, even if the troops naturally relished the line 'Someone had blunder'd.' What seems to have gone wrong is not technique but the poet's attitude:

> 'Forward the Light Brigade!'
> Was there a man dismayed?

Yes; 600 were.

To get the point of view of the soldier is always difficult for a civilian poet, as Lord Wavell pointed out in his introduction to *Other Men's Flowers* (1944). On the other hand, popular songs and street ballads, which might be expected to strike a note of greater reality, usually fail through lack of technical skill. Perhaps the only possible form of dignified patriotic–military utterance was found by Thomas Campbell (1777–1844) in 'Ye Mariners of England'. Campbell, a Scotsman, was a master of poetic decorum, finding the right note (heroic) for the English (or 'British'), plaintive for the Irish. The non-combatant does not purport to speak as himself a 'Mariner'.

Tennyson's masterpiece in patriotic poetry is 'The Revenge'. Here the event commemorated is far away and long ago, already a legend, which is just as well, for even if we take the view of Sir Richard Grenville which A. L. Rowse takes in his 1937 book on him, Grenville is not a sympathetic character, and to appreciate Tennyson's ballad fully we have to desensitise our historical imagination and see Grenville as a fictional figure, merely a symbol of reckless English courage. This is a little chilling. And the first person (the 'we') of the poem arouses misgivings. Some of the best lines in the poem would be hard to imagine as spoken by a sailor-participant:

So Lord Howard past away with five ships of war that day,
Till he melted like a cloud in the silent summer heaven . . .
                                        (R iii, 26, ll. 13–14)

But who could complain about such lines? It is that sense of over-arching spaciousness that makes the poem so memorable. It is all 'seen', not as if it were a memory of something in real life, but as if it were a great nineteenth-century historical painting:

Thousands of their soldiers looked down from their decks and
    laughed,
Thousands of their seamen made mock at the mad little craft
Running on and on, till delayed
By their mountain-like San Philip that, of fifteen hundred tons,
And up-shadowing high above us with her yawning tiers of guns,
Took the breath from our sails, and we stayed .
                                        (ll. 37–42)

In its mastery of metre and rhythm the poem is rivalled in the Victorian age only by Hopkins's *The Wreck of the Deutschland* and Francis Thompson's 'The Hound of Heaven'. The free-ranging move-ment of the lines is from time to time set off against *rallentando* moments of serenity:

And the sun went down, and the stars came out far over the
    summer sea . . .
                                        (l. 56)

There are two rhythmic principles at work in the poem, one ener-getic and staccato, one retarded and gracious, and at the end they come together, when all the rhythmic power is gathered up in the fourteenth stanza as the wind rises and the great wave breaks and the *Revenge* goes down, 'to be lost evermore in the main'.

In the history of poetic forms 'The Revenge' belongs to the period after the vogue of the Lays which we have noted with reference to Scott and Macaulay and Aytoun. It may be that the element of democratic aspiration in them proved to be their undoing as a genre. They were too exalted, had too much literary dignity, to compete with street ballads for the attention of the general public. Historical ballads now moved slightly downmarket, became less ambitious in scope than the Lays, as sophisticated poets used them in an attempt to capture the note of popular feeling. Browning did this in 'Hervé Riel', and Tennyson in 'The Revenge'. Tennyson was well-placed to write 'The Revenge' because his own attitude to foreigners seems to have been the same as that of Sir Richard Grenville in the poem; the same as that of the protagonist of Kingsley Amis's novel *I Like It Here*:

> But he tells 'em '*Obrigado*',
> Full of courtly foreign grace, [a phrase from 'The Revenge']
> 'Cos he's got his homeward voucher
> Safely locked up in his case.[9]

But there was still too wide a gap in historical ballads between the popular tones and rhythms that were used and the poet's own dignity and lofty historical point of view. It is now time to consider how far Tennyson overcame this difficulty in his monologues of common life. An example is 'In the Children's Hospital'. Some readers have thought it unpleasant and sentimental, but it is powerful. The mawkish nurse who is the narrator, and the sadistic doctor, with his traditional red hair (cf. Hugh Walpole's novel *Portrait of a Man with Red Hair*, 1925) are plausible as well as nightmarish. Tennyson's poem, though written round about 1880, seems to belong to the pre-chloroform period. George Orwell in 'How the Poor Die' (1946) relates how it became, long after it was written, a living actuality for him when he lay ill in a French hospital:

> as a child I had had it read aloud by a sick-nurse whose working life might have stretched back to the time when Tennyson wrote the poem. The horrors and sufferings of the old-style hospitals were a vivid memory to her. We had shuddered over the poem together, and then seemingly I had forgotten it. Even its name would probably have recalled nothing to me. But the first glimpse of the ill-lit murmurous room [at the Hôpital X] with the beds so close together, suddenly roused the train of thought to which it belonged, and in the night that followed I found myself remembering the whole story and atmosphere of the poem, with many of its lines complete.[10]

In 'In the Children's Hospital' Tennyson has adopted the manner of George R. Sims ('It was Christmas Day in the Workhouse') and there may be a slightly falsetto effect. More congenial today are the poems in dialect, and some of the versifications of anecdotes he was told, or scraps from newspapers or magazines. It was once thought that his avid search for subjects was a sign of his failing inspiration, but it now seems clear that Tennyson was always by temperament not so much a writer with a 'message' as a *bricoleur*, delighting to apply his skill to the most miscellaneous topics. In this region of his poetry the chauvinist–military tone is rarely heard. Nor is there much of the Laureate in his singing-robes. The attitudes behind the popular poems and versified tales are quite different. They are often written from the point of view of a woman, whereas, as the pacifist C. K. Ogden pointed out many years ago, there is a strong misogynistic element in militarism. Some of these poems have the human warmth and the unsqueamish tenderness, the freedom from all forms of humbug, which Tennyson is often supposed to lack. Insight into personal, social, and regional characteristics is shown in 'The Northern Farmer', 'The Northern Cobbler', and 'The Village Wife'. There is something deep, as well as odd, about that mono-logue by a village spinster who has rejected all her suitors because she thinks they are only after her money, but names her cats after them ('The Spinster's Sweet-Arts'). Down to earth, matter-of-fact, heterogeneous, unpredictable, Tennyson in this vein is more like Hardy than any other Victorian poet.

'Rizpah' seems to me the most notable of these monologues of common life and one of the best of Tennyson's poems of any period. Swinburne eulogised it in the same essay in which he made some cutting criticisms of the *Idylls* and their 'blameless King'. He cites 'Rizpah' as a proof that all great poets are bisexual, making much of the phrase 'the bones had moved in my side' as getting the inward-ness of the old woman's point of view.[11] Along with the oddity there is something psychologically convincing in the deranged legalism of the speaker: the bones she had taken down from the gibbet, her son's bones, had been nourished from her own body, they were her prop-erty, whatever the law might say (and she hates lawyers). The rights to property in a corpse are, from a legal point of view, a controversial subject, and the question has some interest for students of Tennyson's poem. But for the most part 'Rizpah' is a study in dementia, raised to a sombre, tragic height by the hint of something ultimate and uni-versal in the situation: it is an elemental evocation of the maternal. By entitling the poem 'Rizpah' (not the name of the speaker) the poet depersonalises and universalises her.

The passage about Rizpah in II Samuel 21: 10–11, brief and cryptic, sounds like a summary of an Antigone-type tragedy:

And Rizpah the daughter of Aiah took sackcloth, and spread it for her upon the rock, from the beginning of harvest until water dropped upon them [the bones] out of heaven, and suffered neither the birds of the air to rest on them by day, nor the beasts of the field by night. (Authorised Version)

The political edge to the poem is sharpened by the presence as auditor of the supercilious lady, the District Visitor, whom the old woman denounces; there is a link here with 'Lady Clara Vere de Vere' and other poems in that category. But there seems to be another interest at work in the poem, something more personal and subjective. Dr Susan Shatto, the editor of *Maud*, drew my attention to the many echoes of the earlier poem (with which we know Tennyson was always obsessed) in 'Rizpah': the touches of paranoia of the protagonist of Part I of *Maud*, the similar cadences and phrases in both poems, the mad scene in *Maud* II. 5. The preoccupation with bones is characteristic of both poems. I learn from Christopher Ricks's edition that 'Rizpah' was recited as 'Bones' on 5 June 1879. There are, of course, differences between the two poems. In *Maud* the narrator is a troubled young intellectual of the 1850s, not a simple, half-crazed old woman in the eighteenth-century. And 'Rizpah' shows a concern with Christian motifs not found in *Maud*: election, salvation, sin and punishment and repentance, the after-life, the resurrection of the body. But the later poem can plausibly be regarded as a variation on themes from *Maud*. Perhaps we may come to regard this poem, neglected by critics, as in resonance with the Tennyson who matters to us.

Just what that is will be a matter for the hoped-for late twentieth- or twenty-first-century critique. It is doubtful whether we can now look to Tennyson for guidance in philosophical and religious thought. What he says is not uninteresting, but it belongs to his time rather than ours. The mystical element is more tantalising and puzzling than illuminating. In his prettier poems the men and women and children have a waxwork quality. We are uneasy with the Arthurian properties and the classical mythology, and not so thrilled as the Victorians were with the indefatigable onomatopoeia and the delicate colourings of the Nature notes. The Tennyson who still fascinates us is the poet of 'black blood', aware of the divisions and the dissociations that are among the possibilities of the human mind, the poet of 'madness', of the 'weird seizures' in *The Princess*, and the visions and dreams and nightmares of *In Memoriam* and *Maud*: the poet who not only perhaps reveals his own psychological conflicts, but can bring intelligence and insight to bear on them. The road to understanding here is through the study of Tennyson's use of language, with which modern scholarship has helped us. We may be now in a better position to make sense of Eliot's puzzling judgement that Tennyson's surface, his 'technical accomplishment', is 'intimate with his depths';[12] to ponder more closely the association between sound and feeling that gives their haunting quality to 'The splendour falls' or 'To Virgil'. But today, as I hope to have shown, there is matter of great interest in the study of Tennyson as a poet writing for a public: the things in his poetry that move between the surface and the depths.

Notes

1. See his *A Choice of Kipling's Verse* (London: Faber & Faber, 1941), p. 10.
2. See the Introduction to *English and Scottish Popular Ballads*, ed. H. C. Sargent and G. L. Kittredge (Boston: Houghton Mifflin, 1932).
3. This and a subsequent reference are to Chapter 10 of Albert B. Friedman, *The Ballad Revival: Studies in the Influence of Popular on Sophisticated Poetry* (Chicago: University of Chicago Press, 1961).
4. *Fortnightly Review*, May 1870, pp. 551–79.
5. Amis, *The Faber Popular Reciter* (London: Faber & Faber, 1978), Introduction, pp. 15–18. The reference to 'Horatius' is on his pp. 17–18.
6. Graves, *The Crowning Privilege* (Harmondsworth: Penguin, 1959), p. 131.
7. Quoted from *Richmond Times-Despatch*, 7 October 1986.
8. 'Rudyard Kipling', *The Collected Essays, Journalism and Letters of George Orwell*, ed. Sonia Orwell and Ian Angus (Harmondsworth: Penguin, 1970) II, pp. 227–8.
9. Amis, *I Like It Here* (London: Gollancz, 1958), p. 175.
10. 'How the Poor Die', *Collected Essays*, IV, 271–2.
11. Reprinted in *Tennyson: the Critical Heritage*, ed J. D. Jump (London: Routledge & Kegan Paul, 1967), p. 337.
12. Eliot, 'In Memoriam', *Essays, Ancient and Modern* (London: Faber & Faber, 1936), p. 189.

Index